★ THE WEST POINT ATLAS OF WAR ★

WORLD WAR II: EUROPEAN THEATER

Compiled by The Department of Military Art and Engineering
The United States Military Academy

Chief Editor
Brigadier General Vincent J. Esposito, USA

Tess Press

Photo Credits: page 156 left APImages; page 156 center U.S. Signal Corps via APImages;
page 156 right U.S. Army photo/NARA; page 157 left U.S. Army photo/NARA;
page 157 top right U.S. Army photo/NARA; page 157 bottom British Official Photo/NARA;
page 158 left NARA; page 158 top APImages; page 158 bottom APImages; page 159 left APImages;
page 159 top NARA; page 159 bottom U.S. Army/NARA.

Published by Tess Press, an imprint of
Black Dog & Leventhal Publishers, Inc.
151 West 19th Street
New York, NY 10011

Cover and interior design: Lindsay Wolff

The content of this book was originally published in 1959 under the title *The West Point Atlas of American Wars,
Volume I (1689-1900)* and *Volume II (1900-1953)*. Since then, generations of West Point cadets have used the
atlases as an important part of their study of military history in preparation for their service as officers in
the United States Army. While the maps and corresponding text represented the finest military scholarship
available at that time, subsequent scholarship has in some cases altered historical interpretations. Readers of
this book—like West Point cadets—therefore should complement their study with more current works to
develop a complete picture of the history presented.

ISBN-10: 1-60376-023-7
ISBN-13: 978-1-60376-023-2

h g f e d c b a

Printed in China

CONTENTS

★

GERMAN AGGRESSIONS (1936–39)

★

The Europe of 1938 had been sapped by World War I. France and Britain had been bled to exhaustion and could not contemplate any more large scale warfare. The USA was far away and self-absorbed. On the one hand, undue faith was placed in the flimsy apparatus of the League of Nations; and on the other, France tried to wrap itself in a network of protective alliances which, ironically, would drag the world into war.

Hitler had become Chancellor of Germany in 1933 and was determined to redress what many Germans saw as the draconian provisions of the 1919 Treaty of Versailles. In 1935 he denounced the limitation on German rearmament, and in March 1936 remilitarized the Rhineland. In March 1938, he occupied Austria, followed in October 1938 by the Sudeten area of Czechoslovakia, and in March 1939 by the rest of Czechoslovakia. On 23 August 1939 Germany and Russia signed a non-aggression pact. So far he had not had to fire a shot, and Britain and France stood by helplessly. Now it was Poland's turn.

Poland was, for the most part, open and level: great tank country. And in the fall of 1939 the weather, usually wet, smiled on Hitler. The extended dryness made for firm going for his panzer divisions. The rivers were low, and the ground was hard. The Polish high command faced many problems, not least of which was a small army with antiquated weaponry; but it also face a strategic problem: the Danzig Corridor, which led up to the country's only port, Gdynia, was highly vulnerable, sandwiched between Germany and East Prussia; their main industries were in exposed areas in the Lodz–Cracow region, close to the German border. So, if the Poles massed their troops west of the San–Vistula rivers line they would create a salient with exposed flanks. But if they pulled back below those rivers, they forfeited the most productive parts of their country.

Britain and France, still with fresh memories of the slaughter of the Western Front, were not about to intervene directly; but Poland had seen what had happened to Czechoslovakia when it went down without a fight, and they were determined not to go the same way. Hitler was confident that he could crush Poland before France or Britain could react. If they did attempt to intervene, the West Wall, which he had been building as a barrier between German and France, would hold them. A quick victory over Poland would cow the other nations of southeast Europe, guaranteeing Germany continued access to Hungarian wheat and Rumanian oil.

The German invasion plan (so confident was Hitler that he would not even allow his generals to war game it) envisioned a two prong attack. From the north, von Bock's Army Group (Fourth Army under Gen von Kluge, and Third Army under Kuechler) would come down from the Baltic, cut off the Danzig corridor at its base, and then move on to Warsaw where it would link up with von Runsdstedt's Army Group South after it had punched through western Poland via Lodz and Cracow.

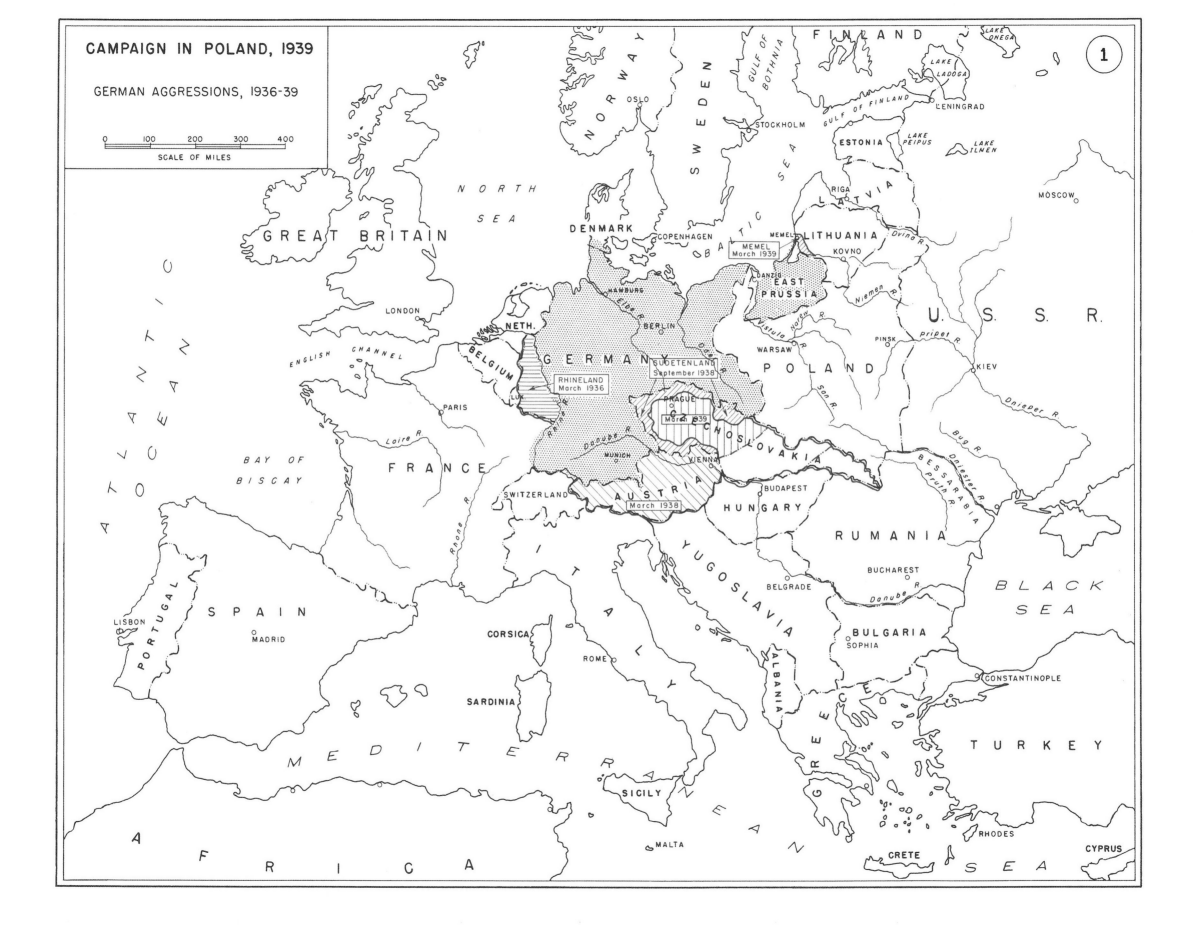

CAMPAIGN IN POLAND, 1939

GERMAN AGGRESSIONS, 1936-39

SCALE OF MILES
0   100   200   300   400

1

RHINELAND
March 1936

SUDETENLAND
September 1938

MEMEL
March 1939

PRAGUE
March 1939

AUSTRIA
March 1938

THE EXPLOITATION

★

Faced with the two pronged German invasion, the Polish plan appears to have been an attempt to hold as much of the country as possible by concentrating most of the available troops along the frontiers in the hope that they could tie down the Germans in a World War I–type deadlock until England and France could come to their aid. Poland had no armored forces, and only the flimsiest of field fortifications had been thrown up at the frontiers.

Without bothering with the formality of declaring war, Hitler struck at 0440 on 1 September 1939. The Luftwaffe raided airfields all across Poland, and the German army surged across the frontier. As though mesmerized, the Poles were taken completely by surprise, and by 3 September the Polish Air Force had been annihilated and the German Third and Fourth Armies had joined hands to cut the Danzig Corridor. The Polish resistance had been tough and desperate, some of the cavalry charging at tanks with lance and saber because, so unofficial contemporary reports suggest, they thought the German tanks were "dummies" made of canvas and papier-mâché.

Bock's Third Army continued its advance toward the Narew River while over on the west, Tenth Army began crossing the Pilica River, with only open country between it and Warsaw. Fourteenth Army (List) was meeting resistance at Cracow, while Eighth Army (Blaskowitz) was pushing across the Warta River. For the Poles it was desperate; most of their reserves had been committed, and their headquarters, forced to move constantly, was continuously and accurately targeted by the Luftwaffe, who had been tipped off by fifth columnists.

On 6 September Rundstedt's Tenth Army continued its relentless advance against Warsaw, despite desperate Polish resistance. On its right, the Fourteenth Army took Cracow, and thereafter Brauchitsch directed that it advance northeast toward Lublin to intercept any Polish units which might escape across the Vistula.

In the north, Bock regrouped his XXI Corps and sent it toward Lomza on the 7th, and on the 9th the leading elements of Guderian's XIX Corps came into action on its left. On the 11th, hearing that the Polish government had moved to Lwow and was trying to set up a new line of resistance and the Bug and San rivers, Brauchitsch directed that Third Army press on to a line below Kock and Wlodawa where it would make contact with Fourteenth Army advancing to Lublin, thus completing the second envelopment of the Polish army.

Continuing German advances on all fronts gave the Poles no chance to reorganize. Third Army closed in on Warsaw; Lwow fell on 21 September, and Warsaw, ravaged by starvation and typhoid, capitulated on 27 September. Russia entered the eastern provinces under a secret deal with Germany which would cede it all territory east of the Bug, and on 6 October the Polish army made its last stand at Kock where, in a two-day fight, Tenth Army took 17,000 prisoners.

The new Luftwaffe-panzer combination had proved itself, although the main burden of combat had fallen on the hard-marching German infantry and its largely horse-drawn artillery.

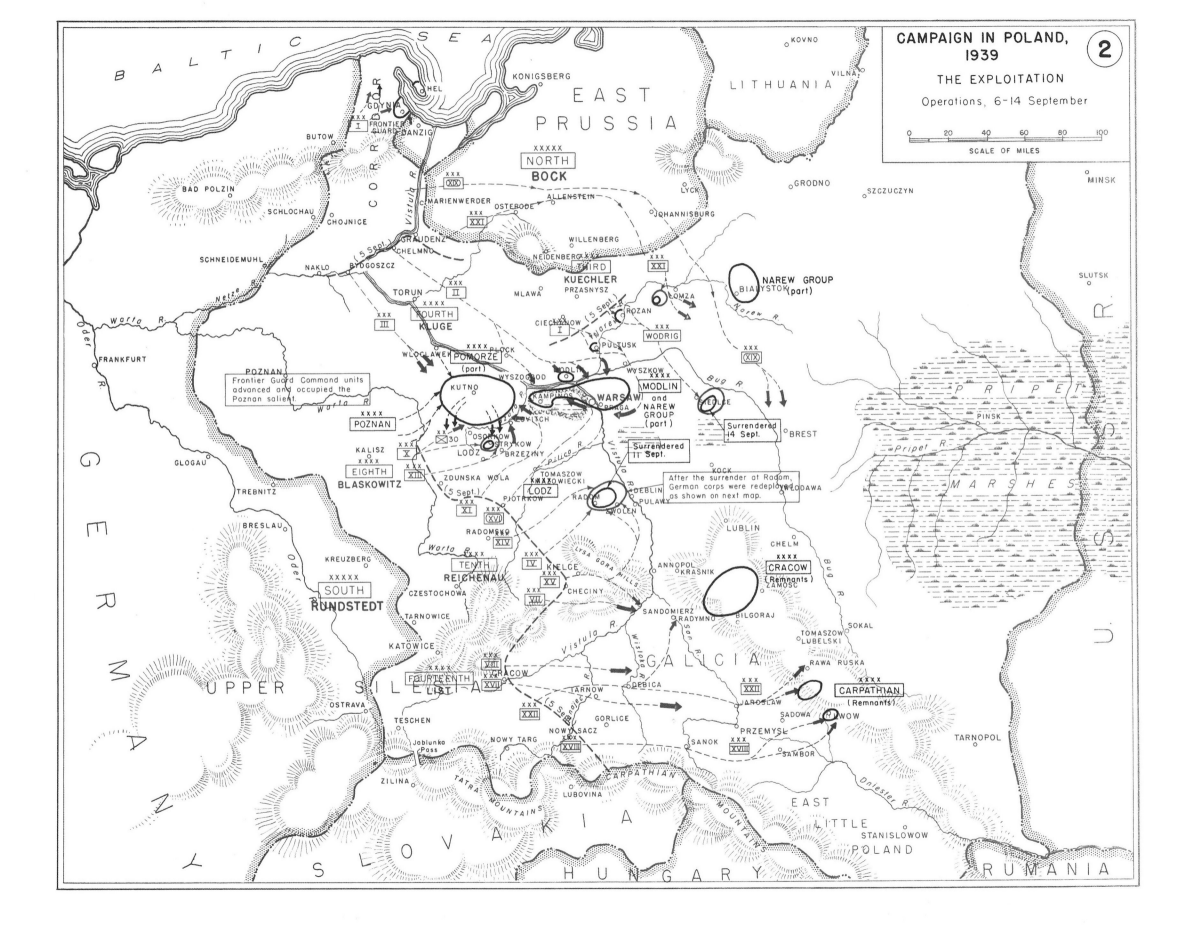

CAMPAIGN IN POLAND, 1939

2

THE EXPLOITATION

Operations, 6-14 September

SCALE OF MILES

0   20   40   60   80   100

BALTIC SEA

EAST PRUSSIA

LITHUANIA

KOVNO

VILNA

KONIGSBERG

GDYNIA

HEL

BUTOW

I
FRONTIER
GUARD
DANZIG

MINSK

SZCZUCZYN

GRODNO

XXXXX
NORTH
BOCK

BAD POLZIN

SCHLOCHAU

CHOJNICE

MARIENWERDER

OSTERODE

ALLENSTEIN

WILLENBERG

NEIDENBERG

LYCK

JOHANNISBURG

SLUTSK

SCHNEIDEMUHL

NAKLO

BYDGOSZCZ

GRAUDENZ (5 Sept.)

CHELMNO

XXX
XIX

THIRD
KUECHLER

PRZASNYSZ

MLAWA

CIECHANOW (5 Sept.)

XXX
XXI

XXX
XXI

NAREW GROUP
(part)

BIALYSTOK

XXX
II

TORUN

FRANKFURT

WARTA R.

Netze R.

XXX
III

FOURTH
KLUGE

WLOCLAWEK

PLOCK

XXXX
POMORZE
(part)

WYSZOGROD

POZNAN
Frontier Guard Command units
advanced and occupied the
Poznan salient.

Warta R.

KUTNO

XXXX
POZNAN

KAMPINOS

KALISZ

XXX
30

OSOROW

OSTRYKOW

LODZ

BRZEZINY

Pilica R.

LOWICH

WARSAW

PRAGA

MODLIN
and
NAREW
GROUP
(part)

MODLIN

PULTUSK

WODRIG

ROZAN

LOMZA

Narew R.

Narew R.

Bug R.

XXX
XIX

PRIPET

Pripet R.

PINSK

MARSHES

XXXX
MODLIN

SIEDLCE

Surrendered
14 Sept.

BREST

KOCK

Surrendered
11 Sept.

After the surrender at Radom,
German corps were redeployed
as shown on next map.

DEBLIN

WLODAWA

PULAWY

CHELM

GLOGAU

TREBNITZ

XXXX
EIGHTH
BLASKOWITZ

XXX
X

XXX
XIII

ZDUNSKA WOLA
(5 Sept.)

TOMASZOW
MAZOWIECKI

RADOM

SWOLEN

KALISZ

PJOTRKOW

XXX
XI

XXX
XVI

PIJOTRKOW

RADOMSKO

XXX
XIV

LUBLIN

BRESLAU

KREUZBERG

Warta R.

Lysa Gora Hills

XXX
IV

KIELCE

ANNOPOL

KRASNIK

XXXX
CRACOW
(Remnants)

ZAMOSC

GERMANY

ODER R.

SOUTH
RUNDSTEDT

XXXXX

CZESTOCHOWA

TARNOWICE

XXXX
TENTH
REICHENAU

XXX
XV

CHECINY

San R.

SANDOMIERZ

RADYMNO

BILGORAJ

Bug R.

TOMASZOW
LUBELSKI

SOKAL

RAWA RUSKA

KATOWICE

OSTRAVA

TESCHEN

Jablunka
Pass

ZILINA

UPPER SILESIA

XXXX
FOURTEENTH
LIST

XXX
VIII

XXX
XVII

CRACOW

Vistula R.

TARNOW

DEBICA

Wisloka R.

GORLICE

Dunajec R.

NOWY SACZ

NOWY TARG

GALICIA

JAROSLAW

XXX
XXII

PRZEMYSL

SANOK

XXX
XVIII

SADOWA

SAMBOR

XXXX
CARPATHIAN
(Remnants)

LWOW

Dniester R.

TARNOPOL

STANISLOWOW

EAST
LITTLE
POLAND

CARPATHIAN MOUNTAINS

TATRA MOUNTAINS

LUBOVINA

SLOVAKIA

HUNGARY

RUMANIA

XXX
XVIII

SOVIET-FINNISH WAR BETWEEN DECEMBER 1939 AND JANUARY 1940

★

Finland, described as a country consisting "almost entirely of natural obstacles to military operations," had been assigned to the Russian sphere of influence by the 1939 Russo–German Treaty, along with Estonia, Latvia, and (later) Lithuania. They were scraps Hitler threw to Stalin to keep him placid while Hitler dealt with Britain and France. Stalin rapidly absorbed Estonia, Latvia, and Lithuania by sending in troops on fake "defense" missions. From Finland Stalin demanded the Karelian Isthmus up to Viipuri, the Finnish portion of the Rybachi Peninsula, and the use of Hango as a Russian naval and air base. The Finns attempted to negotiate, but Stalin, like Hitler in Poland, skipped the niceties and, on 30 November 1939, loosed his air force on Helsinki and Viipuri.

The Finns, with a long history of conflict with Russia, had, to the best of their limited means, prepared themselves. Their armed forces numbered about 300,000 and they were backed up by a Civic Guard (roughly equivalent to the National Guard in America) of 100,000. In addition, there was a women's auxiliary that took on the burden of administration. Although they had little heavy artillery or mechanized equipment, they were sensibly trained, particularly for fighting on their terrain—a land of lakes and forests.

The Mannerheim Line, which blocked off the Karelian Isthmus, consisted of scattered strong points of mutually supporting pillboxes and World War I–type fortifications that had been cleverly constructed to take care of the Isthmus's rugged terrain and heavy woods. In addition, there were lighter fortifications on the southern seacoast and across the roads to the northeast of Lake Ladoga. Along the rest of their eastern border, the Finns could depend only on the rough terrain.

The exact initial Russian plan remains unknown; apparently, it followed the classic Russian style of a mass onslaught along every possible avenue of approach, combined with landings on both the northern and southern coasts; air raids against finish communications, coupled with "terror raids" to break civilian morale; a ground attack all along the frontier, and a Communist revolution within the country.

Attacks against the snow-cloaked Mannerheim Line, pushed with utter disregard for losses, ended in bloody failure in early February. Above Lake Ladoga, the Russians initially broke through on a wide front, but Finnish counterattacks at Pitkaranta forced the surrender of a Russian division and tank brigade in February. In other Russian operations (taken from south to north), two divisions were practically wiped out at Tolvajarvi; the Ilomantsi advance was blocked; the 54th Division, surrounded at Kuhmo, was almost destroyed; Suomussalmi (see next map for detailed description) was a disaster; the 122nd Division reached Kemijarvi, only to be chased back on the 88th Division, and the two stalled at Markajarvi.

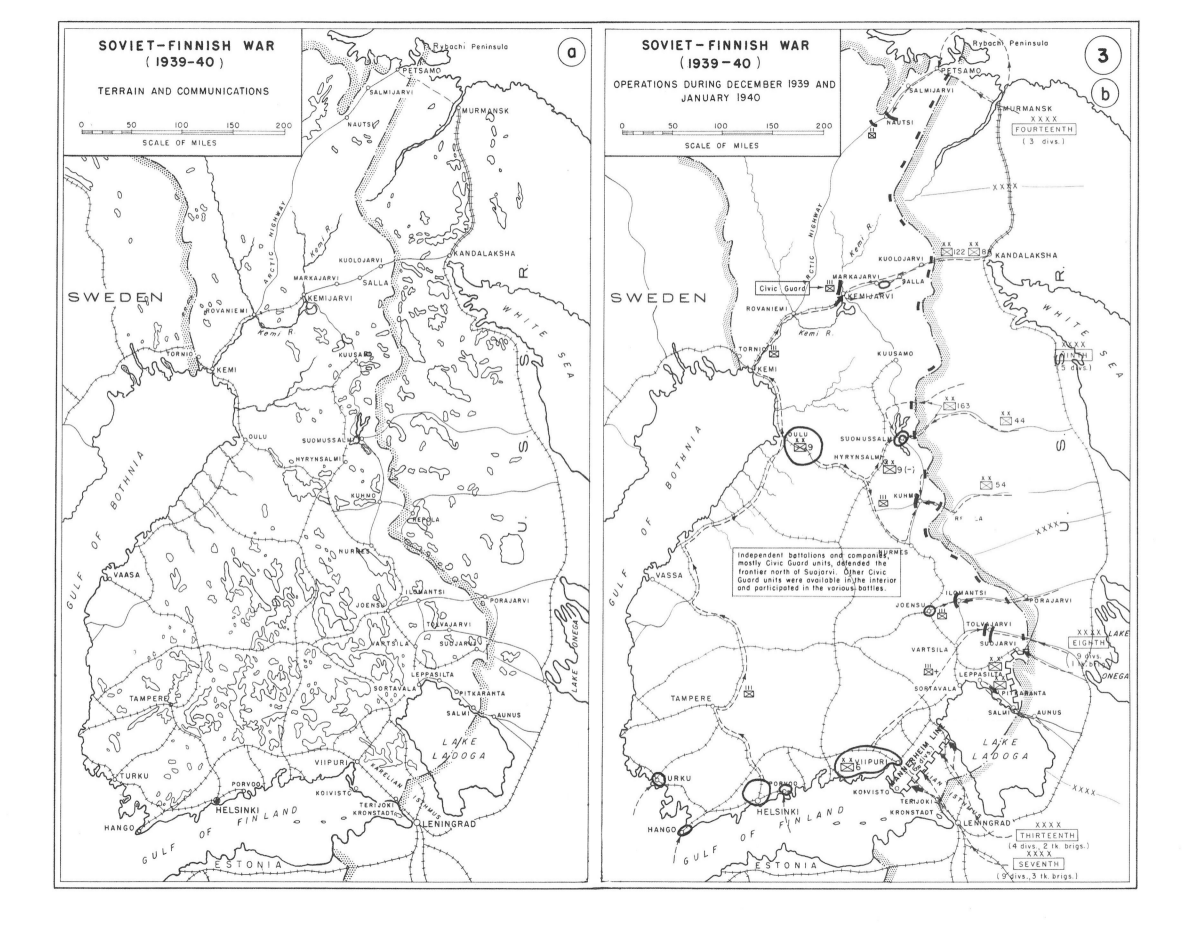

BATTLE OF SUOMUSSALMI

★

The battle of Suomussalmi is one of the great military classics—an astonishing David and Goliath story—that has been unjustly neglected in military histories.

The Russian 163rd Division entered Finland in two columns. Fresh from the Ukraine, it was neither trained nor equipped for sub arctic operations. Its heavy weapons and equipment were handicaps on the poor, narrow Finnish frontier roads. The terrain around Suomussalmi was a monotonous jumble of lake, forest, and swamp, disorienting to anyone but a native. The woods were choked with four feet of snow, restricting movement and visibility; the temperature frequently dropped below minus 40°F; blizzards were common, and daylight lasted for only a few hours. The frozen lakes were the only open spaces. Local Civic Guards units—almost invisible in their white overalls and silent on their skis—hunted the Russian columns, and anything that could give the enemy shelter was burned.

On 7 December, the two columns of the 163rd Division linked up at Suomussalmi, and while the Russians paused, infantry units of the Finnish 9th Division began arriving and attacked on 11 December. The Russians were pounded and ambushed as they tried to escape. On 22 December the Russian 44th Division also arrived at Suomussalmi, and they too became trapped in the killing zone, victim of accurate Finnish artillery. On the 27th, the Finns attacked from all directions. First the 163rd Division was annihilated, and then the Finns turned their attention to the 44th. It was cut up into smaller and smaller groups which, although they resisted tenaciously, were mopped up. The Russians started

the battle with a 3:1 superiority, but when it was over 27,500 were killed or frozen to death, compared to the Finns 900 killed and 1,770 wounded.

After their early defeats, the Russians regrouped. Fighting Finns in the forests would only lead to defeat, whereas the Karelian Isthmus, close enough to Leningrad to assure plentiful supplies, offered a more promising prospect. The resulting operation was not subtle. Beginning on 1 February 1940, there were four or five major attacks every day. Supporting artillery fire was reported to have reached the rate of 300,000 shells each day—one of the heaviest bombardments ever recorded. Large numbers of supporting aircraft, and over thirteen divisions made the main effort between Lake Kuolema and Lake Muola. Although Russian casualties were enormous, the Finns could not take punishment at this level and on 13 February they gave way near Summa. The Russians pushed ahead against stubborn rearguard resistance and cut off the key fortress of Koivisto. By 1 March, the Finnish right wing and center had been pushed back to the outskirts of Viipuri where its exhausted soldiers were threatened by an attack across the ice of the Gulf of Finland from Johannes. Without hope of any foreign intervention on their behalf, the Finns were forced to capitulate. The Finns lost about 25,000 killed or missing, and 43,000 wounded. Russians losses, although not accurately known, were probably at least 200,000 killed and a proportionate number wounded.

Ironically, Russia benefited from her mistakes in Finland because it lulled Hitler into a complacent belief that Russia could be defeated with comparative ease.

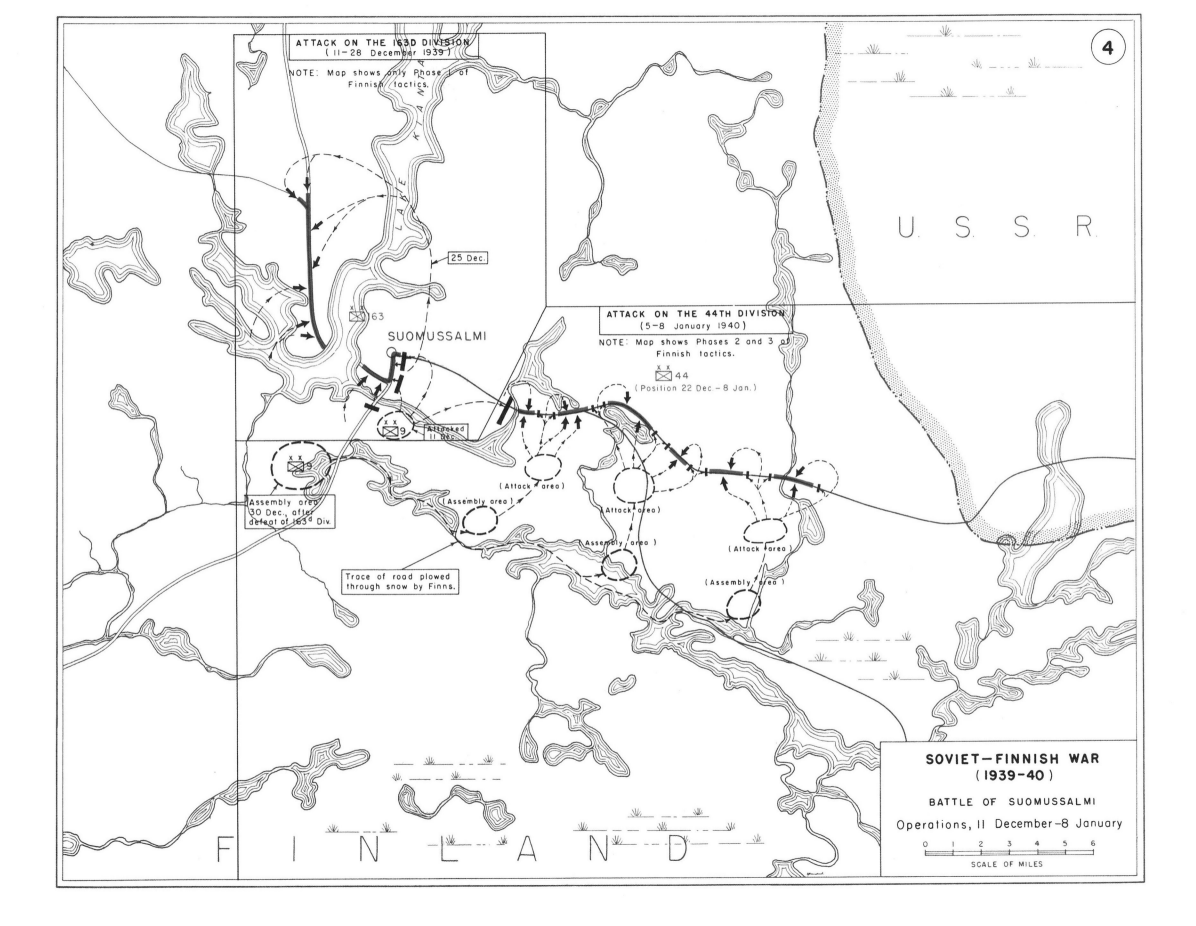

ATTACK ON THE 163D DIVISION
(11-28 December 1939)

NOTE: Map shows only Phase I of
Finnish tactics.

25 Dec.

LAKE KIANTA

XX 163

SUOMUSSALMI

ATTACK ON THE 44TH DIVISION
(5-8 January 1940)

NOTE: Map shows Phases 2 and 3 of
Finnish tactics.

XX 44
(Position 22 Dec.-8 Jan.)

XX 9

Attacked
11 Dec.

XX 9

(Attack area)

(Assembly area)

(Attack area)

(Attack area)

(Assembly area)

Assembly area
30 Dec., after
defeat of 163d Div.

(Assembly area)

(Attack area)

Trace of road plowed
through snow by Finns.

U S S R

F I N L A N D

SOVIET—FINNISH WAR
(1939—40)

BATTLE OF SUOMUSSALMI

Operations, 11 December—8 January

0 1 2 3 4 5 6
SCALE OF MILES

4

CAMPAIGN IN NORWAY, 1940

★

For Germany, Norway offered two great prizes. First, the naval bases along its coast would give the German navy greater freedom of action (the Allied naval blockade of World War I was still fresh in German minds). Second, the German armament industry depended on steady imports of Swedish iron ore, which was shipped by rail to Narvik, and then by freighter down the Norwegian coast to Germany. Ever fearful that the British navy might block this essential traffic, Hitler decided by early February to seize Norway, and on the 21 February 1940, Gen. Nikolaus von Falkenhorst was made commander of the invasion forces.

The German task force weighed anchor late on 7 April, although there were scattered clashes with the Royal Navy, bad weather conditions hindered British reconnaissance. Though warned, the Norwegian government failed to act decisively; coastal units were not alerted, and reservists were only notified of mobilization by regular mail. (It is interesting to note, despite popular belief, that Vidkun Quisling's tiny pro-German party played hardly any part in Norway's downfall.)

Early on 9 April, German warships put lightly armed commando units ashore at Oslo, Kristiansand, Bergen, Trondheim, and Narvik, while parachutists captured Sola airport and Stavanger. In the interim, Denmark had been overrun to provide the Luftwaffe with additional bases.

Though surprised, the Norwegians fought, and the German naval attack on Oslo was bloodily repulsed. But Falkenhorst met the crisis by airlifting troops into Fornebu airport, where they overawed Oslo until the harbor forts were knocked out. Kristiansand and Bergen were captured after heavy fighting. Although German naval forces took heavy punishment at Narvik and elsewhere, the Germans poured in reinforcements, and by 16 April had practically cleared southern Norway. The British navy had been forced by constant air attacks to withdraw its major ships north of Trondheim, while Allied troops, hastily organized and poorly equipped, had landed at the small ports of Andalsnes and Namsos in an effort to recapture Trondheim where, despite stubborn resistance, they were no match for the superior German forces. By 3 May, the Allies had been forced out of central Norway, and the remaining Norwegian troops soon surrendered.

Fighting continued around Narvik, and indeed Allied forces recaptured it and forced the Germans back into the mountains. But by this time the German invasion of northern France had created a desperate situation for Britain and France, and the Allies were forced to withdraw their troops early in June.

The campaign brought Germany immense prestige, insured her supply of iron ore and, by winning air and submarine bases in Norway, had loosened the British naval blockade. Germany had also won a significant psychological victory. It had beaten the Allies on land and at sea, where the potency of German aircraft against Allied shipping had proved decisive. On the other side of the coin, the damage inflicted on the German navy, particularly by Norwegian shore defenses, would take months to repair.

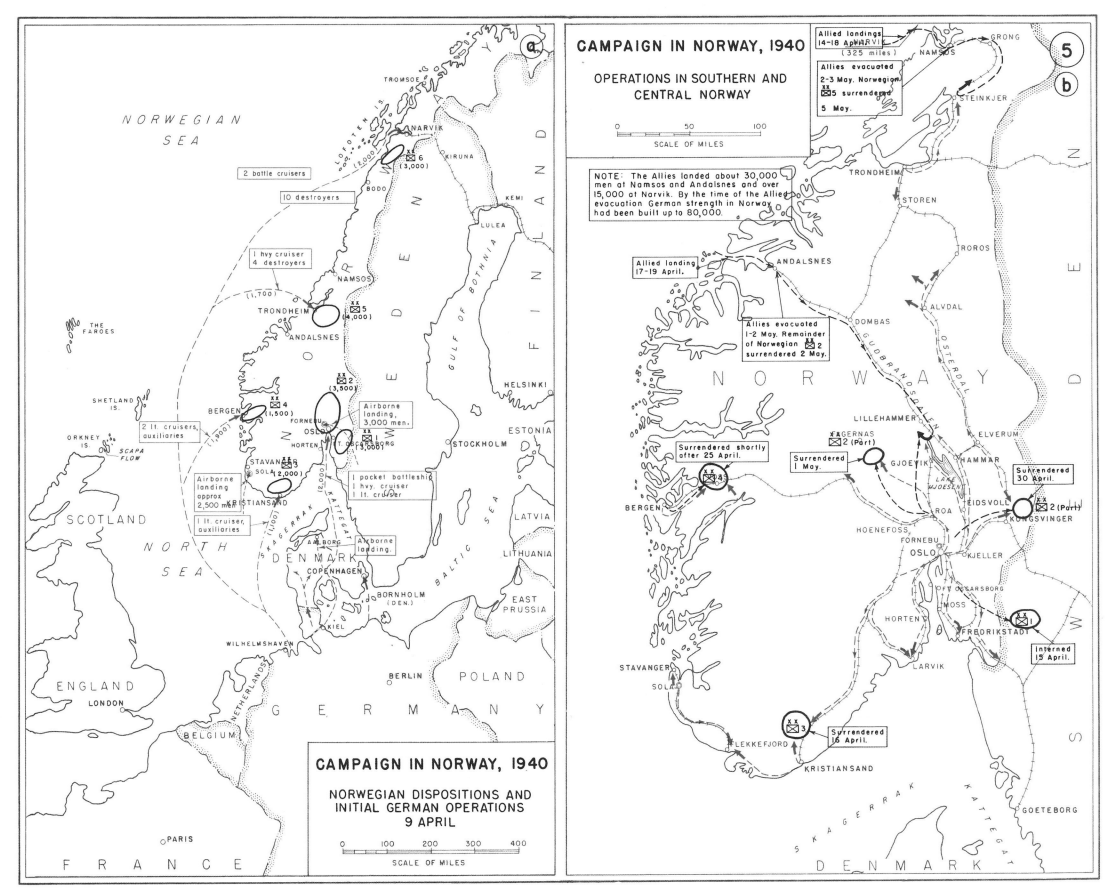

CAMPAIGN IN NORWAY, 1940

OPERATIONS IN SOUTHERN AND CENTRAL NORWAY

Allied landings 14-18 April.
(325 miles)

Allies evacuated 2-3 May. Norwegian 5 surrendered 5 May.

SCALE OF MILES
0   50   100

NOTE: The Allies landed about 30,000 men at Namsos and Andalsnes and over 15,000 at Narvik. By the time of the Allied evacuation German strength in Norway had been built up to 80,000.

Allied landing 17-19 April.

Allies evacuated 1-2 May. Remainder of Norwegian 2 surrendered 2 May.

Surrendered shortly after 25 April.

Surrendered 1 May.

Surrendered 30 April.

Interned 15 April.

Surrendered 16 April.

CAMPAIGN IN NORWAY, 1940

NORWEGIAN DISPOSITIONS AND INITIAL GERMAN OPERATIONS 9 APRIL

SCALE OF MILES
0   100   200   300   400

2 battle cruisers

10 destroyers

1 hvy cruiser 4 destroyers

Airborne landing, 3,000 men.

2 lt. cruisers, auxiliaries

Airborne landing approx 2,500 men

1 pocket battleship 1 hvy. cruiser 1 lt. cruiser

1 lt. cruiser, auxiliaries

Airborne landing.

THE BATTLE OF FLANDERS

★

Hitler's invasion of Poland goaded Britain and France into declaring war. But their mobilization was painfully slow and relied on naval blockade, economic sanctions, fortifications, and a generally defensive strategy. Air power, specifically strategic bombing, was to be the decisive instrument of the new war. Rebuffed in peace talks with the Allies in October 1939, Hitler was determined on a military solution—France and Britain were to be smashed—although many generals in the German high command were decidedly queasy. The major effort, spearheaded by seven panzer and three motorized divisions, was to be made by Army Group A (Rundstedt, with forty-five divisions) through the Ardennes, while Army Group B (Bock, with thirty divisions) applied frontal pressure in the north. Army Group C (Leeb, with nineteen divisions) remained on the defensive in the south . . . The Luftwaffe was to provide tactical support and airborne troops to Bock. Meanwhile, the French were convinced that the Maginot Line was impregnable and that the Ardennes was impassable, and so disposed their forces accordingly. The Allies seem to have expected a repeat of von Schlieffen's plan in World War I and prepared their leftmost armies to move up to the Dyle Line if the Germans came sweeping through Belgium. Numerically the opposing forces were about equal, but the Germans had been combat tested and had, unlike the Allies, placed their faith in tactical air power, the importance of mobility and speed, and the shock impact of massed armor.

Shortly after midnight 9–10 May 1940, Hitler struck with intensive aerial bombardments of air bases in France, Belgium, and Holland, followed by swift ground assaults of Holland (which fell in five days) and Belgium. The bulk of the French Seventh Army began falling back on the 14 May.

Army Group B's main attack was made by the Sixth Army through the Maastricht–Liège area, and in a brilliantly executed airborne operation, the Germans captured the key Belgian frontier fort at Eben Emael and key bridges over the Albert Canal, thus allowing armored divisions to drive toward Liège and the River Dyle.

Between Namur and Antwerp, the Allies had thirty-five of their best divisions, including practically all of the British Expeditionary Force (BEF), in the mistaken belief that the main German thrust would be there. But by the night of the 15 May it was clear that the Ardennes front was the primary target, ad it was here that the weak French Second and Ninth Armies were shredded, forcing the Allies to fall back westward on the Escaut River.

While Bock was overrunning Belgium, the powerful Army Group A moved by the three routes shown to the Meuse, arriving there by nightfall, 12 May. Leading the advance were Gen. Evald Kleist's Panzer Group (five panzer divisions under Guderian and Reinhardt, and three motorized divisions) and Gen. Hermann Hoth's Panzer Corps (two panzer divisions). The Meuse was forced on the 13th and the panzers poured across, throwing off French counterattacks. Gen. André-Georges Corap's Ninth Army, and the left of the Second were shattered. Gen. Maurice Gustav Gamelin (commander in chief of Allied forces) ordered reinforcements to the Ardennes, but they arrived too late.

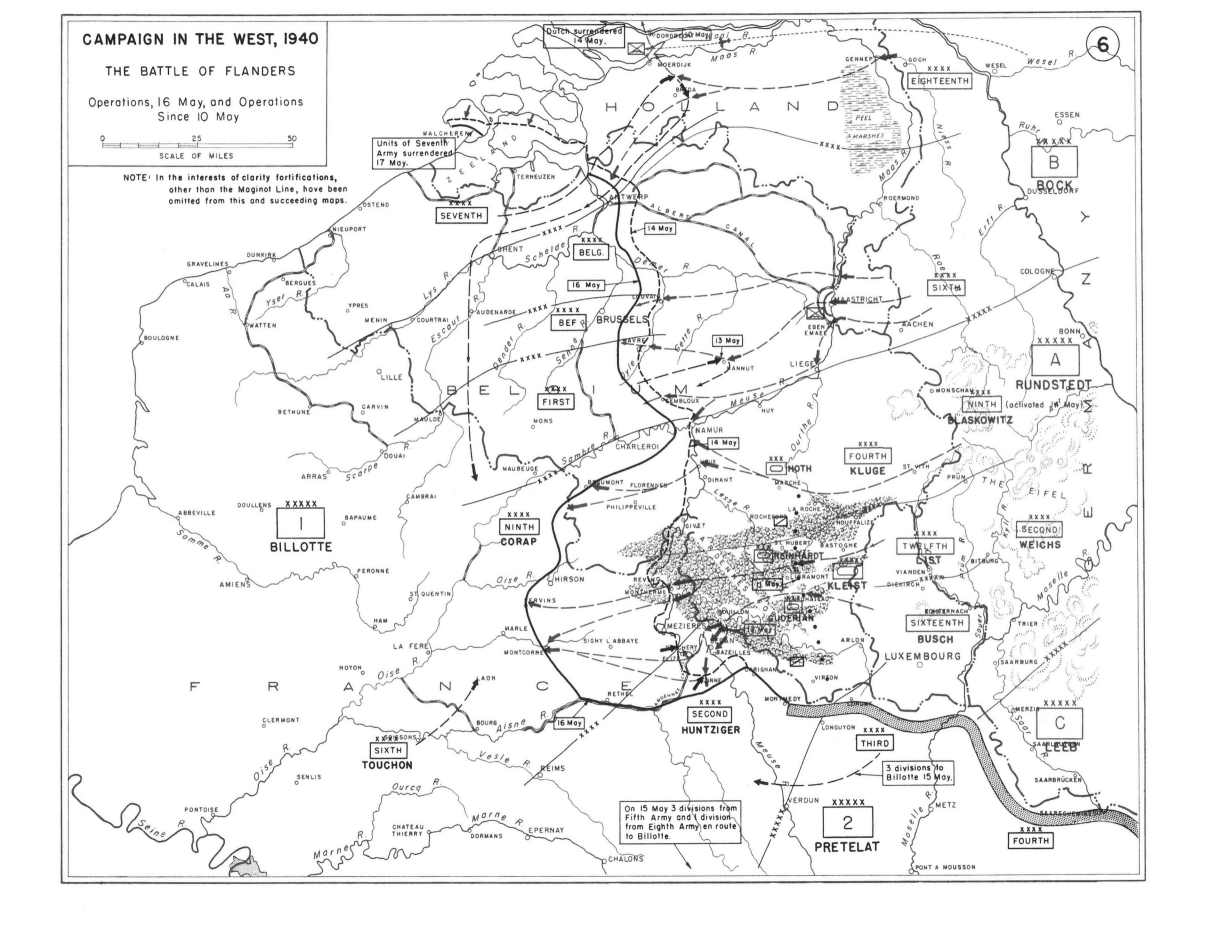

CAMPAIGN IN THE WEST, 1940

THE BATTLE OF FLANDERS

Operations, 16 May, and Operations
Since 10 May

0 — 25 — 50
SCALE OF MILES

NOTE: In the interests of clarity fortifications,
other than the Maginot Line, have been
omitted from this and succeeding maps.

Dutch surrendered
14 May.

Units of Seventh
Army surrendered
17 May.

On 15 May 3 divisions from
Fifth Army and 1 division
from Eighth Army en route
to Billotte.

3 divisions to
Billotte 15 May.

THE BATTLE OF FLANDERS

★

Fear of a French counterstroke from the Verdun–Châlons area unnerved Army Group A, and as a result Guderian was peremptorily ordered to halt. After a violent altercation with Kleist (which List had to mediate), Guderian received permission on 17 May for a "reconnaissance in force," and he hurled his divisions westward; by the 18th he head reached Péronne. It was during this advance that the French Ninth Army made one last futile effort to halt the onslaught. Also, Gen. Charles de Gaulle launched counterattacks against Guderian's south flank, but his weakened armor division could not hold the limited gains made.

Further north, Hoth's Panzer Corps, spearheaded by Rommel's division, drove forward and seized Cambrai (although the French First Army fought well). In Belgium, Bock chased the retreating Allies until, by the 18th, he was at the Dender River. By the 19th, infantry from the Twelfth and Sixteenth Armies had lined the southern flank of the breakthrough as far west as Montcornet, and the German army's high command now lifted the restriction on Kleist's advance. Guderian, closely followed by the motorized infantry corps of Kleist's group, raced along the Somme River toward Abbeville which, late on the 20th, surrendered. Now the corridor to the sea, though tenuous, was a reality. The BEF, its communications with Cherbourg severed, was forced to switch its base to the Dunkirk area. Guderian had seized bridgeheads across the Somme; the motorized infantry had closed up to relieve the panzers on the south flank, and the infantry from Second and Ninth Armies was rapidly moving westward to strengthen the extended south flank.

But on the north side of the penetration, German success was slower and achieved at greater cost. After crossing the Meuse, in contrast to Kleist's drive to the south, Hoth still had to fight his way through the border fortifications. Rommel burst through relatively easily, but Kluge's following infantry had some bloody fighting in the mop-up. Then, as they pushed toward Cambrai, the French First Army put up a vigorous resistance and took a heavy toll. Thus, when Guderian plunged forward on the 19th, Hoth restrained Rommel at Cambrai until more infantry could close up to protect the north flank. Early next morning, Rommel pushed his leading elements to the vicinity of Arras.

Lord Gort, commander of the British Expeditionary Force, had realized that the French First Army could not protect his right and rear. Therefore, he stationed some of his communication-zone troops in the gap between the Somme and the Scarpe, hoping to slow Guderian. He also formed "Frankforce" (parts of two infantry divisions and a tank brigade) and gave it the mission of reinforcing Arras and blocking east-west roads to the south of it.

The Allied command then urged a joint French–British attack south toward the Somme, and the French agreed to aid Frankforce with an attack toward Cambrai, but Frankforce was too weak to do more than bloody Rommel's nose. Hoth massed other divisions and forced the British back to Arras on the 22nd.

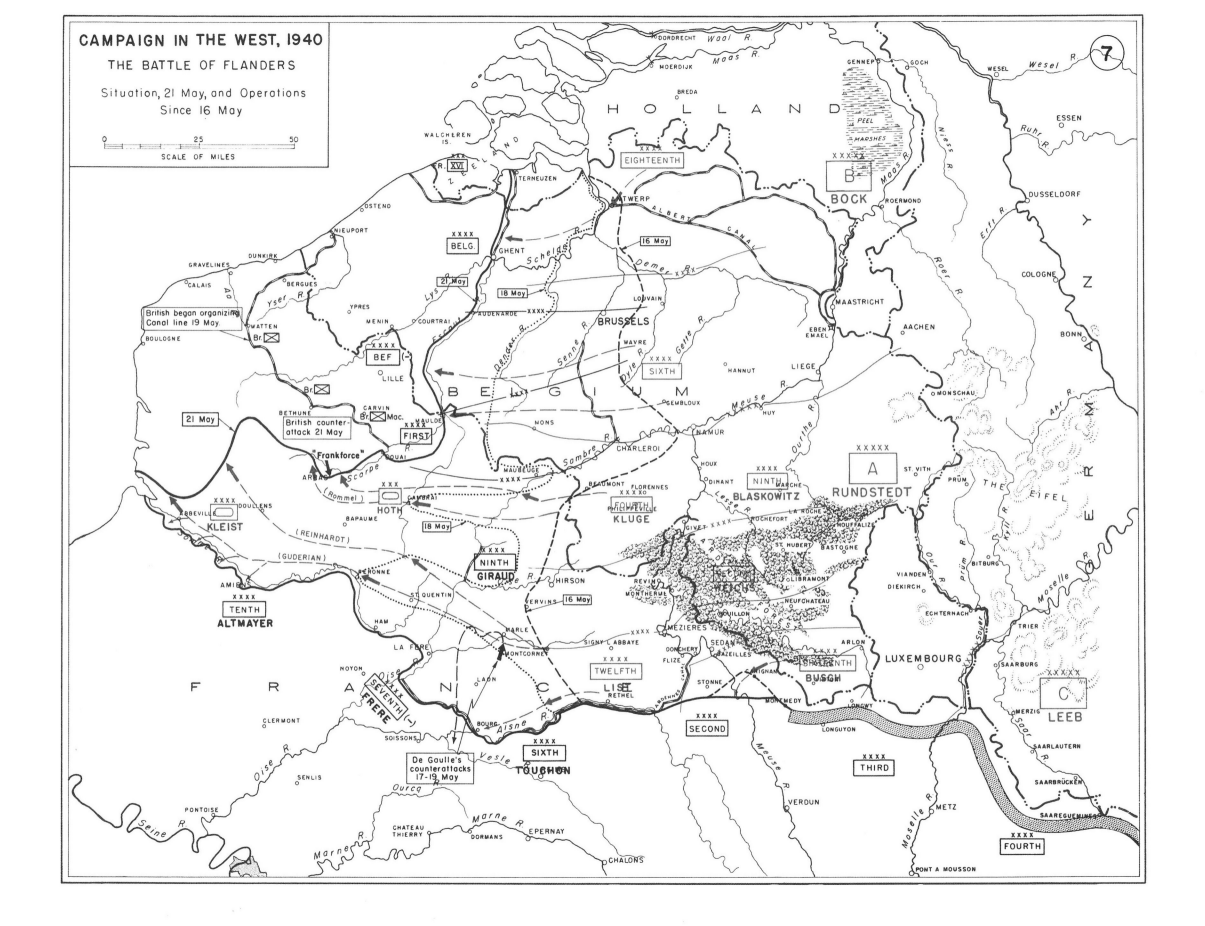

CAMPAIGN IN THE WEST, 1940

THE BATTLE OF FLANDERS

Situation, 21 May, and Operations
Since 16 May

THE BATTLE OF FLANDERS

★

Having driven Frankforce back into Arras on 22 May, Hoth pressed his attack northward, and on the 23rd he had forced the BEF back to Béthune. That day, the French counterattacks on the Somme failed. Meanwhile, Guderian fought his way against stiff resistance northward to Boulogne and Calais. Boulogne was captured on the 23 May, but Calais, recently reinforced from Britain, held out until the 27th. By 24 May, five panzer divisions were exerting pressure on the canal line, which Gort had reinforced, although the chances of holding it appeared slim.

Now, however, Hitler and Rundstedt intervened, and halted the attack of the armored elements for two days, allowing the British to stiffen the canal defenses and to begin a withdrawal to the Dunkirk beachhead. The halt order, one of the most controversial decisions of the war, was issued by Hitler over the protests of his army high command; but the record reveals that Rundstedt, more cautious than the panzer leaders, was concerned with readying his troops for the conquest of the rest of France. Hitler considered the Dunkirk area, with its soft, sandy soil, unsuitable for armor, and perhaps felt the Luftwaffe was a better instrument to finish the job. Furthermore, he seemed almost frightened by the magnitude of his success.

On 24 May, Bock launched a powerful offensive with his Sixth Army which, on the 25th, created a gap between the Belgian right and the British left. Gort now committed all his available forces in an unsuccessful attempt to close the gap. On the 26th, Gort decided to withdraw to Dunkirk, and that night the Royal Navy was ordered to begin the evacuation of the BEF and those French and Belgian forces in the area. On the 28th, Belgium surrendered unconditionally.

Late on 26 May Hitler's halt order was lifted and the panzer divisions attacked the canal line. Near Béthune, Rommel's penetration, linking up with a Sixth Army column, sealed the fate of half of the French First Army, whose leaders had rebelled at the idea of withdrawal. By 30 May most of the British and some of the French were within the Dunkirk perimeter. The previous day, most of the German armor had been withdrawn, and the reduction of the pocket was left to the Luftwaffe and ten infantry divisions under Kuechler's control.

Now the well-organized evacuation proceeded under the cover afforded by the Royal Air Force which, in general, kept the Luftwaffe from having its accustomed free hand. By 5 June, when the Germans finally reached Dunkirk, the Allies had evacuated 338,226 British, French, and Belgian troops.

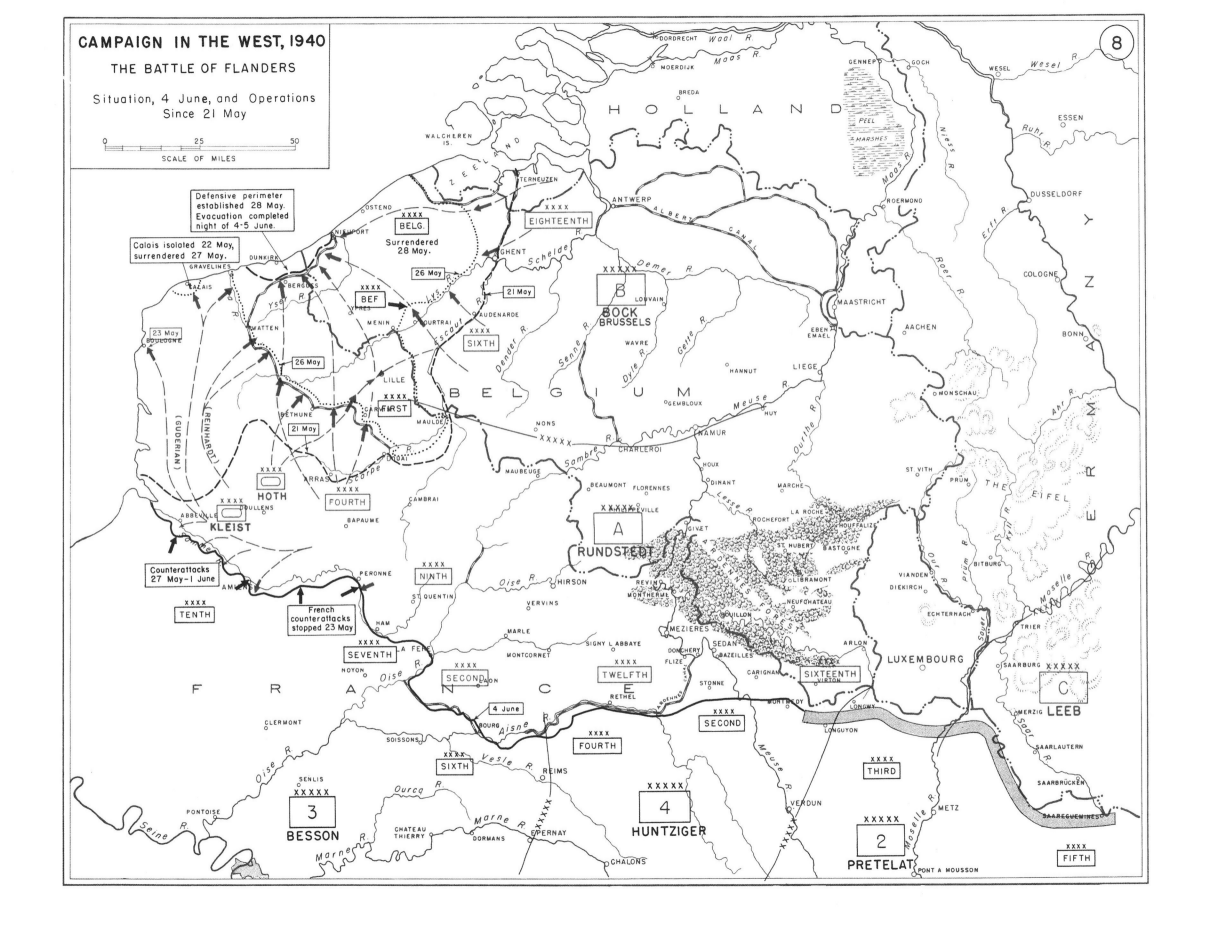

CAMPAIGN IN THE WEST, 1940

THE BATTLE OF FLANDERS

Situation, 4 June, and Operations
Since 21 May

0   25   50
SCALE OF MILES

8

Defensive perimeter
established 28 May.
Evacuation completed
night of 4-5 June.

Calais isolated 22 May,
surrendered 27 May.

23 May

26 May

(REINHARDT)

(GUDERIAN)

Counterattacks
27 May-1 June

French counterattacks
stopped 23 May

21 May

26 May

26 May

21 May

4 June

THE BATTLE OF FRANCE

★

In the short period since the evacuation at Dunkirk, German forces had been redeployed along the Somme and the Aisne and readied for the offensive. It was a remarkable achievement, because in addition to the shifting of forces, considerable reequipping and reorganization were required.

The German battle plan had three main elements. First, Rundstedt, with about forty-five divisions, would make the main attack east of Paris on 9 June to separate French Army Groups 2 and 4 and to pin Army Group 2 against the Maginot Line. Second, Bock was to make the major supporting attack with about fifty divisions. It was to drive rapidly to the Seine. Third, Army Group C, with twenty-four divisions, was to make two attacks; one against the Maginot Line at Saarbrücken, the other at Colmar. Thus, about 120 divisions, backed up by twenty-three others in general reserve, would participate. To combat this seasoned and formidable host, the French had only about sixty-five divisions, many under-strength, and most lacking good morale.

Bock's Fourth Army took one day to establish a firm grip south of the Somme, then plunged headlong for the Seine; by the 9th Manstein's panzers had reached it. Now the German armor was directed westward to cut off French IX Corps, which had been slow in withdrawing from the Somme. Rommel accepted their surrender on 12 June.

The French Fourth Army, defending in depth and making judicious use of local counterattacks, prevented List's Twelfth Army from securing a large enough bridgehead across the Aisne to accommodate the panzers until late in the day, when Guderian was able to cross west of Rethel. There were French counterattacks, but to the west French Sixth Army had been forced back. On the 12th, Guderian broke through at Châlons and raced southward. On Guderian's right, Kleist's armor had crossed the Marne at Château Thierry and was surging southward.

The French retreat had now become a rout, with the Germans hot in pursuit. Bock's armies fanned out to the southwest while Rundstedt moved south and southeast. Hoth's panzers overran Brittany and Normandy. At Cherbourg, Rommel had a brisk encounter with the British, who were evacuating troops debarked there as recently as the 14 June, when hope still flickered for the French cause. Most French troops were south of Paris by the 13 June and the German Eighteenth Army entered the capital on the 14th.

On the 17th, panzer elements from Kleist's and Guderian's groups reached the Loire at Nevers and the Swiss border respectively, isolating the French troops in and behind the Maginot Line. Between Hoth's panzers to the west and Kleist's group to the east, the infantry corps of five German armies pressed southward in a sold mass.

The last week of the campaign was an anticlimax. Pétain asked for an armistice on the 17th, and it was signed on the 22nd, in the same railway carriage at Compiègne that the Germans had signed the armistice after World War I.

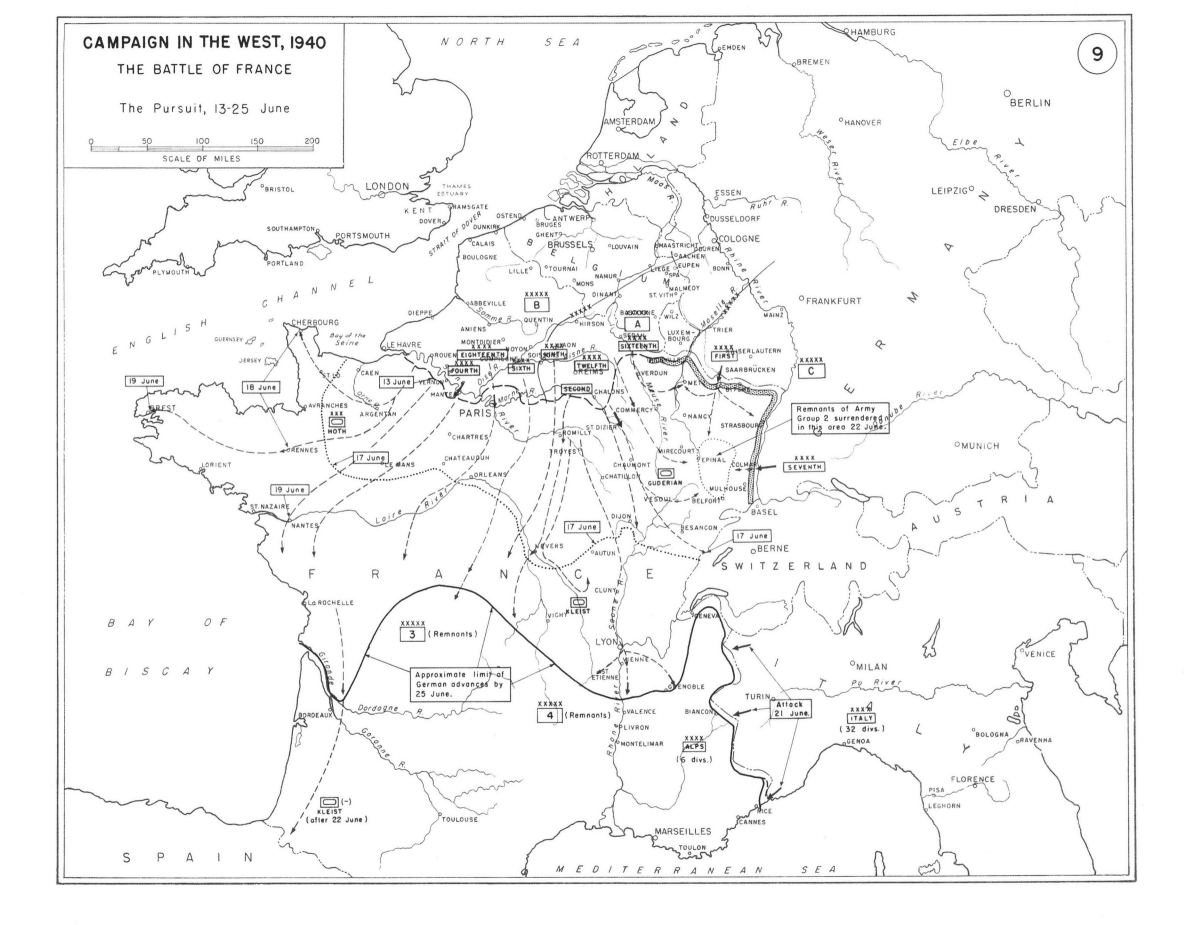

CAMPAIGN IN THE WEST, 1940

THE BATTLE OF FRANCE

The Pursuit, 13-25 June

SCALE OF MILES
0   50   100   150   200

9

Remnants of Army Group 2 surrendered in this area 22 June.

Approximate limit of German advances by 25 June.

Attack 21 June.

ITALY (32 divs.)

ALPS (6 divs.)

KLEIST (-) (after 22 June)

3 (Remnants)

4 (Remnants)

19 June
18 June
13 June
19 June
17 June
17 June
17 June

EIGHTEENTH
FOURTH
NINTH
SIXTH
TWELFTH
SECOND
SIXTEENTH
FIRST
SEVENTH
HOTH
GUDERIAN
KLEIST

A
B
C

NORTH SEA
ENGLISH CHANNEL
BAY OF BISCAY
MEDITERRANEAN SEA

HAMBURG
BREMEN
BERLIN
HANOVER
EMDEN
AMSTERDAM
ROTTERDAM
HOLLAND
LEIPZIG
DRESDEN
ESSEN
Ruhr R.
DUSSELDORF
COLOGNE
AACHEN
DUREN
BONN
EUPEN
MALMEDY
ST. VITH
FRANKFURT
MAINZ
TRIER
LUXEM-BOURG
KAISERLAUTERN
SAARBRUCKEN
MUNICH
AUSTRIA
Wesel River
Elbe River
Rhine River
Moselle R.
Meuse R.
Maas R.
Danube River

LONDON
BRISTOL
SOUTHAMPTON
PORTSMOUTH
PLYMOUTH
PORTLAND
KENT
DOVER
RAMSGATE
Thames Estuary
Strait of Dover
OSTEND
DUNKIRK
CALAIS
BOULOGNE
BRUGES
GHENT
ANTWERP
BRUSSELS
LOUVAIN
LILLE
TOURNAI
MONS
NAMUR
LIEGE
SPA
DINANT
BELGIUM
GUERNSEY
JERSEY
CHERBOURG
Bay of the Seine
LE HAVRE
DIEPPE
ABBEVILLE
Somme R.
AMIENS
MONTDIDIER
QUENTIN
HIRSON
BASTOGNE
WILZ
SEDAN
LAON
SOISSONS
Aisne R.
Oise R.
ROUEN
VERNON
MANTES
PARIS
REIMS
CHALONS
COMMERCY
VERDUN
METZ
NANCY
STRASBOURG
EPINAL
COLMAR
MULHOUSE
BASEL
ST. LO
CAEN
Orne R.
ARGENTAN
AVRANCHES
BREST
RENNES
LORIENT
ST. NAZAIRE
NANTES
CHARTRES
CHATEAUDUN
LE MANS
ORLEANS
Loire River
Seine River
Marne R.
ST. DIZIER
ROMILLY
TROYES
CHAUMONT
CHATILLON
MIRECOURT
VESOUL
BELFORT
BESANCON
DIJON
AUTUN
NEVERS
Saone R.
CLUNY
VICHY
LYON
ST. ETIENNE
VIENNE
GRENOBLE
GENEVA
BERNE
SWITZERLAND
Rhone River
Gironde
Dordogne R.
Garonne R.
LA ROCHELLE
BORDEAUX
TOULOUSE
VALENCE
LIVRON
MONTELIMAR
TURIN
BIANCON
NICE
CANNES
MARSEILLES
TOULON
MILAN
Po River
GENOA
VENICE
BOLOGNA
RAVENNA
FLORENCE
PISA
LEGHORN
ITALY
SPAIN
FRANCE
GERMANY

INVASION OF YUGOSLAVIA AND GREECE

★

Having missed out on any spoils of war from the fall of France, and piqued by Hitler's occupation of Rumania, Mussolini greedily eyed Greece. He had seized Albania in 1939, and on 28 October 1940 his armies invaded Greece, only to be repulsed in November. The Greeks, although short on equipment were very high on morale and mountain-fighting skills. A second Italian offensive on 9 March also failed, but there were ominous indications in Bulgaria of German troop movements.

On 5 March 1941, Britain moved 50,000 troops into Greece from North Africa (she had occupied Crete in October 1940), and on 27 March 1941 Hitler's attempted staged *coup d'état* in Yugoslavia failed. His response was to crush Yugoslavia. On 6 April the bombing of Belgrade paralyzed the Yugoslav high command and shattered communications; the city fell on 12 April, and was followed by Sarajevo on the 17th. During their lightning strike on Yugoslavia the Germans had lost a mere 558 men.

Lt. Gen. Sir Henry Maitland Wilson, commander of British forces in Greece, occupied the Aliakmon Line in the east, and he was well aware how easily it could be outflanked by a concerted drive the Monastir Gap in the center. Ahead of him, the Greek Second Army held the Metaxas Line, which he realized could easily be outflanked on its left, and the Greek First Army, holding a line over to the east in Albania, refused to fall back and block Monastir.

Early on 6 April, the Luftwaffe struck Piraeus, the port for Athens, and quickly destroyed it. By 9 April German troops were driving toward Monastir and Albania, while over at the Metaxas Line, XVIII Corps of List's Twelfth Army, spearheaded by mountain divisions, was fighting its way through; 2nd Panzer rounded the left of the Greek line and entered Salonika. The XXX Corps on the east subdued Thrace, and the entire eastern Macedonian front collapsed with the surrender of the Greek Second Army.

The remainder of the fighting was essentially a pursuit. General Alexander Papagos, commander of Greek forces, left it too late to fall back from his position in Albania, and his dispirited and exhausted First Army, cut off by German elements in its rear, surrendered. Papagos recommended to Wilson that the British evacuate Greece, if they did not intend to surrender, and on 17 April, the British began to withdraw. Although they were mercilessly hounded by the Luftwaffe, most managed to get on to the Peloponnesus and were evacuated by the Royal Navy. By 30 April, the last British troops had been either evacuated or captured.

Total German casualties were 5,100; the British suffered 11,840, and the Germans also took 270,000 Greeks and 90,000 Yugoslavs prisoners. Once again, bold, aggressive tactics and the skillful use of armor had paid handsome dividends. His south flank now secured, Hitler began to redeploy his troops for the imminent invasion of Russia.

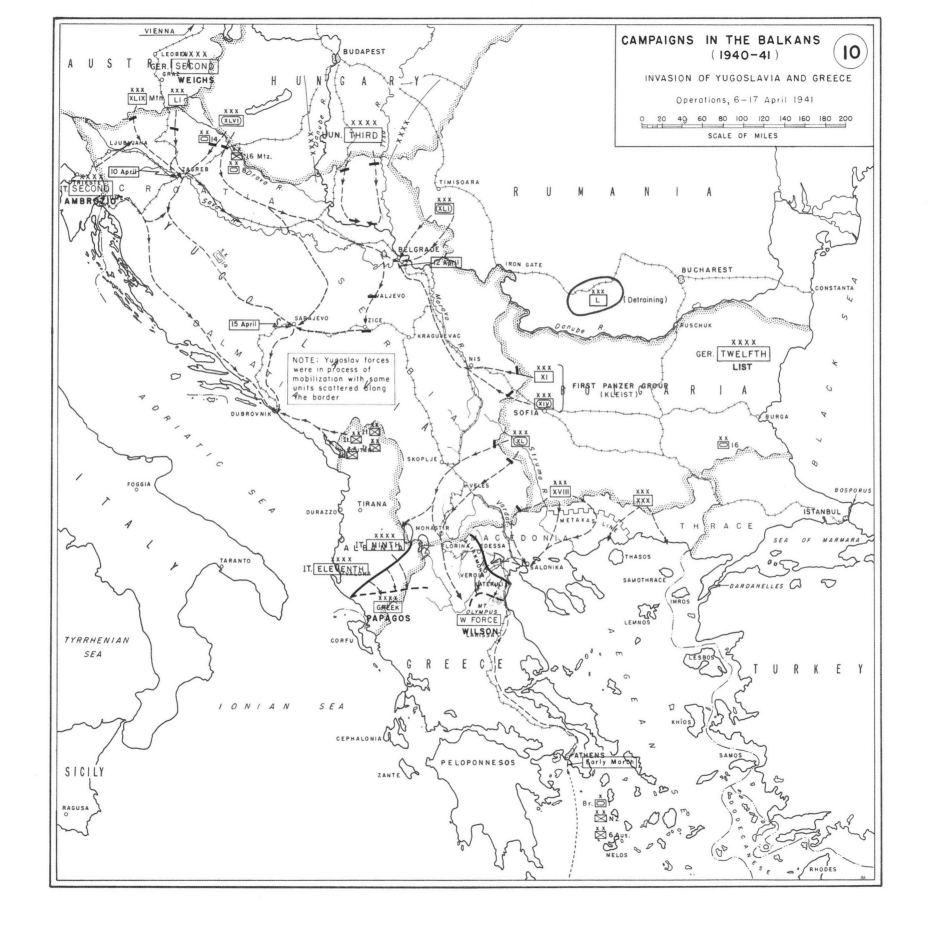

CAMPAIGNS IN THE BALKANS
(1940-41)

10

INVASION OF YUGOSLAVIA AND GREECE

Operations, 6-17 April 1941

0 20 40 60 80 100 120 140 160 180 200
SCALE OF MILES

NOTE: Yugoslav forces were in process of mobilization with some units scattered along the border

CONQUEST OF CRETE

★

The British failure to garrison Crete strongly in early 1941 was not an oversight. They appreciated the importance of the island, but higher priority demands in Cyrenaica and Greece sapped the limited resources available. The original garrison of Crete received no sizable reinforcements until the battered remnants of Wilson's force evacuated from Greece arrived in April 1941. The enlarged garrison, under the command of New Zealander Maj. Gen. Bernard C. Freyberg, had few antiaircraft guns, only about twenty artillery pieces, twenty-four tanks, and no aircraft (the RAF had withdrawn to Egypt in May). Worse still, the loss of air bases in Cyrenaica, 200 miles south, precluded any fighter challenge to the Luftwaffe. Another critical deficiency was lack of transport which, coupled with the bad roads, prevented the creation of a central mobile reserve. Freyberg therefore had to divide his troops between Maleme, Khania, Rethymnon, and Herakleion.

Although Hitler was almost entirely focused on the coming Russian campaign, Göring persuaded him to agree to an airborne assault on Crete with the hope of breaking British control in the eastern Mediterranean. The 7th Parachute Division and 5th Mountain Division were commanded by Lt. Gen. Kurt Student, Germany's leading exponent of airborne warfare. He, and all naval and tactical air support forces, was controlled by Fourth Air Force, in Greece.

After intensive air strikes, Student's assault elements, consisting of two parachute regiments, each preceded by two companies of glider-borne troops, began landing at 0800 on 20 May in the Maleme—Khania area. The defending New Zealanders inflicted heavy casualties on the paratroopers and when night fell remained in control of Maleme airfield and Galatos. Meanwhile, Student's second wave (also two regiments) had been dropped at Rethymnon and Herakleion that afternoon where it suffered even heavier casualties. By the afternoon of 21 May, the German, in desperation, began landing the 5th Mountain Division at Maleme, even though it was under British fire. This tipped the balance, and the airfield was captured, the defenders being driven up into the mountains and toward Khania. Now German reinforcements could flow in freely.

On 28 May, Freyberg ordered a withdrawal to Sfakia on the south coast and ultimate evacuation. When the Germans arrived at Herakleion, the defenders had gone, but the garrison at Rethymnon was forced to surrender on the 30th. Meanwhile, the exhausted British force from Khania withdrew into the mountains, and on the 31st, the Germans closed on Sfakia, only to discover that the Royal Navy had evacuated much of the force.

British casualties totaled 17,325 (including 2,011 naval losses and 11, 835 prisoners). The Germans losses of 5,678 and the shattering of the 7th Division horrified Hitler who never again contemplated the use of airborne forces to any significant level. Concerned with Russia, he withdrew air and ground elements and allowed Britain eventually to regain control over the eastern Mediterranean.

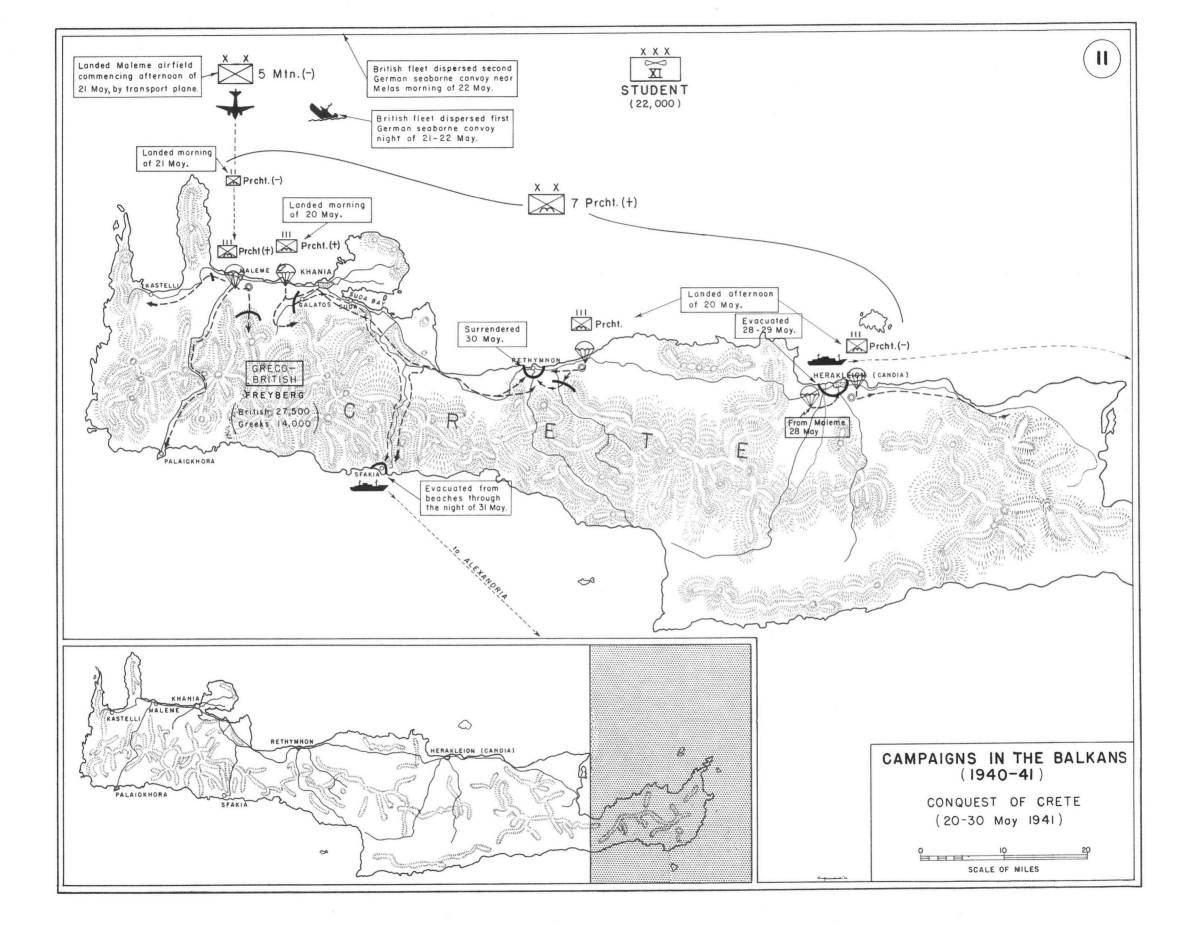

II

XXX
⊠⊠
XI
STUDENT
(22,000)

Landed Maleme airfield commencing afternoon of 21 May, by transport plane.

⊠⊠ 5 Mtn. (−)

British fleet dispersed second German seaborne convoy near Melas morning of 22 May.

British fleet dispersed first German seaborne convoy night of 21-22 May.

Landed morning of 21 May.

⊠ Prcht. (−)

Landed morning of 20 May.

⊠⊠ 7 Prcht. (†)

⊠ Prcht (†)   ⊠ Prcht. (†)

KASTELLI

MALEME   KHANIA

GALATOS

SUDA BAY

SUDA

Landed afternoon of 20 May.

⊠ Prcht.

Surrendered 30 May.

RETHYMNON

Evacuated 28-29 May.

⊠ Prcht. (−)

HERAKLEION (CANDIA)

GRECO-BRITISH
FREYBERG
(British 27,500)
(Greeks 14,000)

C   R   E   T   E

From Maleme 28 May

PALAIOKHORA

SFAKIA

Evacuated from beaches through the night of 31 May.

TO ALEXANDRIA

KHANIA
KASTELLI   MALEME
RETHYMNON
HERAKLEION (CANDIA)
PALAIOKHORA
SFAKIA

CAMPAIGNS IN THE BALKANS (1940-41)

CONQUEST OF CRETE
(20-30 May 1941)

0   10   20
SCALE OF MILES

TERRAIN AND COMMUNICATIONS

★

It is ironic that neither the German nor Russian armies began this campaign—probably in sheer size, the greatest in history—with any definite overall strategic concept. Russians dispositions remain a puzzle. Troops were massed at the border as though for eventual offensive action (as may have been Stalin's intention) with few, if any, plans for defense in depth. It was only after the war that the great patriotic myth was put in place that Stalin had somehow always meant to retreat and draw the German armies to their eventual doom deep in the hinterland.

Hitler's directive of 18 December 1940 had stressed that Russia was to be crushed with lightning speed, with the bulk of the Russian army to be destroyed in place, to prevent organized units retiring into the vastness of the Russian interior. Army Group South (Rundstedt), operating below the Pripet Marshes would advance toward Kiev with the intention of cutting off all Russian forces in the western Ukraine before they could escape across the Dnieper River. Army Group Center (Bock) would make the main attack up the traditional Warsaw–Smolensk–Moscow invasion route, using its two panzer groups to envelop and destroy the large Russian forces massed on its front. Army Group North (Leeb) was to destroy the Russian forces in the Baltic area and then advance on Leningrad.

Beyond these initial missions, there seems to have been little agreement between Hitler and his military commanders. Hitler's objectives were largely dictated by political and economic factors. Leningrad was important to him because it meant the Baltic would fall under German control; Ukraine would provide wheat; the Caucasus, oil. The German general staff wanted a single-minded push on Moscow, the political center of Russia, and the site of much of its armament industry. For these reasons, the generals thought the Russians would commit the flower of their army to the city's defense, giving the Germans an opportunity to destroy it in a short period of aggressive warfare. No definite agreement was ever reached, and often the German advance was managed on a day-to-day basis reflecting Hitler's vacillations.

Hitler had increased the number of his panzer divisions, largely by cutting the number of tanks in each one, which reduced their capability for sustained combat. At the same time Germany's armament industry had not been geared up to full-scale wartime output, while many factories were being diverted from army over to naval and air force requirements in preparation for the planned invasion of Britain that would follow the triumphant conquest of Russia. Meanwhile, the Navy and much of the Luftwaffe were still engaged in fighting the British, which meant that Hitler would be fighting on two fronts.

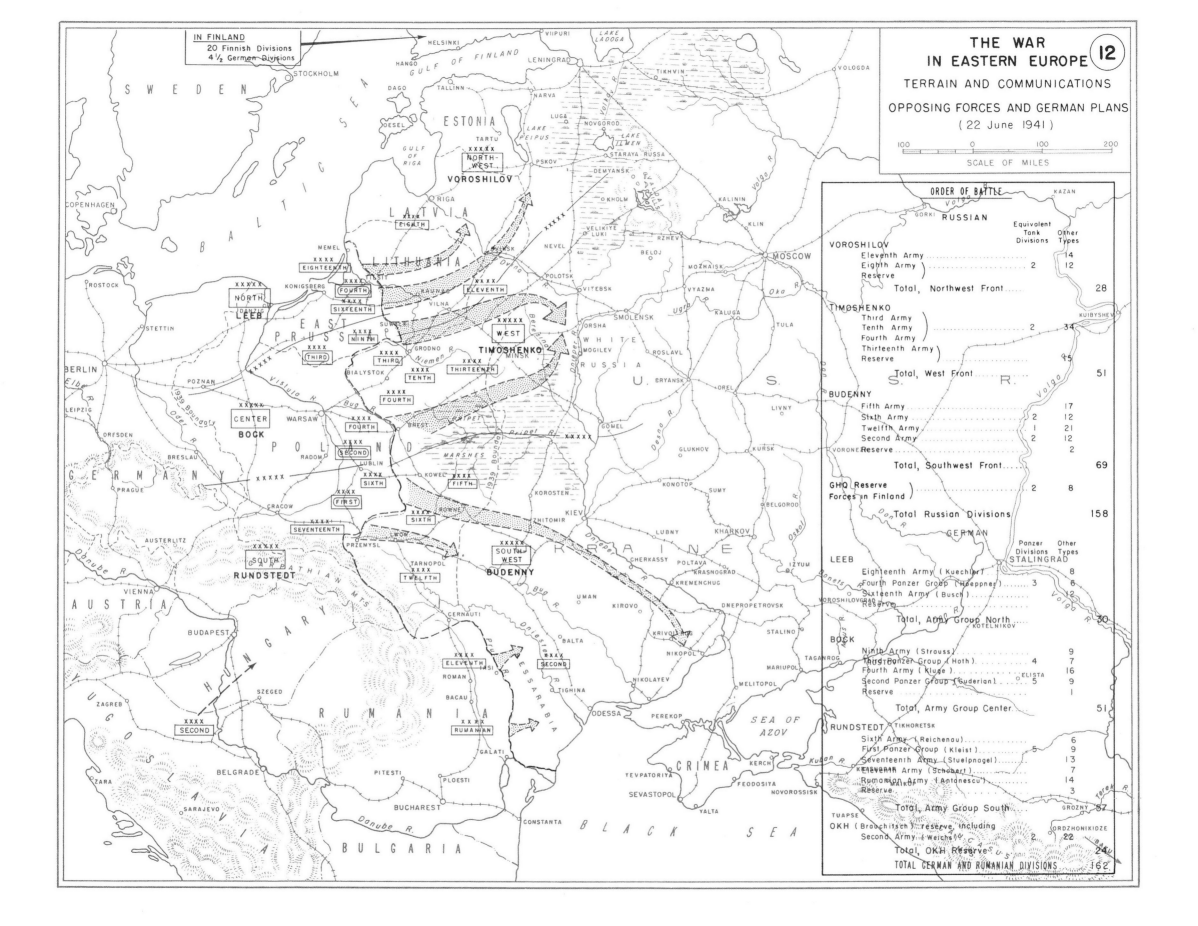

THE WAR IN EASTERN EUROPE 12

TERRAIN AND COMMUNICATIONS

OPPOSING FORCES AND GERMAN PLANS

(22 June 1941)

100   0   100   200

SCALE OF MILES

ORDER OF BATTLE

RUSSIAN

	Equivalent Tank Divisions	Other Types
VOROSHILOV		
Eleventh Army		14
Eighth Army)	2	12
Reserve)		
Total, Northwest Front		28
TIMOSHENKO		
Third Army)		
Tenth Army)	2	34
Fourth Army)		
Thirteenth Army)		
Reserve		15
Total, West Front		51
BUDENNY		
Fifth Army		17
Sixth Army	2	12
Twelfth Army	1	21
Second Army		12
Reserve		
Total, Southwest Front		69
GHQ Reserve)	2	8
Forces in Finland)		
Total Russian Divisions		158

GERMAN

	Panzer Divisions	Other Types
LEEB		
Eighteenth Army (Kuechler)		8
Fourth Panzer Group (Hoeppner)	3	6
Sixteenth Army (Busch)		12
Reserve		
Total, Army Group North		30
BOCK		
Ninth Army (Strauss)		9
Third Panzer Group (Hoth)	4	7
Fourth Army (Kluge)		16
Second Panzer Group (Guderian)	5	9
Reserve		1
Total, Army Group Center		51
RUNDSTEDT		
Sixth Army (Reichenau)		6
First Panzer Group (Kleist)	5	9
Seventeenth Army (Stuelpnagel)		13
Eleventh Army (Schobert)		7
Rumanian Army (Antonescu)		14
Reserve		3
Total, Army Group South		57
OKH (Brauchitsch) reserve, including Second Army (Weichs)		22
Total, OKH Reserve		24
TOTAL GERMAN AND RUMANIAN DIVISIONS		162

IN FINLAND
20 Finnish Divisions
4½ German Divisions

GERMAN SUMMER OFFENSIVE OF 1941

★

Another peculiarity of the war was that Russia, despite its elaborate spy network, and although warned by Britain, got the whole thing terribly wrong; when the German attack started at 0300 on 22 June, the Russians were completely wrong-footed. Though many units rallied and fought stubbornly (particularly against Army Group South where Russian Fifth Army counterattacks southward of the Pripet Marshes were particularly effective), at command level there was almost a complete loss of control.

By contrast, Army Group Center was highly successful from the start. With effective Luftwaffe support, its two panzer groups smashed through the confused Russians to link up east of Minsk. The trapped masses made desperate but uncoordinated efforts to break out. Some escaped through the panzers' encircling net, but the German infantry, moving closely behind the tanks, efficiently mopped up any remainders. The Minsk pocket yielded 290,000 prisoners, 2,500 tanks, and 1,400 artillery pieces. By mid-July, a second lunge forward by Army Group Center was closing another trapping the vital Smolensk–Orsha–Vitebsk area, which controlled the "dry" route to Moscow between the headwaters of the Dnieper and Divina rivers.

Army Group Center likewise advanced steadily in a series of penetrations and envelopments which destroyed between twelve and fifteen Russian divisions west of the Dvina. Not only had the Russian air force been comprehensively destroyed, but also her tank armies were shattered, reversing the numerical superiority they had originally enjoyed.

By 19 July Army Group Center had closed its trap near Smolensk, taking 100,000 prisoners and 2,000 tanks. The Russians here were highly disorganized, and all sorts of make-shift formations were thrown into the line as desperate stop-gaps. But by now the Germans were also beginning to discover that speedy advances brought supply problems, not made easier by the dusty, rough roads that disabled large numbers of tanks and vehicles.

On 19 July Hitler did something remarkable. Just as things were going so splendidly in the center, he ordered Second Panzer Group from Army Group Center to Army Group South, and Third Panzer, also from Army Group Center, to Army Group North. So, in one move he defanged the most successful part of his attack. Finally, on 21 August, Hitler decided that Moscow was not the central focus of the invasion; it could be taken care of *after* Leningrad had been taken, the Donets Basin occupied, and the Caucasus secured. Hitler's astounding failure to let Army Group Center press home its victorious advance was, for the Russian high command, nothing short of a miracle.

In the meantime, during early August 1941 Army Group South had scored its first major successes, destroying between sixteen and twenty divisions near Uman, and thereafter cleared the pocket that lay within the great sweep of the Dnieper Bend. Von Runstedt now swung his First Panzer Group north to meet Guderian's Second Panzer Group coming south.

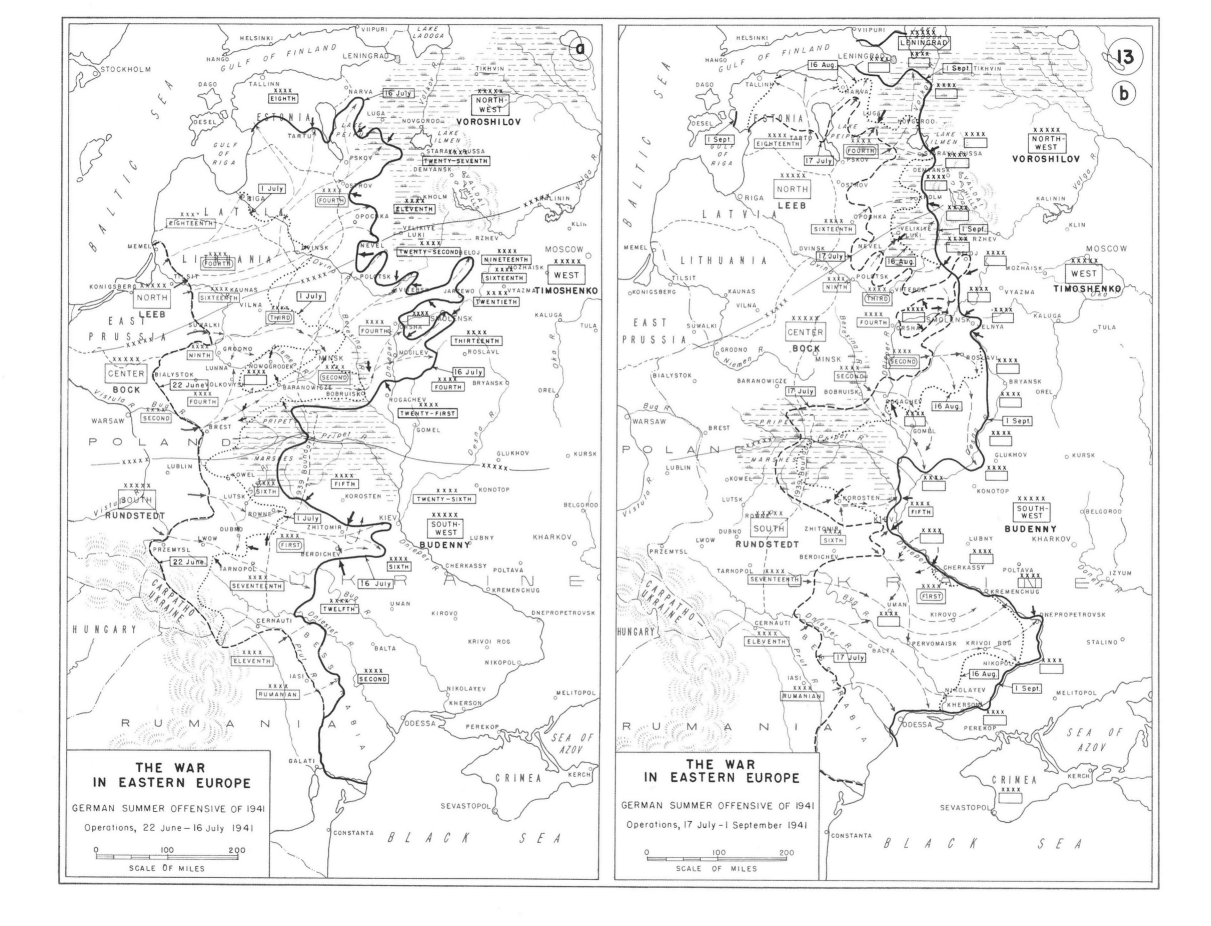

THE WAR
IN EASTERN EUROPE

GERMAN SUMMER OFFENSIVE OF 1941

Operations, 22 June - 16 July 1941

0   100   200
SCALE OF MILES

THE WAR
IN EASTERN EUROPE

GERMAN SUMMER OFFENSIVE OF 1941

Operations, 17 July - 1 September 1941

0   100   200
SCALE OF MILES

GERMAN SUMMER OFFENSIVE OF 1941

★

The southward movement of Guderian's Second Panzer Group was risky because it exposed his left flank to Russian attacks, and his progress was hampered by heavy rain that made the Russian roads into "mud canals." But once Rundstedt and Guderian met up, Kiev fell on 19 September 1941, amid considerable confused fighting, with encircled Russian units attempting to break out while fresh Russian forces tried to break in to rescue them. It was not until the 26th that the surviving Russian pockets of resistance were mopped up. In all, 665,000 prisoners were taken.

As a tactical operation, the reduction of the Kiev pocket was outstanding. The greater part of the Russian forces in the zone of Army Group South had been destroyed, clearing the way for Rundstedt's subsequent drives on Kharkov and Rostov. But, from a strategic point of view, Hitler's diversion of forces to achieve this victory was a major blunder. It delayed the advance on Moscow, which gave the Russians six weeks to strengthen their defenses, and it crippled Second Panzer Group, whose tanks were worn out.

During early September the Russians continued their furious counterattacks in the Smolensk–Vyazma–Yelna area, making slight gains at excessive cost, but giving the Ger-

man command some anxious days. Bock had been stripped of reserves to assist Rundstedt and Leeb, and increased partisan activity was beginning to hamper his supply system.

Leeb's advance, during early September, had finally closed up to Leningrad, which Hitler had regarded as the "birthplace" of Bolshevism and was convinced that once it fell so would Stalin, but once Leeb reached the city's inner defenses Hitler forbade an assault, preferring to reduce it through starvation and artillery fire. Leeb tried to seize the hills south of Leningrad but was frustrated by the terrain and Russian counterattacks. Of Leeb's various shortcomings in this campaign, it was his failure to wipe out the isolated Eighth Army that would prove most damaging.

In the far north, Falkenhorst's XXXVI and Mountain Corps had made initial gains, but soon stalled in the frontier wilderness, where climate and terrain were more formidable enemies than the Russians. By early October, Mannerheim's Finnish troops had regained the territory lost in 1939, and the Finnish government decided to halt. The Russian supplied Leningrad sketchily across Lake Ladoga by boat during the summer and by building a railroad on the lake's ice during the winter.

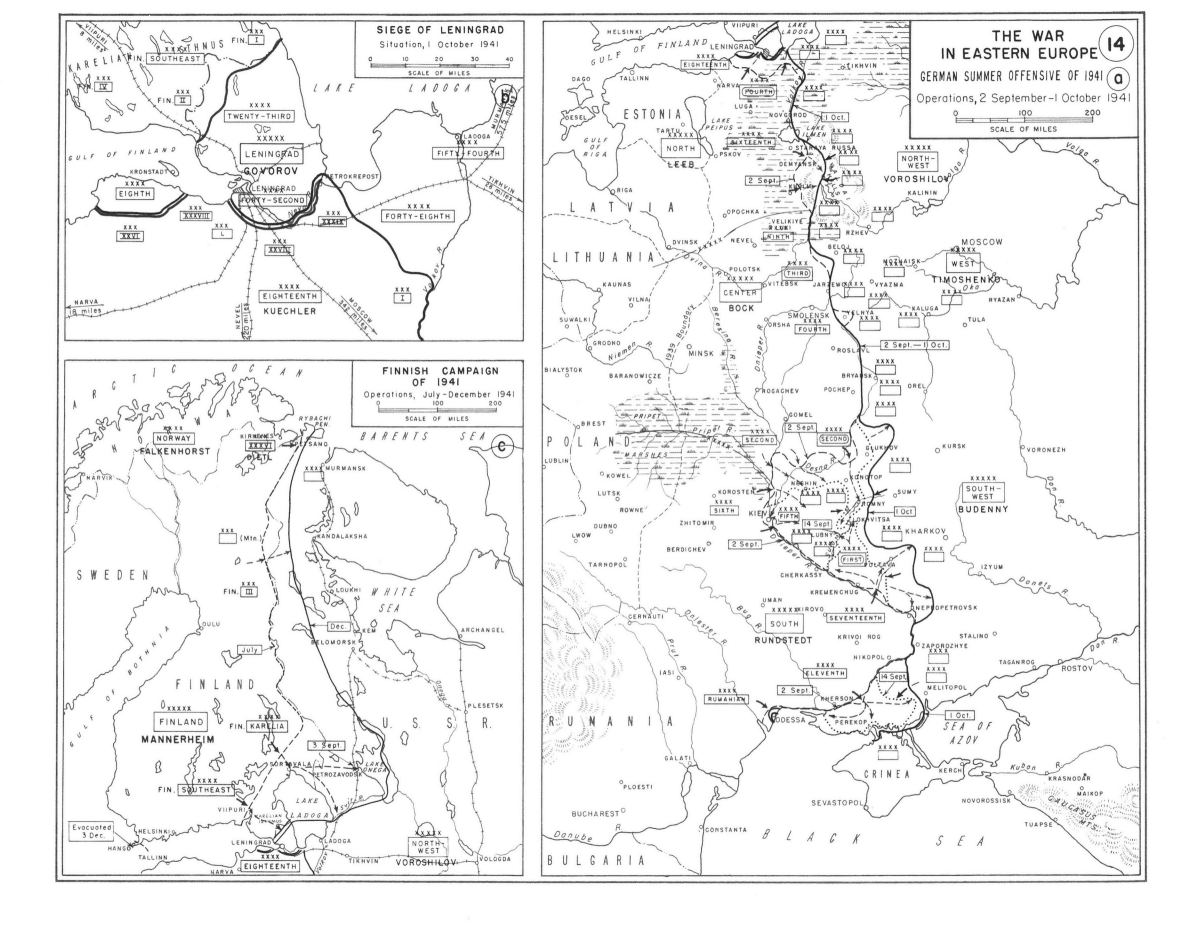

SIEGE OF LENINGRAD
Situation, 1 October 1941

SCALE OF MILES
0 10 20 30 40

THE WAR IN EASTERN EUROPE
GERMAN SUMMER OFFENSIVE OF 1941
Operations, 2 September–1 October 1941

14
a

SCALE OF MILES
0   100   200

FINNISH CAMPAIGN OF 1941
Operations, July–December 1941

SCALE OF MILES
0   100   200

GERMAN SUMMER OFFENSIVE OF 1941

★

With Army Group North and the Finns tightening their grip on Leningrad, the Kiev pocket beginning to develop, and the Eleventh Army approaching the Crimea, Hitler at last became more willing to listen to his army commanders. Plans were drawn up for a decisive offensive against Moscow.

Toward the end of September 1941, in preparation of the offensive, panzer and Luftwaffe units which had been temporarily transferred from Army Group Center to Army Group North were recalled. The Second Army and Second Panzer Group, previously transferred to Rundstedt likewise reverted to Army Group Center. These movements, made as far as possible during darkness to ensure security, consumed considerable time. Many of the panzer divisions had to march several hundred miles to reach their assembly areas. (Guderian, for example, moved 400 miles.) Army Group Center's supply situation was becoming worse, and guerrilla activity in its rear was increasing. Furthermore, the season was growing late, a fact that haunted the more conscientious German commanders.

On 30 September, Guderian's Second Panzer Group attacked, and two days later, the Third and Fourth Panzer Groups jumped off. The Russians were completely surprised. Bock's assault quickly shattered their well-established defensive positions, and in less than a week masses of Russians were hopelessly trapped in pockets at Bryansk and Vyazma. Although these required hard fighting to liquidate, the cache of Russian prisoners—658,000—was enormous. While the infantry cleared the pockets, Bock thrust his panzers forward to keep the offensive going. The Second Panzer Group was to advance through Tula on Moscow; the Third Panzer Group would move on Kalinin, preparatory to an attack on the capital from the northwest; between them, the Fourth Panzer Group would spearhead a secondary frontal attack. Meanwhile, Army Group South was advancing steadily on Rostov, while Eleventh Army methodically reduced the defenses of the Perekop Isthmus.

Then Russia's traditional ally, the weather, intervened. On 7 October the autumn rains began, gradually slowing but certainly not halting the German advance. The Russians threw in all available units to block the Moscow road, but Mozhaisk, the last town before Moscow, fell on 20 October. By early November Guderian was approaching Tula. But it was on their flanks that the Germans made the most progress. In an attack through very difficult terrain, Leeb captured the bauxite-producing area of Tikhvin. Army Group South had taken Kharkov and Taganrog, and was on the outskirts of Rostov, the "gateway to the Caucasus." Furthermore, Eleventh Army, under the skilled leadership of Manstein, had driven superior Russian forces out of their Perekop defenses on 8 November and was now clearing the Crimean peninsula.

With his troops only forty miles from Moscow, Hitler began his plans for its envelopment. Naturally, he ignored the mud in which his troops were floundering; somehow, he and his immediate staff had inspired themselves with the idea that the Russians were about to retreat from the Moscow front in order to save as many as they could of their remaining troops.

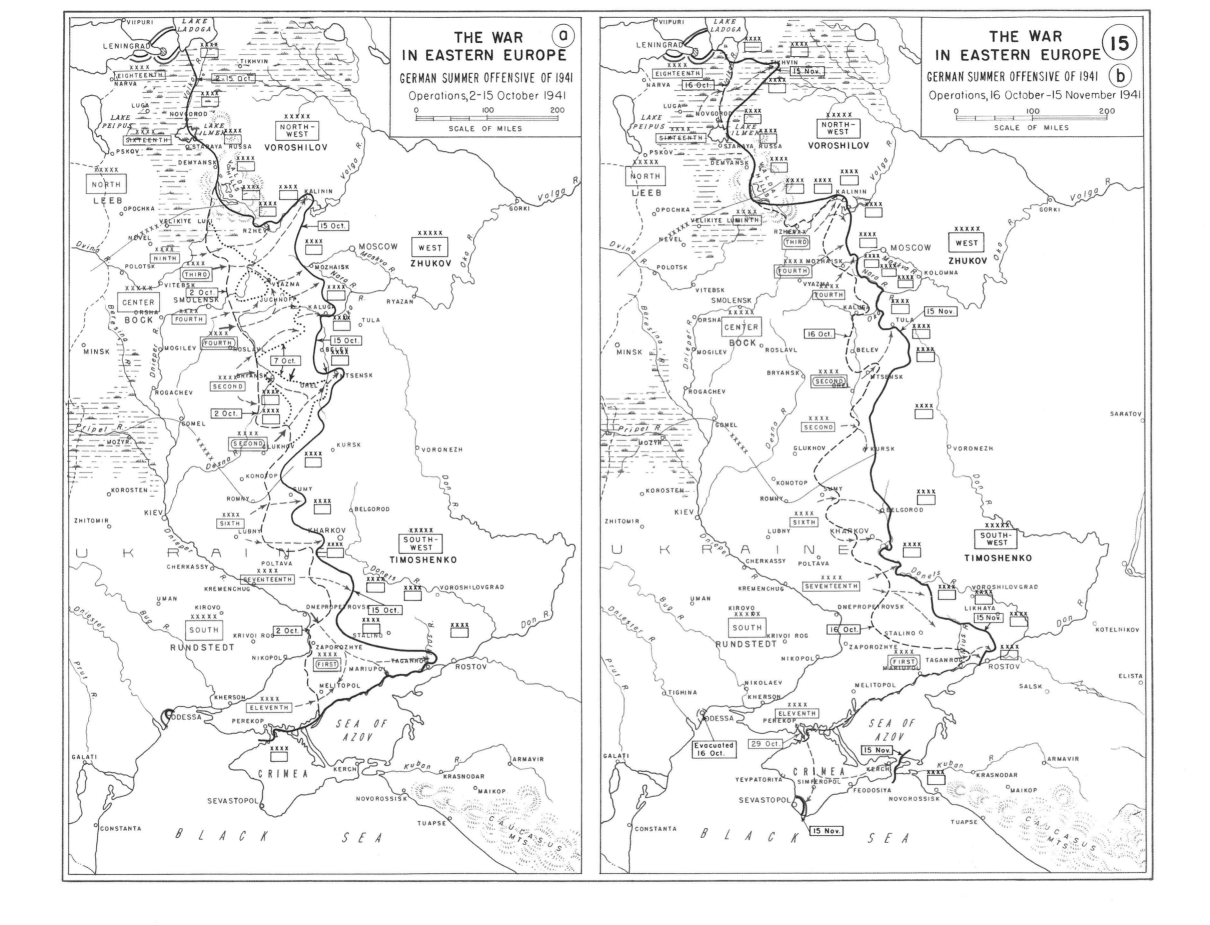

THE WAR
IN EASTERN EUROPE ⓐ
GERMAN SUMMER OFFENSIVE OF 1941
Operations, 2–15 October 1941

THE WAR
IN EASTERN EUROPE ⑮
GERMAN SUMMER OFFENSIVE OF 1941 ⓑ
Operations, 16 October–15 November 1941

THE FINAL DRIVE ON MOSCOW

★

Early in November, the rains dwindled, ushering in a short period of relatively clear, cold weather that proceeded the savage Russian winter. The Germans had but a few weeks to win a decisive victory in 1941.

The German armies were actually drawing on their last reserves of strength and resolution. They had just finished the greatest sustained offensive in military history, killing or capturing Russians in numbers at least equal to their own strength at the beginning of the campaign. But now their infantry divisions had only some 65 percent of their original combat efficiency, their panzer divisions little more than 50 percent. Their tank strength was less than one-third of normal (probably due more to Russian terrain than Russian armed resistance). Officer casualties had been very heavy, and supply was practically on a hand-to-mouth basis. All of Army Group Center's reserves had been committed.

Under these conditions, many German leaders urged the adoption of flexible defensive tactics until reinforcements and supplies could be accumulated for a renewed offensive. Hitler and his supporters spurned the idea. The Russians, they claimed, were almost exhausted, and one more hard blow would finish them off. Moscow was only forty miles away. Second Panzer Group, on the right, was to advance northward from Tula, enveloping Moscow from the southwest. Third Panzer Group would move up to the Volga Canal, and then turn in on Moscow from the northwest, using the canal to cover its left flank. Fourth Panzer Group and the Fourth and Ninth Armies would attack due east.

Army Group Center began its offensive on 15 November with Third Panzer Group and the Ninth Army. Two days later, Guderian attacked, bypassing Tula; on his right, the Second Army likewise began to pile up considerable gains. Astride the Mozhaisk–Moscow road, however, the Russians threw in attack after attack against Fourth Army, holding it on the defensive until 1 December. One Russian unit committed against it was of evil portent for the Germans—an armored brigade equipped with British tanks, evidence that British and American aid was beginning to reach Russia in appreciable amounts.

Russian resistance now stiffened throughout the Moscow area. The Russian Air Force, including several improved types of aircraft previously held in reserve, had been increasing active for some time. Large numbers of Siberian troops, hardened by informal border clashes with the Japanese in Manchuria, were now in action, as were substantial numbers of the new Russian T-34 tank, which was superior to even the best the Germans had. It was the winter, however, that really crippled the German offensive. Temperatures suddenly fell to minus 40°F and below. And because Hitler had planned for a short war, there were no supplies of winter clothing or of winter lubricants for the vehicles. Frostbite casualties soared. A final push carried Third and Fourth Panzer Groups to within twenty-five miles of Moscow, but there, on 5 December 1941, the great offensive ground to a halt.

In the meantime, the Russians had scored their first solid successes. Rostov was encircled and Runstedt advised Hitler that it could not be held. Hitler fired Runstedt, but the city was nevertheless abandoned on 28 November.

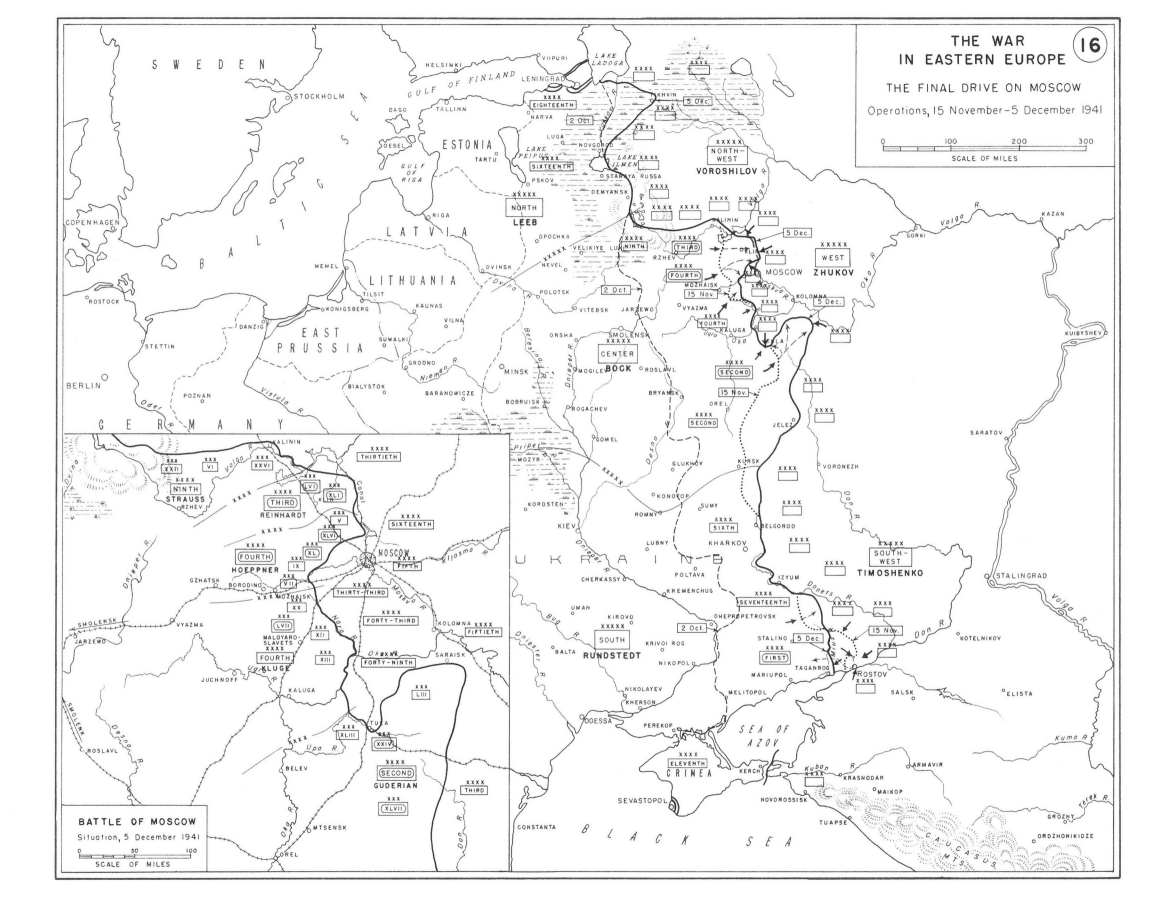

THE WAR
IN EASTERN EUROPE

16

THE FINAL DRIVE ON MOSCOW

Operations, 15 November–5 December 1941

100   200   300

SCALE OF MILES

BATTLE OF MOSCOW

Situation, 5 December 1941

0   50   100

SCALE OF MILES

RUSSIAN WINTER COUNTEROFFENSIVE

★

On 6 December 1941, the Russians opened their counteroffensive against over-extended, freezing, disheartened Army Group Center. Army Group North and Army Group South were already under great pressure. By 8 December, as this Russian drive gained momentum, Hitler approved orders placing the German army generally on the defensive for the winter. Panzer and motorized divisions were to be taken out of the line for rehabilitation. Incessant Russian local attacks, however, made that impossible. The Russian commanders had hordes of troops, accumulated for just this purpose, and no compunction whatsoever about expending them. Their supply lines in the Moscow area were short and in good condition, their troops in high morale and reasonably well equipped for winter fighting. However, this was in large part a raw, new army, hastily assembled and short of all types of heavy weapons. Its commanders lacked the skill to carry out large scale, coordinated operations; also, they had a healthy respect for their opponents.

Hitler at first allowed some freedom of choice as to defensive tactics. But, on 18 December, irked by the loss of weapons and equipment during some local withdrawals, he ordered every inch of ground contested. He also took over direct command, forcing Brauchitsch, Leeb, Guderian, and others, to join Rundstedt in retirement.

Late December 1941 and early January 1942 were times of crisis. Russian attacks had gradually eroded gaps between Second Panzer Army and the Fourth Army, and along the boundaries between Army Group North and Army Group Center. Attacks against Army Group North continued; and Russian amphibious operations poured troops into the Crimea, forcing Eleventh Army to fight for its life. On 15 February, Hitler finally agreed to "dignified" withdrawals by Army Group Center. Then, in late January, the Russians penetrated Army Group South's front near Izyum. In the north, the situation steadily worsened with two corps of Sixteenth Army being almost surrounded at Demyansk. Hitler chose to leave them in place and supplied by air as a magnet for Russian forces that might otherwise have pushed on south and west.

Almost suddenly, in late February, the Russian offensive ran out of steam. Army Group South had managed to contain the Izyum penetration, and Army Group Center had stabilized its right flank. The Russians were in logistical difficulties and had lost heavily in their assaults against the German "hedgehogs"—positions organized for all-around defense. German losses were also great, but they had not yet suffered a major defeat. Their primary misfortune, which was not immediately apparent, was that Hitler now credited his own will power and his order to wage a static defense with having saved the German army.

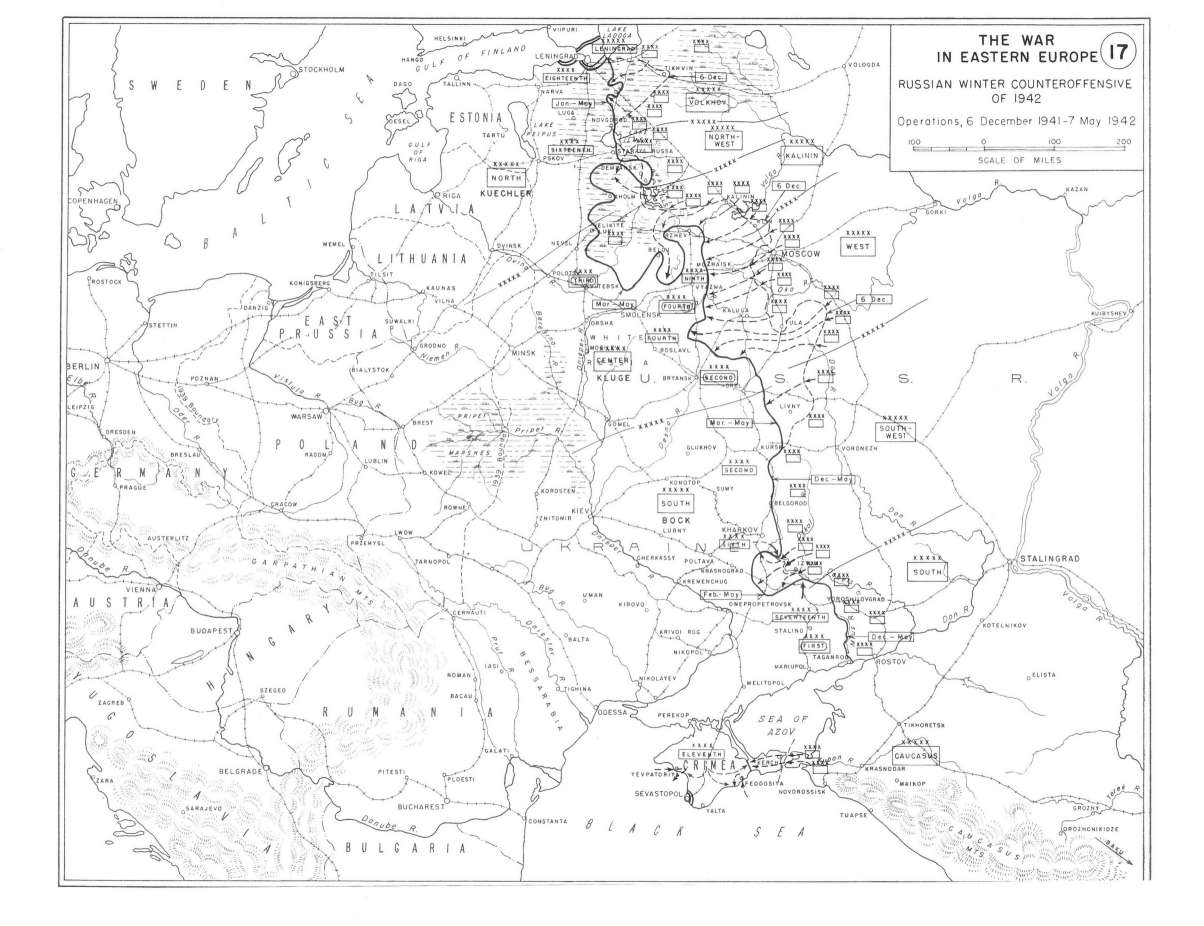

THE WAR
IN EASTERN EUROPE ⑰

RUSSIAN WINTER COUNTEROFFENSIVE
OF 1942

Operations, 6 December 1941-7 May 1942

100   0   100   200
SCALE OF MILES

SWEDEN

STOCKHOLM

BALTIC SEA

COPENHAGEN

ROSTOCK

GERMANY

BERLIN

LEIPZIG

DRESDEN

PRAGUE

AUSTERLITZ

VIENNA

AUSTRIA

HUNGARY

BUDAPEST

ZAGREB

YUGOSLAVIA

BELGRADE

SARAJEVO

ZARA

BULGARIA

SOFIA

BUCHAREST

RUMANIA

HELSINKI

VIIPURI

GULF OF FINLAND

HANGO

TALLINN

ESTONIA

DAGO

OESEL

LAKE PEIPUS

TARTU

GULF OF RIGA

LATVIA

RIGA

LITHUANIA

MEMEL

KONIGSBERG

TILSIT

EAST PRUSSIA

DANZIG

STETTIN

POZNAN

POLAND

WARSAW

BRESLAU

CRACOW

LWOW

PRZEMYSL

TARNOPOL

CARPATHIAN MTS

UKRAINE

VILNA

KAUNAS

SUWALKI

GRODNO

BIALYSTOK

MINSK

BREST

LUBLIN

KOWEL

KOROSTEN

ROWNE

ZHITOMIR

KIEV

LENINGRAD

EIGHTEENTH

Jan.-May

NARVA

LUGA

NOVGOROD

SIXTEENTH

PSKOV

STARAYA RUSSA

NORTH-WEST

DEMYANSK

KHOLM

NORTH

KUECHLER

VELIKIYE LUKI

RZHEV

BELOI

THIRD

VITEBSK

Mar.-May

SMOLENSK

ORSHA

FOURTH

CENTER

KLUGE

ROSLAVL

FOURTH

MOGILEV

POLOTSK

DVINSK

NEVEL

U. S. S. R.

VOLOGDA

TIKHVIN

6 Dec.

VOLKHOV

KALININ

6 Dec.

MOSCOW

WEST

MOZHAISK

VYAZMA

KALUGA

TULA

6 Dec.

GORKI

KAZAN

KUIBYSHEV

BRYANSK

SECOND

OREL

LIVNY

Mar.-May

KURSK

SOUTH-WEST

VORONEZH

WHITE RUSSIA

PRIPET MARSHES

GOMEL

SECOND

KONOTOP

SUMY

GLUKHOV

BELGOROD

Dec.-May

SOUTH

BOCK

LUBNY

CHERKASSY

POLTAVA

KHARKOV

SIXTH

KRASNOGRAD

KREMENCHUG

Feb.-May

DNEPROPETROVSK

SEVENTEENTH

STALINO

FIRST

TAGANROG

VOROSHILOVGRAD

SOUTH

STALINGRAD

Dec.-May

ROSTOV

KOTELNIKOV

UMAN

KIROVO

KRIVOI ROG

NIKOPOL

MARIUPOL

MELITOPOL

NIKOLAYEV

ODESSA

PEREKOP

SEA OF AZOV

CRIMEA

ELEVENTH

YEVPATORIYA

SEVASTOPOL

YALTA

KERCH

FEODOSIYA

NOVOROSSISK

BLACK SEA

TIKHORETSK

CAUCASUS

KRASNODAR

MAIKOP

TUAPSE

CAUCASUS MTS

GROZNY

ORDZHONIKIDZE

ELISTA

BAKU

TEREK R.

Volga R.

Don R.

Dnieper R.

Desna R.

Oka R.

Donets R.

Bug R.

Vistula R.

Oder R.

Elbe R.

Danube R.

Dniester R.

Prut R.

Niemen R.

Dvina R.

Berezina R.

BESSARABIA

IASI

ROMAN

BACAU

GALATI

TIGHINA

BALTA

PLOESTI

PITESTI

CERNAUTI

SZEGED

CONSTANTA

LAKE LADOGA

LAKE ILMEN

GRODNO

SEGED

GERMAN SUMMER OFFENSIVE OF 1942

★

March 1942 brought the spring thaws and the mud which, until early May, enforced a general truce. The Russians were practically exhausted and, despite the increase in Lend-Lease supplies, were often short of basic weapons. The Germans too were in an equally bad way when, on 5 April Hitler, who was probably its author, announced the plan for the 1942 offensive. In it, Army Group South would destroy all Russian forces in the bend of the Don River preparatory to seizing the Caucasus oil fields (a pet project of the Fuhrer's for some time). Because of a lack of rail facilities sufficient to get all the troops into position for a simultaneous advance, the offensive would be carried out in four principal phases (indicated by circled red numerals on the map below). First, a two-pronged envelopment of Voronezh was to be followed by the establishment of a strong defensive line from Voronezh toward Orel; second, an advance down the Don from Voronezh to link up with a second German force advancing from Kharkov; third, a continuing advance down the Don to meet a third a third column which would drive eastward from the Mius River, simultaneously making secondary attacks southward to seize bridgeheads over the lower Don; four, to seize Stalingrad while the main attack prepared to move southeast into the Caucasus. Army Group Center would remain on the defensive but, if Army Group South was successful, Army Group North would seize Leningrad.

The German army of 1942 was far inferior to that of 1941. Only the divisions assigned to Army Group South had received the necessary number of replacements; elsewhere the average German division was little over half strength. Fifty-one satellite divisions (Rumanian, Hungarian, Italian, and Slovak) and another of Spanish volunteers had been added, but their quality was generally poor. The German war industry, still operating at low levels of productivity, had failed to replace many of the vehicles lost during the winter.

Preliminary operations began on 8 May with Manstein's attack on the Kerch peninsula. By the 19th, he had driven the Russians into the sea, inflicting 150,000 casualties. Meanwhile (12 May), the Russians broke through on either side of Kharkov, employing tanks en masse. Hitler countered by beginning the attack on the Izyum salient (17 May). After several weeks of confused fighting, the salient was cut off and mopped up. The Russians lost 240,000 men and 1,249 tanks, but managed to withdraw the troops which had struck at Kharkov from the north. Manstein, in the meantime, had opened his attack against Sevastopol where Russian defenses were strong and resistance stubborn. To the end, reinforcements were pumped into the city; submarines being used after surface vessels were driven off. Supported by the Luftwaffe and super-heavy siege artillery, the German assault teams fought their way to the north shore of Sevastopol harbor on 20 June, and on the night of the 28th, made a surprise amphibious assault across it, taking the defenses south of the city from the rear. Fighting ended on 1 July, the Russians having lost about 100,000 men.

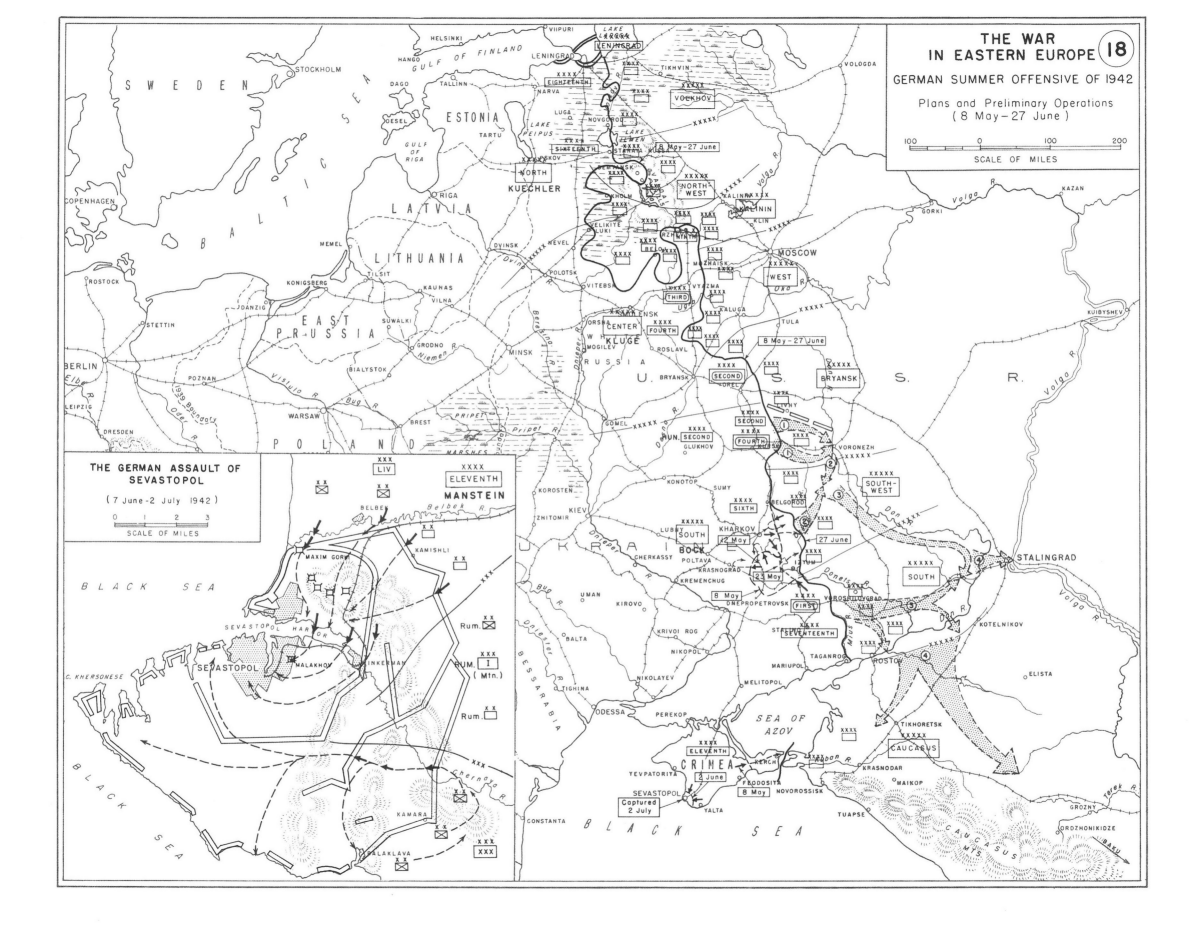

THE WAR
IN EASTERN EUROPE 18
GERMAN SUMMER OFFENSIVE OF 1942

Plans and Preliminary Operations
(8 May – 27 June)

100   0   100   200
SCALE OF MILES

THE GERMAN ASSAULT OF
SEVASTOPOL

(7 June-2 July 1942)

0 1 2 3
SCALE OF MILES

GERMAN SUMMER OFFENSIVE OF 1942

★

Although the impending attack on Voronezh (the first phase of the plan) was known to the Russians through captured documents, when it actually came, on 28 June, they seem to have been taken by surprise. But they recovered rapidly, and counterattacked vigorously, using several tank brigades of which German intelligence had been unaware. Nevertheless, the Germans reached Voronezh on 2 July and captured it on the 6th.

The second phase attack advanced on 30 June and by 7 July had linked up with fourth Panzer Army. During this period Army Group South was reorganized as Army Group A, under List, and Army Group B under Weichs; Bock was relieved. Panzer Groups were also reorganized into Armies.

List's attack, which initiated the third phase was wildly successful, but Hitler, perversely, changed plans, and ordered List to wheel south and cross the Don, leaving Sixth Army alone to continue the advance toward Stalingrad and opened up a gap between Sixth Army and Fourth Panzer through which approximately two-thirds of the Russians in the bend of the Don were able to escape.

German supply problems and Hitler now came to Russia's aid. By 25 July, both panzer armies had been stalled by gasoline shortages, and in the time thus gained the Russians worked frantically to fortify Stalingrad. Hitler's meddling in the plan also aided the Russians. On 23 July he ordered Eleventh Army north to Leningrad. It meant traversing the whole depth of Russia, and having sent his only available reserve on a massive trek, now proceeded to scatter his attacking forces piecemeal across south-central Russia. In addition, he now suddenly detached a panzer corps from Fourth Panzer Army and sent it back toward Stalingrad. Army Group A's new mission was to destroy the Russians who had escaped across the Don from Rostov; neutralize the Black Sea Fleet by capturing its bases, and then push along the southeast shore of the Caspian Sea toward the oil-production center of Baku. Army Group B was to capture Stalingrad and create a defensive front between the Don and Volga rivers and, finally, send a mobile column down the Volga to Astrakhan.

So far the German offensive, despite logistical problems, had been highly successful, so much so that Russia was clamoring for the western Allies to open a second front to relieve the pressure. During late July the Russian retreat along the Caucasus front continued, despite Stalin's order to stand to the last, but List's advance was hampered by Hitler's insistence that Fourth Panzer by detached and sent to Weichs. In addition, lack of gasoline slowed the advance on all fronts. With resistance stiffening, especially in the Caucasus mountain passes, Army Group A was badly overextended, with twenty under-strength divisions spread out over a front of more than 500 miles. Army Group B, supported by most of the available Luftwaffe, cleared the Don bend by 18 August against growing Russian opposition. On 23 August the Germans crossed the Don, repulsed Russian counterattacks, and reached the Volga north of Stalingrad.

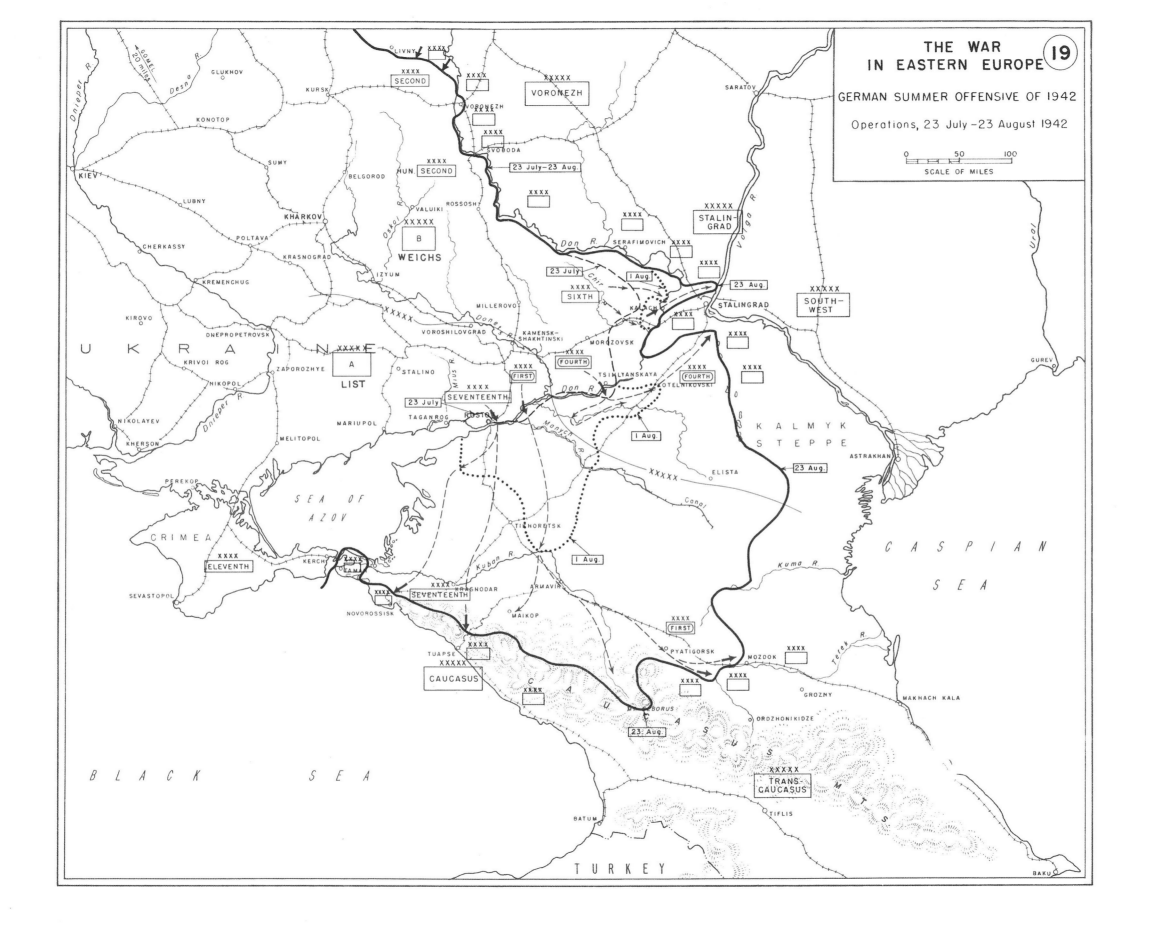

THE WAR
IN EASTERN EUROPE 19

GERMAN SUMMER OFFENSIVE OF 1942

Operations, 23 July – 23 August 1942

0   50   100
SCALE OF MILES

THE BATTLE OF STALINGRAD

★

During the late August, September, and October 1942 the momentum of the German offensive died away. In the Caucasus, for example, List's panzer units were without fuel for weeks at a time. By the end of August, the Russian Trans-Caucasus Front ("Front" was the Russian term for army) once more got its forces organized and, digging in with their usual skill and speed, the Russians held the mountain passes, and occasionally counterattacked. Nevertheless, in early September, German troops from the Crimea made an assault crossing of the Kerch Straights, driving down the coast to take Novdrossisk.

Hitler, however, was becoming increasingly irritable with his military staff and army commanders, whom he accused of "intellectual conceit" and "complete incapacity to grasp essentials." Halder, chief of staff of the army, was fired, and List was relieved for lack of aggressiveness. Hitler himself took over direct command of Army Group A, in addition to his roles as commander in chief and head of state!

In contrast to the Caucasus stalemate, the battle for Stalingrad grew in fury. At Warsaw and Leningrad, Hitler had avoided street fighting because of the heavy casualties it invariably involved, but now he pulled more and more troops away from the Caucasus in order to feed them into the Stalingrad meat grinder.

Stalingrad and its suburbs stretched for thirty miles along the west bank of the Volga, and during the last days of August 1942 the Germans had moved up through the suburbs against only light opposition, which stiffened in September as more and more Russian troops streamed into the city, finally checking the German advance in the business and industrial center near the river.

Vicious hand-to-hand fighting continued through September and October, with the Germans slowly gaining ground, but at a considerable price. The Russians, with the Volga at their backs, fought with phenomenal determination and sacrifice, but by 1 November their position had been split into four separate bridgeheads, which could only be reinforced by boat across the mile-wide river under relentless German artillery fire. On 12 November a final German attack reached the Volga south of the city.

While this pointless battle of attrition raged, German intelligence officers warned of a major build up around Saratov, and of increasing activity around the Russian bridgehead on the south bank of the Don at Serafimovich. Luftwaffe reconnaissance flights failed to confirm these reports because the Russians were skilled at camouflage. On 12 November German intelligence definitely predicted an impending offensive against the Rumanian Third Army, but the attack on Stalingrad continued. As of 0700 19 November, most of the German elements of Army Group B were engaged around Stalingrad. To the north of the city, a screen of troops from client countries (mostly without armor or effective anti-tank guns) watched from the east bank of the Don. South of Stalingrad, the Rumanian Fourth Army covered Army Group B's right flank, and between it and Army Group A stretched a 240-mile gap, guarded only by a single motorized division at Elista. In addition, the logistical situation of both army groups was worsening, as they depended on a single rail link that crossed the Dnieper at Dnepropetrovsk.

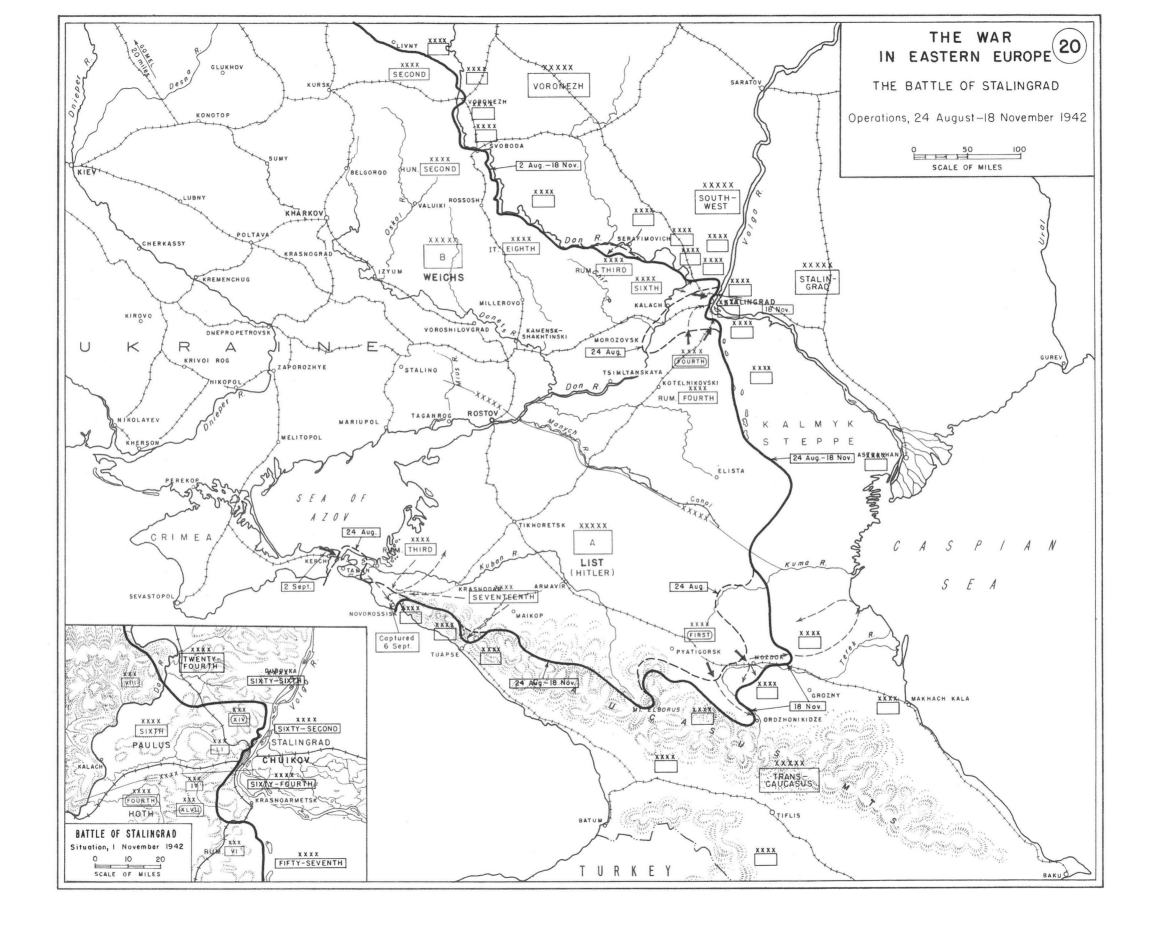

THE WAR
IN EASTERN EUROPE (20)

THE BATTLE OF STALINGRAD

Operations, 24 August–18 November 1942

0   50   100
SCALE OF MILES

BATTLE OF STALINGRAD
Situation, 1 November 1942

0   10   20
SCALE OF MILES

THE BATTLE OF STALINGRAD

★

Hitler had obligingly jammed his troops into a tight corner at Stalingrad where they could be trapped by attacks the Rumanians on either flank. The Russian counteroffensive waited only for freezing weather to permit cross-country tank movements, and the Anglo-American landings in North Africa that would tie down any potential German reinforcements.

About 0720 on 19 November Russian artillery fire suddenly deluged the Rumanian Third Army. At 0850, Russian infantry, massed by divisions into human battering rams, surged out of the Serafimovich bridgehead. They were followed by tank columns and cavalry that swarmed through the broken Rumanian lines. The tanks headed directly for the vital bridge at Kalach, west of Stalingrad, while the cavalry fanned out to the northwest. More infantry and armor cut southeast to isolate Stalingrad. In all, it was the most expertly planned and executed Russian offensive to date.

South of Stalingrad, the Russians struck on 20 November, totally routing the Rumanian Fourth Army. Part of the Fourth Panzer Army was cut off and crowded into the city; the rest escaped, largely because if inept Russian staff work. Tanks from the northern Russian attack reached Kalach on the 21st, and when the southern attack linked up with them the next day, the trap was firmly closed.

Late on the 22nd, Paulus had requested Hitler's permission to fight his way out, but it was denied and he was ordered to hold the city and would be supplied by air. (Göring had grandiloquently pledged that the Luftwaffe would deliver 500 tons of supplies a day; in the event, he was lucky if he could deliver seventy tons.)

Meanwhile, on 20 November Hitler had appointed Manstein commander of the newly formed Army Group Don comprised of Fourth Panzer Army, Sixth Army, plus Third and Fourth Rumanian Armies, and ordered him to "recapture the positions formerly held by us." Arriving on the 26th, Manstein found himself almost without troops. Fortunately for him, though, the Russians had committed all their forces to Stalingrad, but bad weather, the slow arrival of reinforcements, and Russian pressure delayed Manstein's attempt to mount a relief expedition. The situation in Stalingrad grew desperate. At last a forlorn hope expedition drove northeastward from Kotelnikovski, wrecking one Russian unit after another. It got to within thirty-five miles of Stalingrad by the 19 December, and Manstein ordered Paulus to break out and link up; but Paulus, ever fearful of Hitler's reaction, quibbled and, during this period of indecision, the front collapsed. On the 24th, fresh Russian tank units converged on the relief column, which only fought its way back with the greatest difficulty.

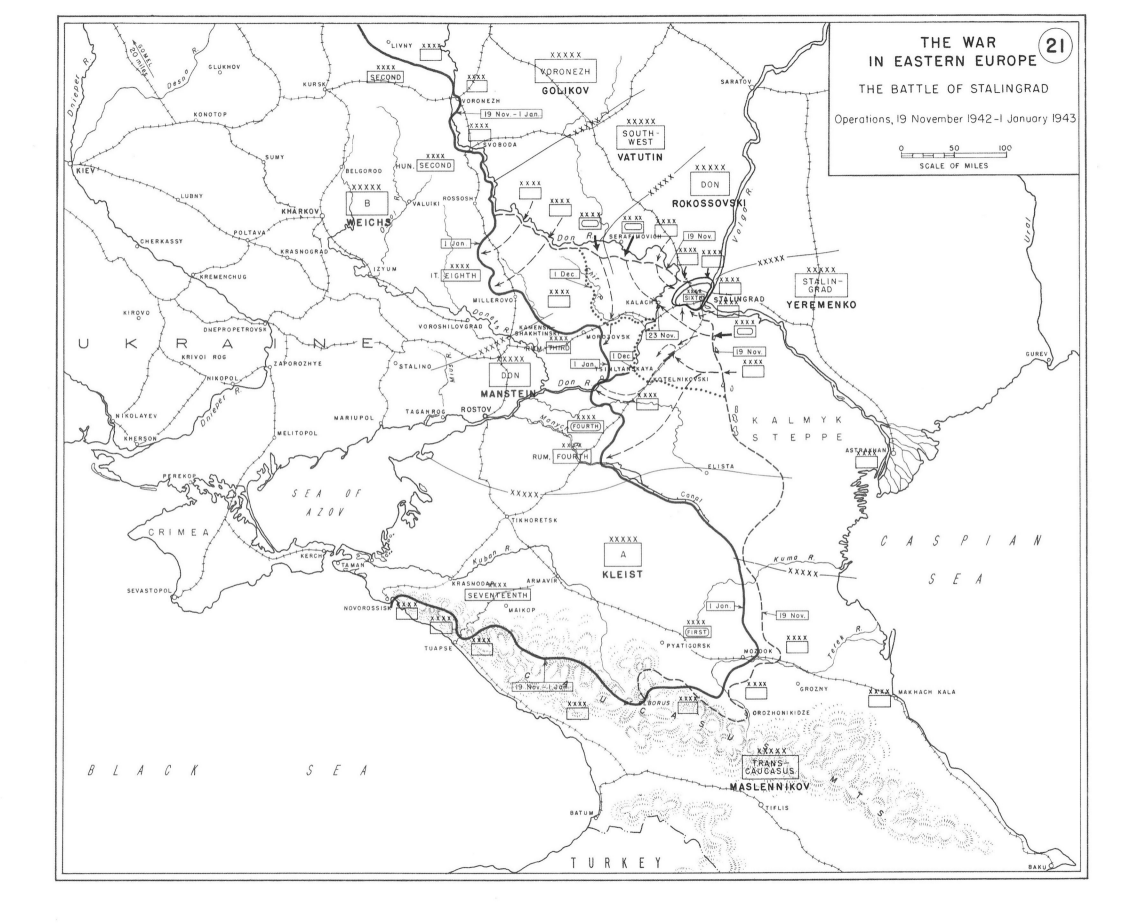

THE WAR
IN EASTERN EUROPE ㉑

THE BATTLE OF STALINGRAD

Operations, 19 November 1942-1 January 1943

SCALE OF MILES
0   50   100

RUSSIAN WINTER OFFENSIVE OF 1943

★

Disaster now faced all the German forces in southern Russia. The furious offensive of the Russian Southwest Front threatened to turn the left flank of Army Group Don, seize the Donets and Dnieper river crossings behind it, and drive on to Rostov. Such a move would cut Army Group A's line of retreat through Rostov and pin Army Group Don against the Sea of Azov; the result would be a second, and greater, Stalingrad.

If Paulus had been courageous enough to defy Hitler, he could probably have extricated the greater part of Sixth Army in a breakout; and by thus reinforcing Manstein, a successful defensive-offensive operation could have been waged between the Don and Donets. But now, with Paulus cooped up, Manstein, Weichs, and Kleist simply lacked sufficient troops to halt the Russians. Most of the Rumanians had been withdrawn, too shaken to be of use, and the Italian Eighth Army had evaporated. Large parts of the German "lines" were held only by improvised formations, created out of service troops and stray detachments.

In this swelling crisis, Paulus could render Germany one last service—to hold out, and thereby tie up as many Russian troops as possible while Army Group A could extricate itself from the Caucasus. This Paulus did; and although his earlier conduct has been criticized, few generals in history faced so grim a set of alternatives as he.

Stalingrad's story is quickly told. After the original Russian November offensive, Sixth Army had had little trouble beating off Russian infantry attacks. Early in January, the Russian Don Front, with considerable air support, was concentrated around Stalingrad. After Paulus had rejected two surrender ultimatums, the Russians attacked on 10 January. Short of ammunition, food, and fuel, Sixth Army resisted stubbornly, but by the 21st, both airports had been lost. On the 23rd, Paulus requested permission to capitulate, but Hitler ordered him to fight on. At 0840 on 2 February 1943 the last pockets of resistance gave up. Stalingrad cost Hitler approximately 300,000 men, which left a gap in the German army that could never be refilled.

In the meantime, Manstein had been fighting Russians, weather, and Hitler to hold the Rostov gateway open for Kleist. The last of those three was by far the most dangerous and illusive. Hitler protested and delayed every backward step, even when he had previously authorized it. On 14 January, the situation was extremely tense. A Russian attack south of Voronezh dispersed most of the Hungarian Send Army, and on the 25th, a second offensive caught the German Second Army retiring from Voronezh and mauled it badly. This shocked Hitler into transferring the First Panzer Army to Manstein.

Manstein was now fighting in three directions, against odds estimated at seven to one. Only by keeping his battered panzer units concentrated for counterattacks against Russian penetrations was he able to keep his front intact. By 1 February, however, a massive Russian armored offensive was crossing the Donets east of Voroshilovgrad, while another was threatening to break into the German rear near Izyum to the northwest.

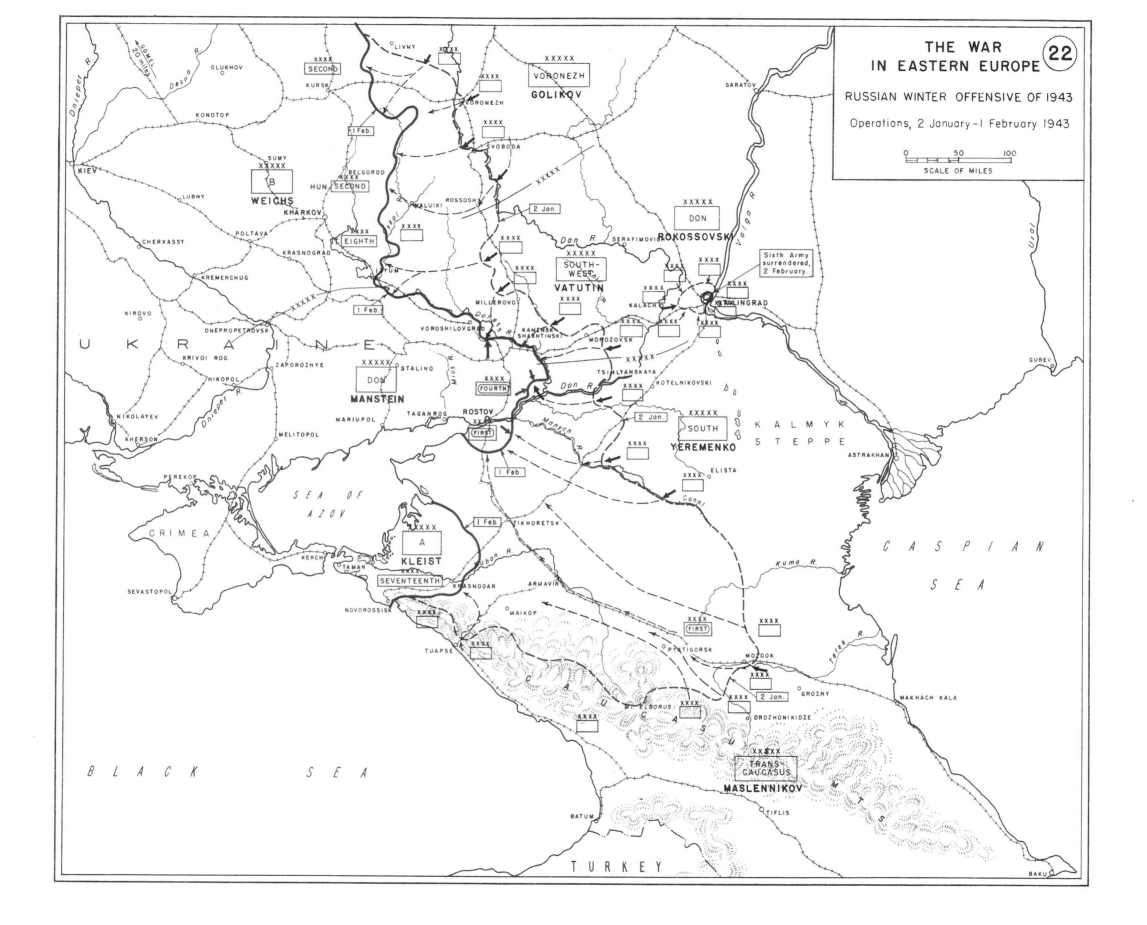

THE WAR
IN EASTERN EUROPE 22

RUSSIAN WINTER OFFENSIVE OF 1943

Operations, 2 January-1 February 1943

0   50   100
SCALE OF MILES

RUSSIAN WINTER OFFENSIVE OF 1943

★

By early February, there appeared little hope for the Germans in southern Russia, especially since Russian units released by the fall of Stalingrad were now joining in the attack. The defeat of the German Second Army near Voronezh had left a gap over 200 miles wide, extending south to Izyum (which fell on 5 February). Vigorously prodded by Manstein, Hitler finally agreed that forces in the salient between Voroshilovgrad and Rostov might withdraw to the Mius River, which was completed by 18 February.

Farther north, Hitler had been attempting to concentrate the SS Panzer Corps at Kharkov, with the far-fetched notion of sending them to rescue Stalingrad, but they were forced out of Kharkov and a flood of Russian tanks, cavalry, and motorized corps flooded southward. By 20 February, Russian spearheads had cut the railroad into Stalino, thus severing Manstein's supply line. Other Russian offensives had cracked the Mius River front at various places.

On 12 February, Hitler had abolished Army Group B and redistributed the remnants of its troops to Army Group Center and Army Group Don (now renamed South). Manstein shifted his efficient Fourth Panzer Army headquarters westward to Dnepropetrovsk to take over the SS Panzer Corps (two divisions) and other available troops in the area. Hitler, finally shaken into action, ordered Kleist to airlift as many troops as he could spare across the Sea of Azov to reinforce Manstein, and, in addition, seven divisions from the West were sent.

On 18 February the Fourth Panzer Army began its counterattack, some divisions striking south and east from Krasnograd, while others attacked north and west. The advancing Russians had failed to keep their forces concentrated, so many units were picked off by the counterattack, while others simply panicked, and yet others ran out of fuel. By 7 March, the Germans were racing toward Kharkov, which fell on the 14th, followed by Belograd immediately after. Except for the large bulge around Kursk the Germans had restored the line from which they had begun their 1942 advance. Manstein's counteroffensive was a masterpiece of mobile warfare, and it is sobering to think what he might have achieved if given a free hand from the beginning.

Fighting elsewhere in Russia during 1942 had been bloody, if less spectacular. Army Group North had weathered a series of crises. The projected attack on Leningrad had been abruptly halted by a major Russian penetration of Eighteenth Army south of Lake Ladoga. Although the Russian spearhead had been destroyed by 21 September, the Leningrad offensive was abandoned. On 12 January, the Russians again attacked in this area and spent 270,000 casualties to carve out a six-mile wide corridor, all of it subject to German artillery, along Lake Ladoga into Leningrad. Two hundred miles south, the Germans trapped in the Demyansk pocket were finally given permission by Hitler to break out, which they did successfully by 18 March.

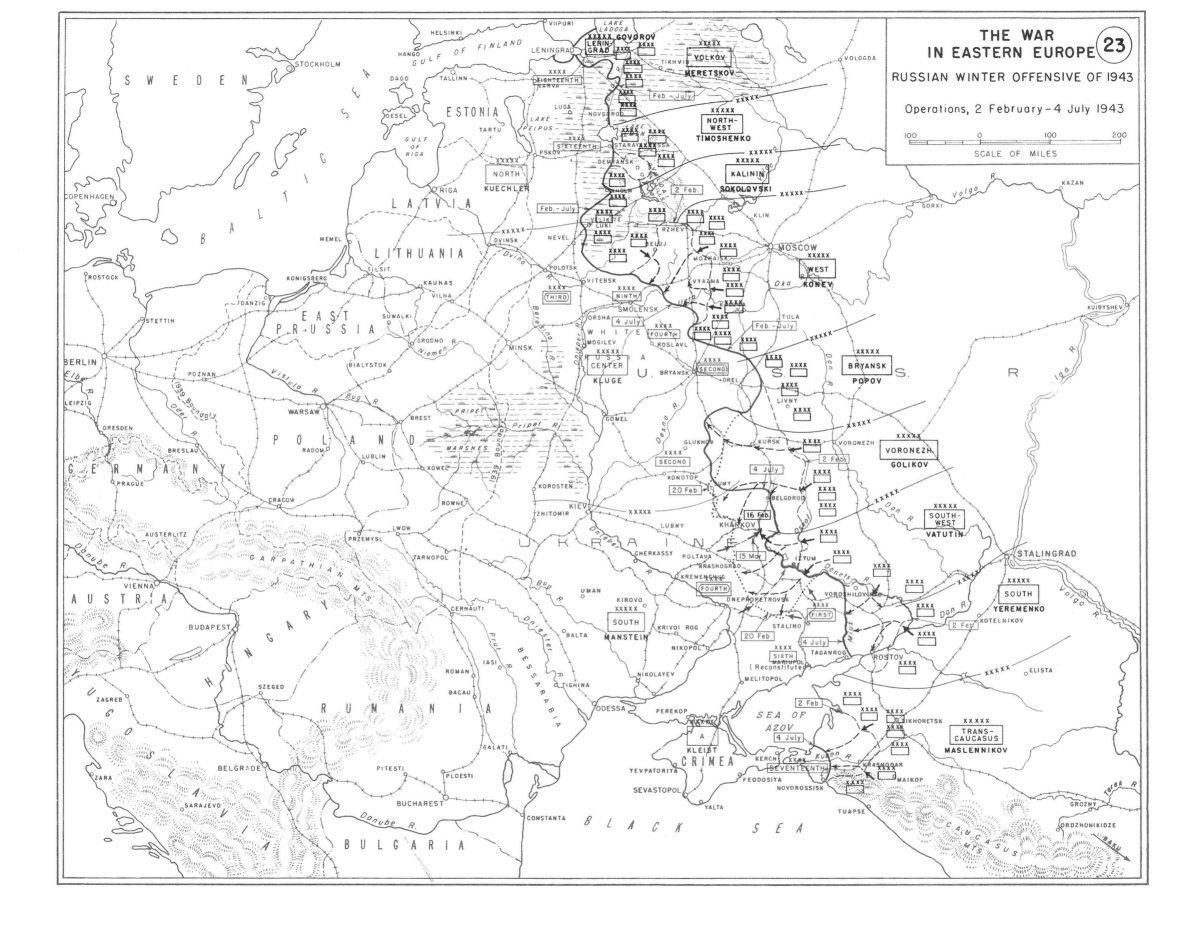

THE WAR
IN EASTERN EUROPE (23)
RUSSIAN WINTER OFFENSIVE OF 1943

Operations, 2 February – 4 July 1943

100   0   100   200
SCALE OF MILES

RUSSIAN SUMMER OFFENSIVE OF 1943

★

During the spring of 1943, both armies reorganized. The Germans gave special attention to re-equipping their panzer divisions with more power tanks . . . The Russians had vastly increased their artillery, their air force, and their armored units; in overall numerical strength, they now enjoyed a four-to-one superiority, and their morale was high.

Hitler and his generals realized that another major offensive was beyond their capabilities and that they did not have sufficient manpower for a purely static defense of the Eastern Front. Rejecting Manheim's proposal to retreat and draw in the South Front Army, and then smash it against the Sea of Azov, Hitler agreed to a quick blow to inflict maximum casualties on the Russians and upset their plans. The location selected was the Russian-held salient east of Kursk. Massed panzers would attack north and south to cut off the salient and trap considerable numbers of Russians. The operation had been originally scheduled for early May, but Hitler postponed it in order to complete the re-equipment of his panzers. The Russians learned of the plan, and prepared an in-depth elastic defense. In their turn, the Germans knew of these preparations, and both Kluge and Manstein tried to persuade Hitler to abandon the offensive. But Hitler would not hear of it, and the attacks were to go ahead on 5 July.

Ninth Army's attack in the north from the Orel salient made slow progress at considerable loss, until it finally came to a halt altogether. On 11 July, the Russians struck the salient from the north and northeast, making considerable gains. In the south, the German attack also met with stiff resistance. Intensive Luftwaffe support for both attacks was met by massive Russian air activity that inflicted severe losses on German fliers.

On 13 July, Hitler announced that the Allied invasion of Sicily would necessitate moving troops out of the Russian theater, and therefore the Kursk attack would have to be terminated immediately. The Russians now seized the initiative and pressure on the Orel salient became intense. Hitler approved its evacuation (apparently to provide troops for Italy), as well as allowing Ninth Army to withdraw behind the Desna River. He insisted, however, that Manstein hold his larger, more exposed, salient in the south.

On the 17 July, the Russians forced the Mius River, captured Taganrog, and made some gains against the First Panzer Army. Manstein shifted his reserves south and defeated the Russians on the Mius, but this transfer weakened his left flank, and the Russians broke through toward Kharkov, and Hitler ordered that the city be held at all costs. Manstein, however, abandoned it on 23 August, and through a series of rapid counterattacks succeeded in reestablishing his front. On 31 August, Hitler finally consented to limited withdrawals by Manstein's Sixth Army and First Panzer.

In Army Group Center's sector, the Russians gained considerable ground against the Second Army, pushing west of Glukhov and making appreciable advances southeast of Smolensk. The northern front remained static.

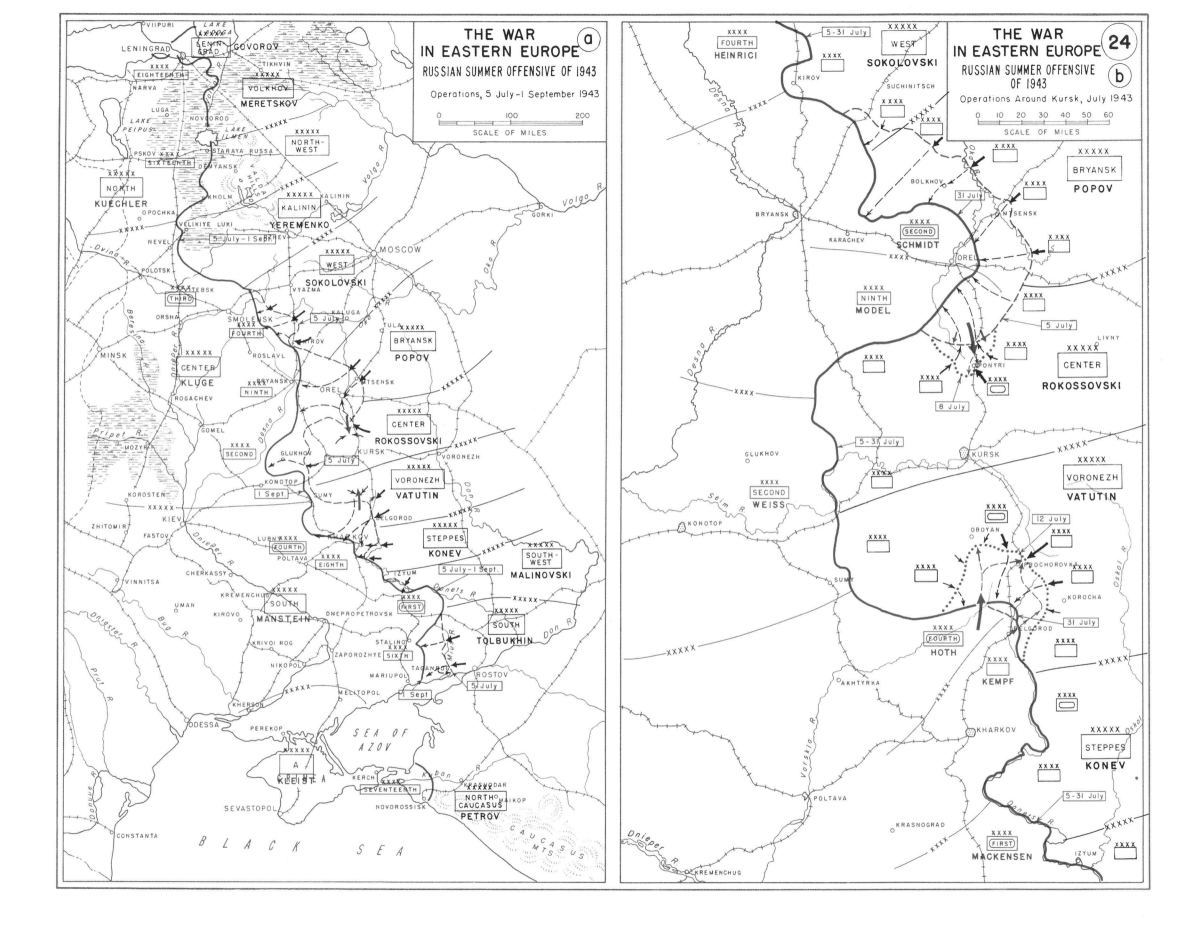

THE WAR
IN EASTERN EUROPE (a)
RUSSIAN SUMMER OFFENSIVE OF 1943

Operations, 5 July–1 September 1943

0   100   200
SCALE OF MILES

THE WAR
IN EASTERN EUROPE (24)
RUSSIAN SUMMER OFFENSIVE
OF 1943 (b)

Operations Around Kursk, July 1943

0 10 20 30 40 50 60
SCALE OF MILES

RUSSIAN WINTER OFFENSIVE OF 1944

★

At this stage in their war against Germany, the Russians were able to exploit their supremacy in manpower and materièl by striking massive blows against widely separated sectors of the German front. When successful, these enveloped and destroyed considerable German forces; when unsuccessful, they merely attacked elsewhere with massed infantry and huge phalanxes of tanks and artillery; appalling losses were accepted stoically. The open terrain in the south offered the Germans few natural defensive positions, and their panzer reserves, for ever switching from one hot spot to the next, wore themselves out.

On 8 September, Hitler finally approved a withdrawal to the Dnieper–Melitopol line, but delayed it so much that Fourth Panzer' s situation became desperate. But Manstein forced his hand, and Army Group South began a desperate race to get behind the Dnieper before its overextended divisions were shattered. Good staff work and hard fighting saved it, though there were only five available crossing sites on Manstein's 440-mile front.

The west bank of the Dnieper was unfortified (except for some light defenses constructed by Army Group South) and ungarrisoned. Consequently, aggressive Russian spearheads were able to cross and establish bridgeheads south of Kremenchug and north and south of Kiev before Manstein's troops could finish deploying along the west bank.

Although the Russian bridgeheads were quickly contained, they could not be eliminated. Army Group Center fell back from the Smolensk area under heavy pressure, but kept its front intact.

Repeated Russian attempts to break out of their Dnieper bridgeheads were bloody failures except at the boundary between Army Group South and Center, where they made appreciable gains. Finally, during October, the Russians drove out of their Kremenchug bridgehead, threatening to envelop First Panzer. Counterattacks by the German reserves threw them back but, south of the Dnieper bend, Sixth Army was defeated and withdrew rapidly. Next, the Russians attacked out of their Kiev bridgeheads and mauled Fourth Panzer. The Russians entered Kiev on 6 November. Manstein replied with a panzer counterattack that smashed the Russians back onto Kiev, but an unexpected thaw halted operations. Meanwhile, five successive Russian offensives struck Army Group Center, concentrating on Fourth Army, but for the small gains, they paid a heavy price.

During early December, Manstein's panzers made several spoiling attacks northwest of Zhitomir. Hitler, when advised to evacuate the Crimea, reacted angrily; the Crimea must be held because its loss would provide air bases for Russia for attacks on the vital Ploesti oil fields.

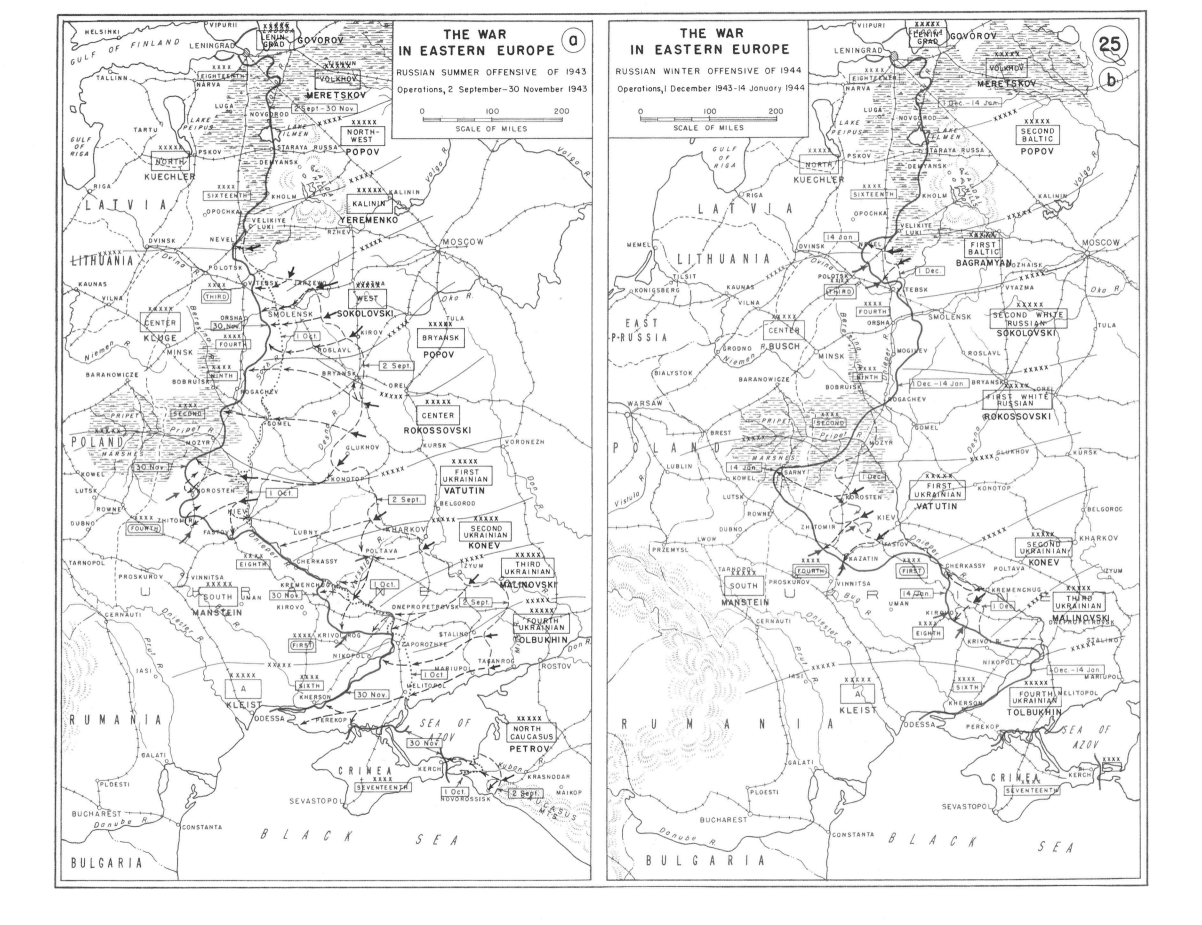

THE WAR IN EASTERN EUROPE **a**

RUSSIAN SUMMER OFFENSIVE OF 1943

Operations, 2 September–30 November 1943

0   100   200
SCALE OF MILES

THE WAR IN EASTERN EUROPE **b**

RUSSIAN WINTER OFFENSIVE OF 1944

Operations, 1 December 1943–14 January 1944

0   100   200
SCALE OF MILES

25

RUSSIAN WINTER OFFENSIVE OF 1944

★

The German Eighteenth Army had been on the Leningrad front for about a year. Most of its reserves had been transferred elsewhere, and it had grown lax. The Russians, sensing an opportunity, now shifted eight armies and a mass of artillery to the Leningrad sector. Their plan was clever: the force to the west of Leningrad, that had never been eradicated, would become the springboard for the counterattack. On 15 January, they attacked southwest out of the bridgehead while, simultaneously, a converging attack came across frozen Lake Ilmen and its surrounding swamps . . . Surprise was total, and the German lines were quickly penetrated. But the Germans soon rallied, withdrew, and established a new front through Luga where they stopped the Russian drive.

The Leningrad offensive, however, was secondary to that in the south. Late in January, the converging attacks of the First and Second Ukrainian Fronts cut off the Korsun salient, trapping two German corps. First Panzer and Eighth Army at once counterattacked, but alternating blizzards and thaws bogged them down. Manstein then ordered them to break out, which about two-thirds managed, although most of the wounded and all of the artillery had to be abandoned. Other Russian attacks drove Sixth Army out of the Nikopol area and seriously threatened the railroad near Lwow.

Manstein now side-slipped his forces westward in order to build up the Fourth Panzer Army in the Lwow area, though he was hampered by having to maintain contact with the dangerously exposed Sixth Army. The Russians, profiting from the greater maneuverability of their broad-tracked tanks and American trucks, still drove vigorously forward in the Dubno–Tarnopol area and against Uman, where a German corps was badly defeated. On 11 March, Eighth Army was ordered to withdraw, only to be overrun by a furious Russian pursuit, that also forced back First Panzer's right wing. Only the Fourth Panzer held firm, and eventually the surviving units of the Sixth and Eighth Armies crossed the Dniester.

The Russian drive to the Dniester had isolated First Panzer, and Manstein requested reinforcements for a rescue attempt. Hitler eventually acquiesced, but then replaced Manstein and Kleist with Model and Schoerner. On 5 April, Fourth Panzer drove southeast to extricate First Panzer which, fighting front, flank, and rear, broke out, bringing all its heavy equipment with it.

In early April, the Russians unleashed a well-organized assault on the isolated garrison of the Crimea. Repulsed by German troops at the Perekop Isthmus, they succeeded in an amphibious attack across the lagoon to the east, where the front was held by Rumanians. Advancing from this beachhead and from the Kerch peninsula, they drove the Germans within the Sevastopol fortifications, which they attacked on 7 May, supported by 300 guns per mile of front, and cleared the town within two days. However, the failure of the Russian Black Fleet to be more aggressive meant that the Germans were allowed to evacuate most of their garrison.

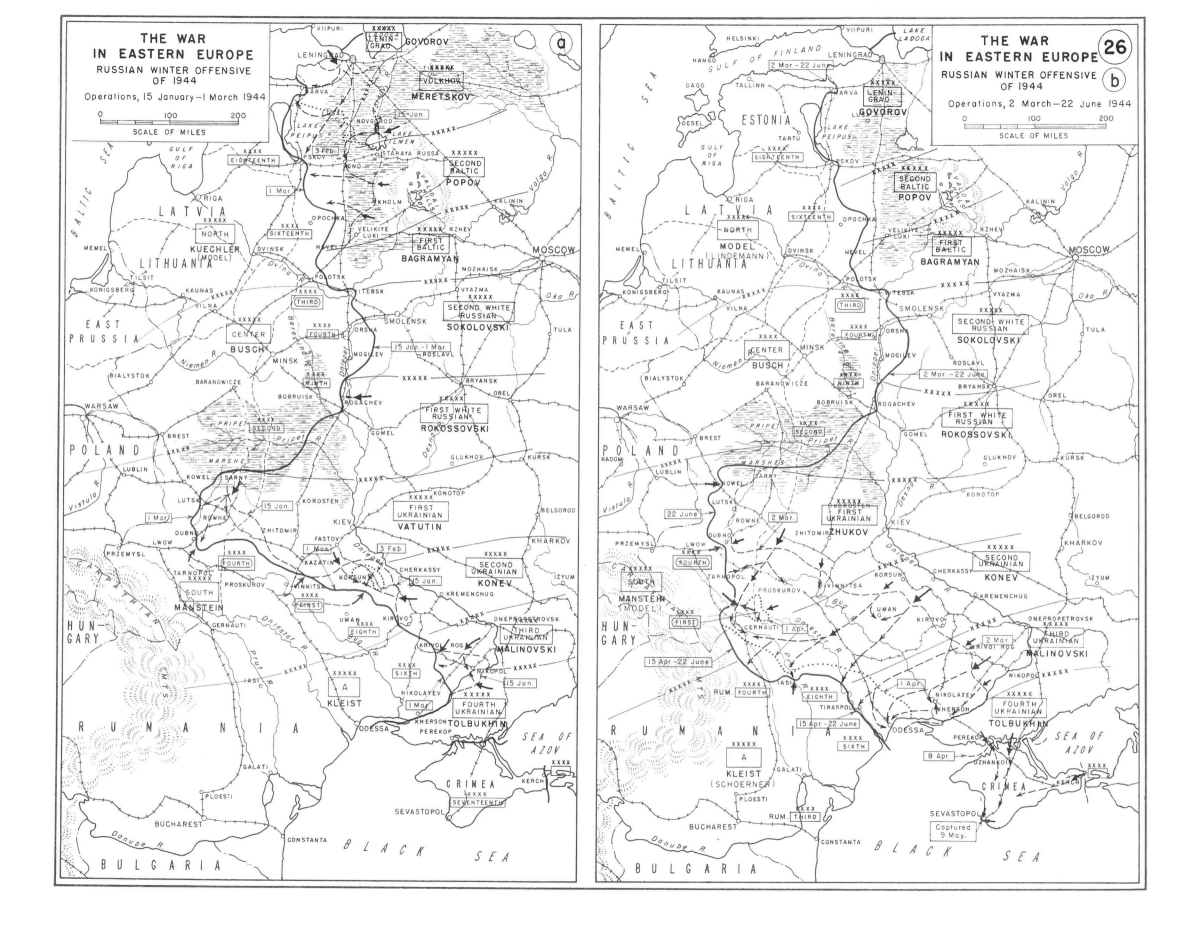

THE WAR IN EASTERN EUROPE

RUSSIAN WINTER OFFENSIVE OF 1944

Operations, 15 January–1 March 1944

SCALE OF MILES
0   100   200

THE WAR IN EASTERN EUROPE

26

RUSSIAN WINTER OFFENSIVE OF 1944

Operations, 2 March–22 June 1944

SCALE OF MILES
0   100   200

RUSSIAN SUMMER OFFENSIVE OF 1944

★

The spring thaws gave the Germans one last chance to reestablish their Eastern Front. They needed to shorten their lines along the Riga–Lwow–Dniester, in order to fortify it in depth. This would make it possible to take enough divisions out of the line to create a large mobile reserve, which could be stationed in a central position, such as Warsaw. Hitler rejected the idea. He wanted to create "fortresses" that were to be held to the last man. No fortified zones in the rear were to be allowed (they encouraged defeatism), and he refused to recall any troops from Norway, Greece, or Crete. He seems to have expected the Russians to continue to make their main effort between the Pripet Marshes and the Carpathian Mountains, and so concentrated most of his panzers in that area.

The Russians, however, had other plans. The thinly defended German salient north of the Pripet Marshes invited a converging attack. It had been agreed at the Teheran Conference in November 1943 that there would be coordination between Allied attacks on northern France and Russian assaults on the Eastern Front. D-Day was on 6 June, and on the 22 June there was an outbreak of guerrilla activity in the rear of Army Group Center, crippling its communications. And then the heavy action started.

On the 23rd, supported by almost hub-to-hub artillery (reportedly 400 big guns per mile), the Russian army rolled forward on a 350-mile front.

Most of Army Group Center's forces were soon drawn into the defense of Hitler's fortresses, where they were rapidly encircled, as Russian armor poured past and around them. In ten days of wild and confused fighting, the Russians bludgeoned a 250-mile wide gap in the German front, overrunning twenty-five divisions, the worst defeat the Germans had yet suffered. Field Marshal Model, "the Fuhrer's fireman," was thrown in to rescue the situation and, gathering up the remnants of Third Panzer and Second Army, he counterattacked successfully near Radzymin.

Meanwhile, on 12 July, the Russian offensive spread to include Army Group North. In Estonia the German front stood firm, but a flanking thrust by Russian Second and Baltic Fronts drove them toward the sea near Riga. On 14 July, the Russians opened their attack south of the Pripet Marshes. Lwow fell on the 27th, and by 1 August the Russians had reached the Vistula, south of Warsaw. Most of the Germans here, thanks to their higher proportion of panzer units, avoided encirclement and fought their way out. By 7 August, most of the front was momentarily stabilized, but the Germans now had new troubles. On 1 August, as the Russian advance guard approached Warsaw, the Polish underground seized control of most of the city, but were suppressed by SS and police units in brutal house-to-house fighting.

THE WAR IN EASTERN EUROPE (27)

RUSSIAN SUMMER OFFENSIVE OF 1944

Operations, 23 June – 7 August 1944

SCALE OF MILES
0   100   200   300

RUSSIAN SUMMER OFFENSIVE OF 1944

★

The destruction of most of Army Group Center was a mortal wound, which was compounded by the assassination attempt on Hitler on 20 July 1944. Hitler's previous distrust of his military leaders now turned to downright hatred. Guderian, who had been appointed chief of the General Staff on 21 July, knew he had to take a more realistic attitude than his ever-optimistic and ever-aggressive Fuhrer, and so sought to fortify Germany's eastern frontier, without seeking Hitler's approval.

With the German forces in Poland still attempting to recover from their recent defeat, and the Russians in that area having outrun their logistical support, Stalin now looked to his flanks. To the north, the German forces in the Baltic states were in a dangerously exposed position, but both sides were regrouping after their battles in the Riga area. With the Germans now obviously powerless to attempt a major counteroffensive, Stalin could now proceed with the acquisition of his Baltic empire.

On 20 August, the Russians launched a major offensive in Rumania. It was so successful that most of the Rumanian army defected to the Russians and sixteen German divisions were trapped. The Russians entered Bucharest on 1 September. Since 26 August, Bulgaria had withdrawn from the war and begun negotiations (somewhat foreshortened by Russia's invasion of the country). Now the Russians turned toward Budapest.

Guderian was desperate to shorten his line of defense and build up a mobile reserve, and Hitler finally consented to recall troops from the Aegean. Guderian ordered Gen. Schoerner to evacuate Estonia and Latvia, but Hitler intervened and suspended it. On 10 October the Russians broke through in the Baltic, leaving Schoerner and twenty divisions stranded in northern Latvia. In the last half of October the Russians launched an offensive against East Prussia, where it ran into fierce resistance.

The Russian's drive northwest across the Balkans continued, and Belgrade was captured on 20 October, cutting the main major north-south railroad available to Weichs's Army Group F in Yugoslavia, forcing it to take the more western route through Sarajevo. Josip Broz Tito's partisans and the Bulgarians were given the mission of driving the Germans out of Yugoslavia, while the Russians concentrated on the drive toward Budapest which they reached on 24 November.

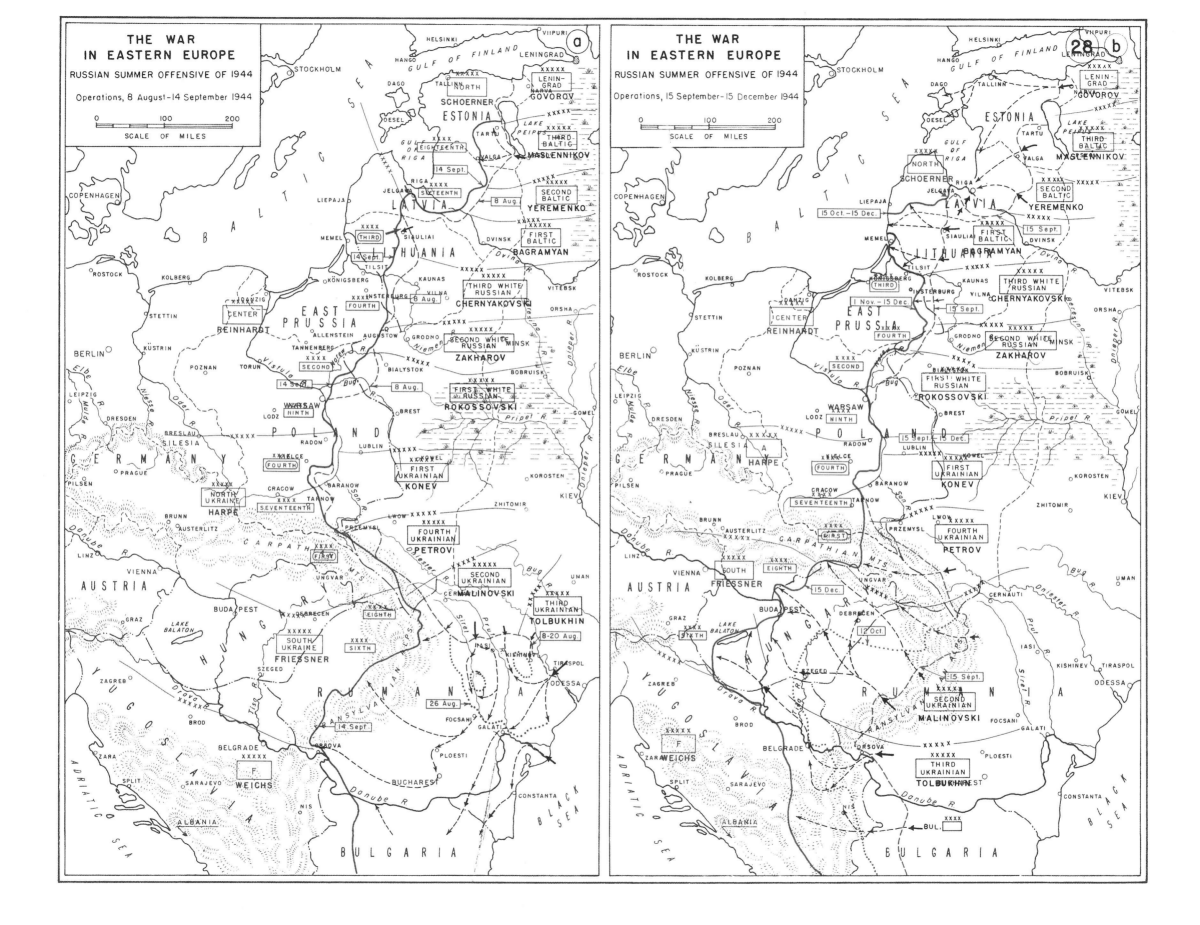

RUSSIAN WINTER OFFENSIVE OF 1945

★

North of the Carpathian Mountains there was little fighting during November and December. While the Russians regrouped in preparation for their next offensive, the Germans began fortifying their front, although Hitler again prevented a defense in depth. Meanwhile, he transferred the pick of his panzer units to the Western Front for his Ardennes offensive. He also insisted on maintaining Army Group North, with its twenty or so veteran divisions, in its splendid isolation in northern Latvia (ostensibly to protect submarine training bases!).

South of the Carpathians, fighting was constant and vicious. Here, the Germans used Budapest as a defensive outpost, but by the 24 December the Russians had surrounded it. On 13 February it was entirely in Russian hands.

Indications increased that the Russian offensive in Poland would soon be renewed; German intelligence predicted that it would begin around 12 January, and that the Russians would be able to muster a superiority of eleven-to-one in infantry, seven-to-one in tanks, and twenty-to-one in both artillery and aircraft. Hitler, now living more than ever before in his own dream world, derided this estimate. Even his own personal military staff preferred to commit the few available reserves in an abortive attack in Alsace-Lorraine. And to add to the dismal picture, from the German point of view, Allied bomber offensives had steadily wrecked the German communications and petroleum industries, creating huge fuel shortages on the Easter Front.

On 12 January Marshal Konev broke out of the Baranow bridgehead in overwhelming strength, with the Fronts on his right and left joining in the offensive during the following few days. Outnumbered and lacking a secondary defense line, the Germans could only attempt to maintain some semblance of order as they fell back. On 26 January the Russians broke through to the Baltic east of Danzig, and five days later Marshal Zhukov's leading units reached the Oder River near Küstrin, only forty miles east of Berlin, some five days later.

Temporarily stalled along the Oder–Niesse Rivers, the Russians turned northward and overran East Prussia. The German defense was grim, especially at Danzig (captured 30 March) and Königsberg (9 April). Thousands of Germans were evacuated by sea, despite the Russians navy's largely amateur efforts at interdiction. Russian forces now overran much of southern Germany. Early in January, Hitler ordered the crack Sixth Panzer (somewhat rehabilitated since the battering of the Ardennes campaign) transferred to Hungary, because he felt it was essential to safeguard the oilfields around Lake Balaton, but progress was slow (the railroad system had been badly shot up) and it was not until early March that a counterattack got underway—although it was successful and almost reached the Danube, except a shortage of fuel checked it at the critical moment. These were all last-ditch efforts, and Russian leviathan rolled on, capturing Vienna on 13 April 1945.

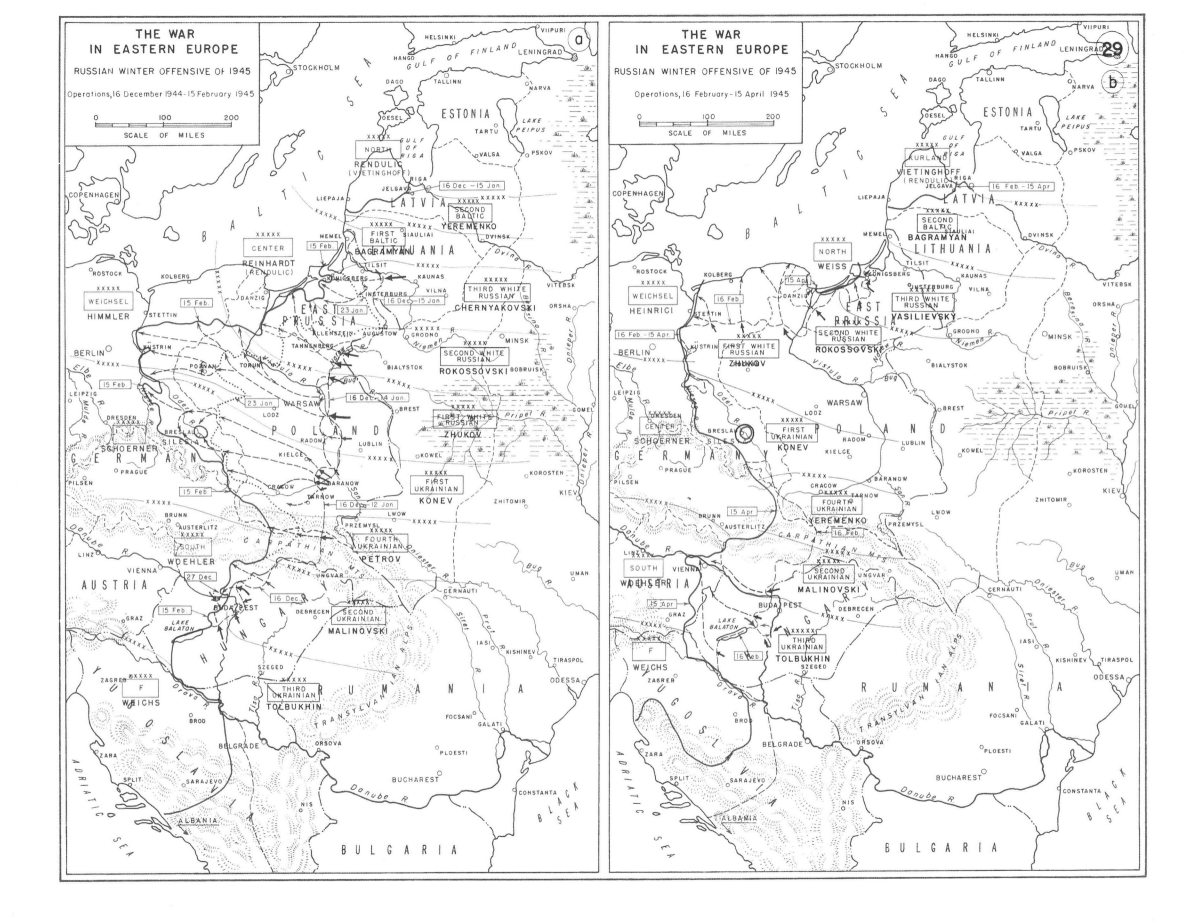

FINAL RUSSIAN CAMPAIGN IN CENTRAL EUROPE

★

From late February until 16 April, there was an uneasy lull along the Oder–Niesse front. The Russians had secured several bridgeheads on the west bank, including one at Küstrin, before halting their drive. Some, but not all, were knocked out by German counterattacks. Farther south, the Russian advance ground slowly forward across Austria and Czechoslovakia, slowed by mountainous terrain and supply difficulties. The German divisions cut off in Latvia held their front, but otherwise remained helpless spectators. Hitler could have withdrawn them at any time, if he had been willing to sacrifice some of their heavy equipment, but he chose not to. In Yugoslavia, the Germans held on successfully through January and February, but after the failure of Sixth Panzer's counteroffensive, were forced to withdraw northward.

On 16–17 April, the northern Russian fronts renewed their advance. There was no hope of successful resistance, with Allied forces pouring across western Germany. All German leaders, including Hitler, realized the war was lost, but the Fuhrer had long ago insulated himself from the reality. The last stages of scattered German resistance were doomed but desperate. The Russian advance reached Berlin on 22 April; the city was surrounded on the 25th, and Hitler was believed to have committed suicide on the 30th. It was not until the 2 May that the last stubborn embers of resistance were put out.

In the meantime, also on 25 April, American and Russian units had made contact near Torgau on the Elbe River. (General Eisenhower and the Russian high command had agreed on the line of the Elbe and Mulde Rivers as a general boundary between their forces in Germany to prevent incidents.) On 2 May the Russians reached Wismar, which British troops had just occupied, and the East and West Fronts soon came together along the length of the boundary with Germany. In Czechoslovakia and Austria, the Russian advance remained slow, in part because of determined German rearguard actions. Nevertheless, the Russian high command insisted that the Americans should not advance appreciably eastward of Pilsen. On 7 May, Admiral Doenitz, Hitler's successor, capitulated.

The war in Russia had been marked by sufferings and a personal brutality rarely approached in the West. Only the war against Japan shared the same ferocity. The major wonder is that, handicapped by Hitler, the German commanders accomplished so much with so relatively little for so long a period. Even in defeat, the German was frequently the more deadly fighter. Statistics are fragmentary or untrustworthy, but it looks as though there were three Russian casualties for every German.

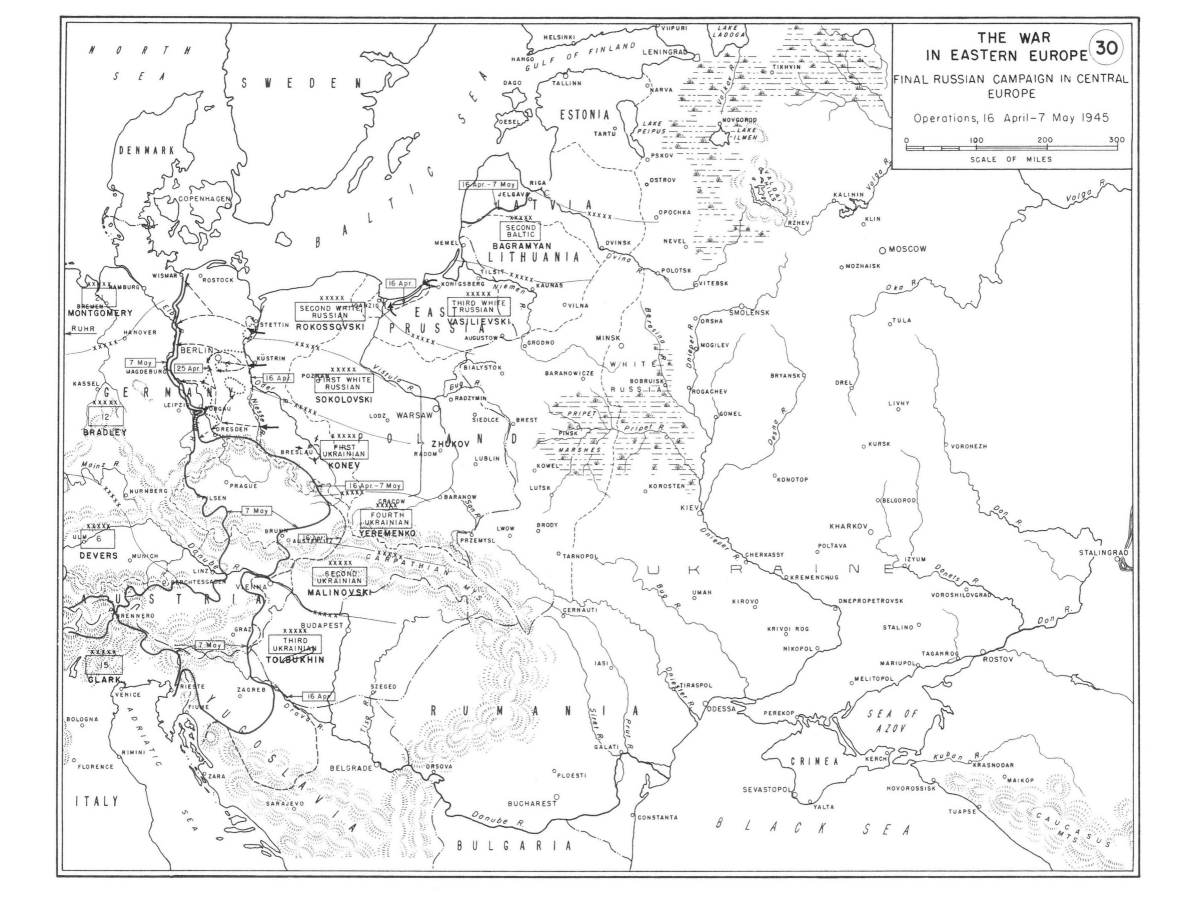

THE WAR
IN EASTERN EUROPE (30)

FINAL RUSSIAN CAMPAIGN IN CENTRAL
EUROPE

Operations, 16 April–7 May 1945

0   100   200   300
SCALE OF MILES

THE COMBINED BOMBER OFFENSIVE,
D-DAY, JUNE 6, 1944
★

It was not until 1943 that the Allies could say they had begun to win the battle of the Atlantic. For the first time during the war new tonnage began to outweigh tonnage lost to German U-boat attacks, and by the end of that year German submarine losses skyrocketed. By the end of the war 781 U-boats would be sunk, and 14,154,838 tons of Allied and neutral shipping lost. It had been a close run thing. Germany, despite the lessons of World War I, had started with only 57 submarines, and as Grand Admiral Karl Doenitz noted, it would be interesting to speculate what might have happened had she started the war with 1,000 U-boats.

As the battle of the Atlantic was being fought, a similar battle raged in the skies of western Europe, except the roles were reversed; Allied strategic air power struck at German industry, while the Luftwaffe played the part of defender.

When the British army was kicked out of Europe at Dunkirk, a new impetus was given to strategic bombing, and in May 1942 British Bomber Command mounted a 1,000 bomber raid on Cologne, which achieved considerable success without prohibitive cost.

Whereas the British believed in area targets and night bombing, the Americans favored high altitude precision bombing during the day. In March 1942 the Eighth Air Force was formed in England as the nucleus of the American strategic air arm, and in the following August, in a small raid against Holland, the feasibility of daylight bombing was tested, with modest success. By June of 1943 a plan for coordinated strategic bombing (Combined Bomber Offensive) had been implemented. The key targets are indicated by the hatched areas on the map below.

The Combined Bomber Offensive gathered momentum in 1943. In an effort to gain air superiority, the Allies hammered at the German aircraft industry by day and cities by night. But in early 1944, new techniques and equipment began to roll, and by April air superiority had been achieved. By now the U.S. Fifteenth Air Force, based in Italy, was participating in the air strikes, and the Allied successes were due, in some part, to the German failure to concentrate on fighter production, particularly on their promising jet fighter program.

At the Cairo–Teheran Conference in November 1943, the final plans for the Allied invasion of Europe—OVERLORD—was finally approved and given a target date. General Eisenhower, now in the Mediterranean theater, was designated supreme commander. In February, the planning group was absorbed into Supreme Headquarters Allied Expeditionary Force (SHAEF), where the plan was honed. Eisenhower's three immediate subordinates were British. Gen. Sir Bernard L. Montgomery, recently returned from Italy, initially commanded all ground forces as head of 21st Army Group; Admiral Sir Bertram Ramsay, headed the Allied naval forces, and Air Chief Marshal Trafford Leigh-Mallory, the air forces. The U.S. Ninth Air Force was to support Lt. Gen. Omar N. Bradley's American First Army while the British Second Air Force supported the British Second Army.

The map below shows the German dispositions and SHAEF's planned limits of advance seventeen, thirty-five, sixty, and ninety days after the landings.

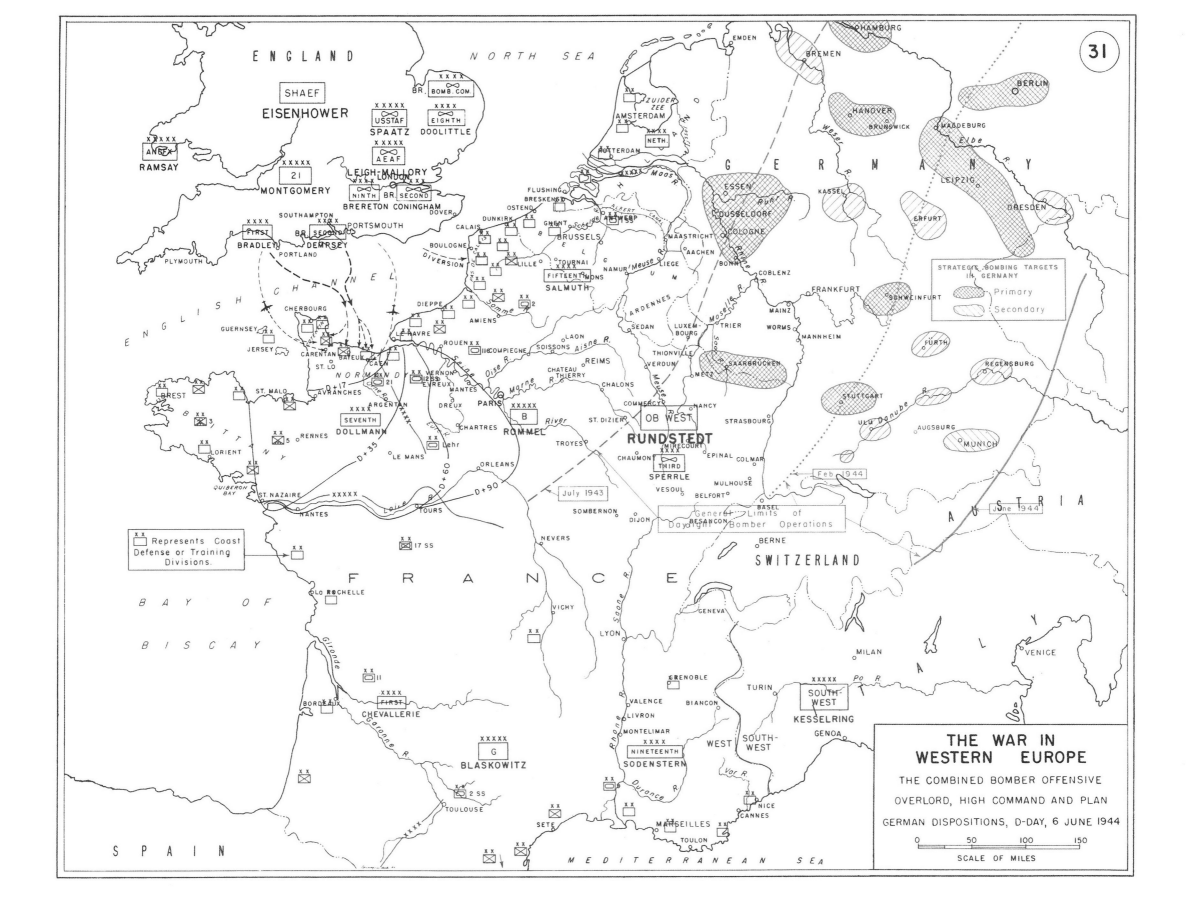

THE WAR IN WESTERN EUROPE

THE COMBINED BOMBER OFFENSIVE
OVERLORD, HIGH COMMAND AND PLAN
GERMAN DISPOSITIONS, D-DAY, 6 JUNE 1944

0   50   100   150

SCALE OF MILES

STRATEGIC BOMBING TARGETS IN GERMANY

Primary

Secondary

Represents Coast Defense or Training Divisions.

General Limits of Daylight Bomber Operations

July 1943

Feb 1944

June 1944

ALLIED INVASION FORCE AND GERMAN DISPOSITION, JUNE 6, 1944

★

Eisenhower was not satisfied with the preliminary plans for the invasion. Both he and Montgomery agreed that the three ground and one airborne divisions the plan had allocated to the initial assault were inadequate; they wanted five and three, respectively. Such an increase would require additional beaches, landing craft, and transport aircraft. So strong was Eisenhower's conviction that the assault had to be strengthened, he postponed the landings for a month. Consequently, in the final OVERLORD plan, the landing area was widened by including Utah Beach, thus causing the beachhead to be split by the estuary above Carentan. It would also, however, force the Germans to defend a greater area.

On 6 June, the strength of the Allied forces (all services) was 2,876,000. The organization of the ground component (forty-five divisions), is shown on the map below; only those divisions in the assault and follow-up forces are specifically indicated. The task of equipping and supplying this tremendous force had been staggering, but by virtually converting the United Kingdom into one huge military base, it had been accomplished.

Meanwhile, the Combined Bomber Offensive had intensified, and tactical air strikes were delivered at German defenses and communications in France (Eisenhower demanded that SHAEF control strategic bombing for OVERLORD, something that did not sit too well with the strategic air commanders). Bridges, roads, and railroads leading toward the landing area were targeted, and by the time of the landings the vicinity had been virtually isolated.

On the Continent, the German forces waited, edgy and not nearly as well prepared as Nazi propaganda had proclaimed. Their divisions were understrength, short of equipment, and filled out with second line troops. In contrast to the Allies, the German command structure teetered on chaos. Rundstedt, nominally the commander in all France, had no control over Luftwaffe, anti-aircraft, or naval forces, and only limited control over SS and parachute elements. Rommel had been sent to France by Hitler ostensibly to "inspect the Atlantic Wall." He had begun to overhaul the coastal defenses and subsequently had received command of Seventh and Fifteenth Armies, and by mutual agreement had partially subordinated himself to Rundstedt, but the two generals disagreed on the best defense. Rundstedt wanted to hold the coast lightly and create a mobile striking force. Rommel, on the other hand, was fearful that Allied air superiority would rampage in the interior, and wanted strong coastal defenses backed up by local reserves. Hitler agreed with Rommel but established no policy. Thus, on 6 June, Rommel controlled three panzer divisions, Hitler four, Blaskowitz three, and Rundstedt none.

Nor was the fabled Atlantic Wall very strong. In Rundstedt's opinion, these coastal fortifications were "sheer humbug." Some of the cities, especially those likely to be Allied supply ports, were garrisoned by hardened troops with orders to resist to the last man. Finally, the German dispositions indicate that the attack was expected in the Boulogne–Calais–Dunkirk area, a perception underpinned by brilliant Allied deception work.

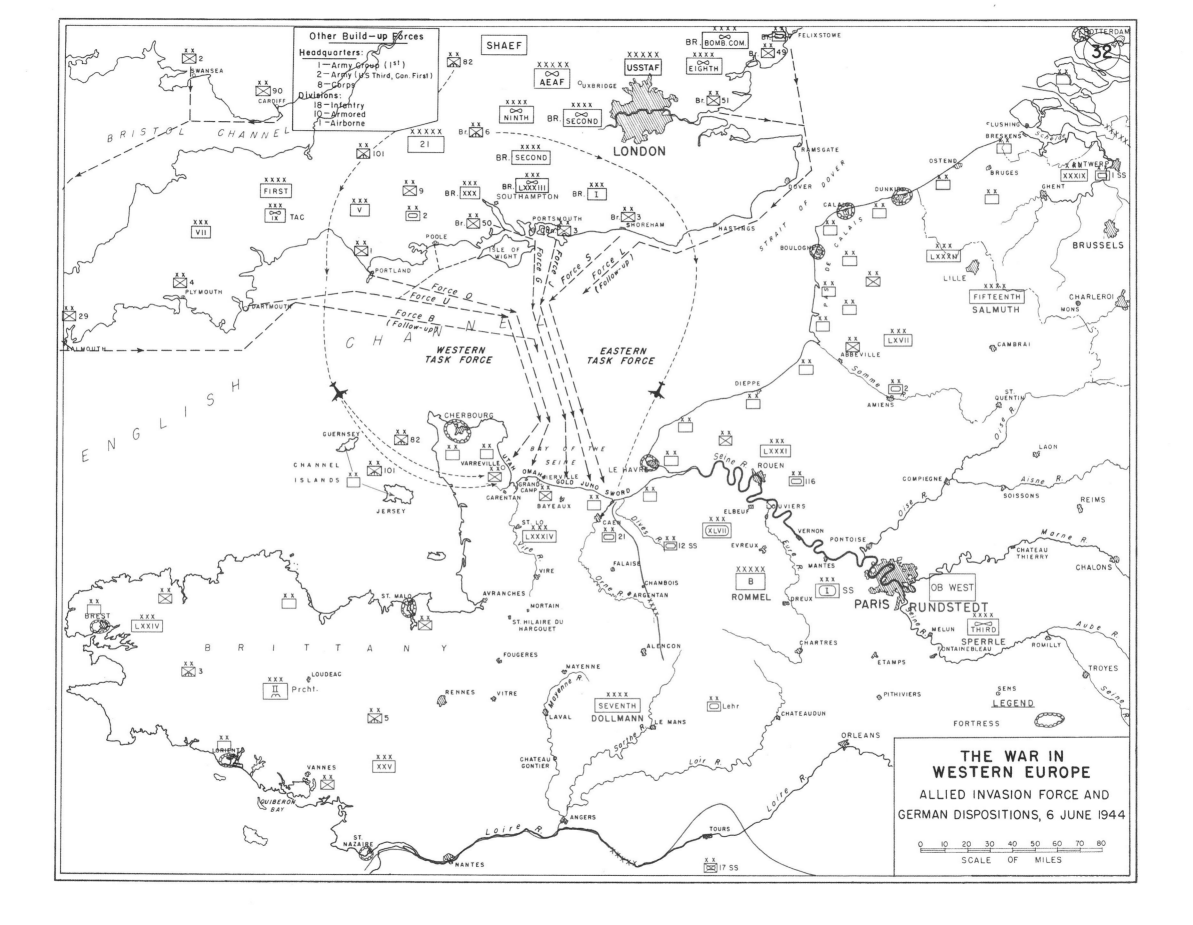

Other Build-up Forces

Headquarters:
  1 — Army Group (1st)
  2 — Army (US Third, Can. First)
  8 — Corps
Divisions:
  18 — Infantry
  10 — Armored
  1 — Airborne

SHAEF

BR. BOMB. COM.

USSTAF

EIGHTH

AEAF

UXBRIDGE

NINTH

BR. SECOND

LONDON

FELIXSTOWE

Br. 49

Br. 51

FLUSHING

BRESKENS

Scheldt R.

OSTEND

ANTWERP

I SS

XXXIX

BRUGES

GHENT

BRUSSELS

2

SWANSEA

90

CARDIFF

BRISTOL CHANNEL

82

21

Br. 6

BR. SECOND

SOUTHAMPTON

BR. LXXXIII

BR. I

RAMSGATE

DOVER

DUNKIRK

CALAIS

PAS DE CALAIS

LXXVII

LILLE

FIFTEENTH

SALMUTH

CHARLEROI

MONS

101

FIRST

9

IX TAC

V

2

Br. 50

PORTSMOUTH

3

Br. 3

SHOREHAM

HASTINGS

STRAIT OF DOVER

BOULOGNE

CAMBRAI

VII

1

POOLE

ISLE OF WIGHT

Force G

Force S

Force L
(Follow-up)

ABBEVILLE

LXVII

Somme R.

2

AMIENS

ST. QUENTIN

POOLE

PORTLAND

Force O

Force U

Force B
(Follow-up)

WESTERN
TASK FORCE

EASTERN
TASK FORCE

DIEPPE

4

PLYMOUTH

DARTMOUTH

29

FALMOUTH

C H A N N E L

E N G L I S H

BAY OF THE SEINE

LE HAVRE

LXXXI

ROUEN

Seine R.

116

Oise R.

LAON

SOISSONS

AISNE R.

REIMS

CHERBOURG

GUERNSEY

82

CHANNEL
ISLANDS

101

JERSEY

VARREVILLE

UTAH

OMAHA

GRAND
CAMP

CARENTAN

BAYEAUX

GOLD

JUNO

SWORD

ST. LO

LXXXIV

Vire R.

VIRE

CAEN

21

Dives R.

12 SS

XLVII

ELBEUF

LOUVIERS

VERNON

PONTOISE

COMPIEGNE

Oise R.

Eure R.

EVREUX

MANTES

B

ROMMEL

DREUX

I SS

PARIS

OB WEST

RUNDSTEDT

CHATEAU
THIERRY

Marne R.

CHALONS

ST. MALO

AVRANCHES

MORTAIN

ST. HILAIRE DU
HARCOUET

FALAISE

CHAMBOIS

ARGENTAN

CHARTRES

MELUN

FONTAINEBLEAU

THIRD

SPERRLE

ROMILLY

Aube R.

Seine R.

BREST

LXXIV

B R I T T A N Y

FOUGERES

ALENCON

MAYENNE

ETAMPS

PITHIVIERS

SENS

TROYES

3

II Prcht.

LOUDEAC

RENNES

VITRE

Mayenne R.

LAVAL

SEVENTH

DOLLMANN

Lehr

LE MANS

CHATEAUDUN

LEGEND

FORTRESS

ORLEANS

LORIENT

VANNES

XXV

CHATEAU
GONTIER

Sarthe R.

Loir R.

QUIBERON
BAY

ST.
NAZAIRE

NANTES

Loire R.

ANGERS

Loire R.

TOURS

17 SS

**THE WAR IN
WESTERN EUROPE**

ALLIED INVASION FORCE AND

GERMAN DISPOSITIONS, 6 JUNE 1944

0 10 20 30 40 50 60 70 80

SCALE OF MILES

ROTTERDAM

32

THE INVASION

★

Many factors influenced the selection of the date and the hours of the landings in Normandy. The major ones were tidal conditions (important to minimize the effectiveness of beach obstacles), the moonlight requirement for airborne drops, and acceptable weather. After much deliberation, the period 5–7 June was selected. The troops were already loaded and preparations initiated for landing on 5 June when unfavorable weather forecast forced Eisenhower to postpone. Continuing predictions of bad weather put Eisenhower in an excruciating position. Should he postpone again, and risk unhinging the whole operation, or go, and perhaps have the invasion fail because of bad weather? At 0415 on 5 June, Eisenhower gave the green light for the next day.

Shortly before midnight, 5 June, airborne units began taking off for their scheduled assaults. The U.S. 82nd Airborne was to secure the bridgehead across the Merderet River; the 101st was to secure the Utah Beach exits so that the U.S. 4th Division could break out from the beach; and the British 6th Airborne Division was to secure crossings over the Orne River and protect the Allied eastern flank.

Elements of five divisions made the OVERLORD amphibious assault landings. The initial follow-up divisions, and the dates on which they came ashore, are shown on the map. At dawn of 6 June, Allied air power (including 1,083 heavy bombers of Eighth Air Force) struck hard at German beach defenses, which were also pounded by naval gunfire shortly afterward.

By the end of D-Day, the Allies had established the beachheads, but nowhere had they reached their planned objectives. They had footholds, but Omaha was a decidedly precarious one. The assault at Utah had met the least resistance, but the greatest success was achieved in the British zone where, landing in greater strength and against moderate resistance, they had made sizable gains.

To the Germans, the landings came as a complete surprise. Air attacks had destroyed much of their radar, and the German navy considered the weather too rough for a landing. None of the German higher commanders predicted the place of the Allied landings, because they assumed it would come over the shortest Channel crossing, in the Calais area.

Learning of the Allied landings, Rundstedt, at 0400, ordered the 12th SS and Panzer Lehr divisions to the Caen area, but OKW, the German army high command, temporarily restrained them. The fury of the assault fell on the six divisions of LXXXIV Corps which, in the confusion of the day, launched only one (unsuccessful) counterattack. No attempt was made to wipe out the tenuous Allied hold at Omaha, because corps headquarters was erroneously advised that the landing there had been repulsed, and because the Germans were more concerned about the British advance toward Caen.

The expansion of the beachhead through 12 June entailed bitter fighting around Caen and Carentan. During this period, as the Allies built up their beachhead strength to sixteen divisions and feverishly poured supplies ashore, the Germans, concentrating their armor at Caen, were never able to launch a major counterattack, and by 12 June, the center of the German line at Caumont was almost ruptured. The remnants of the 352nd Division fell back toward St. Lô.

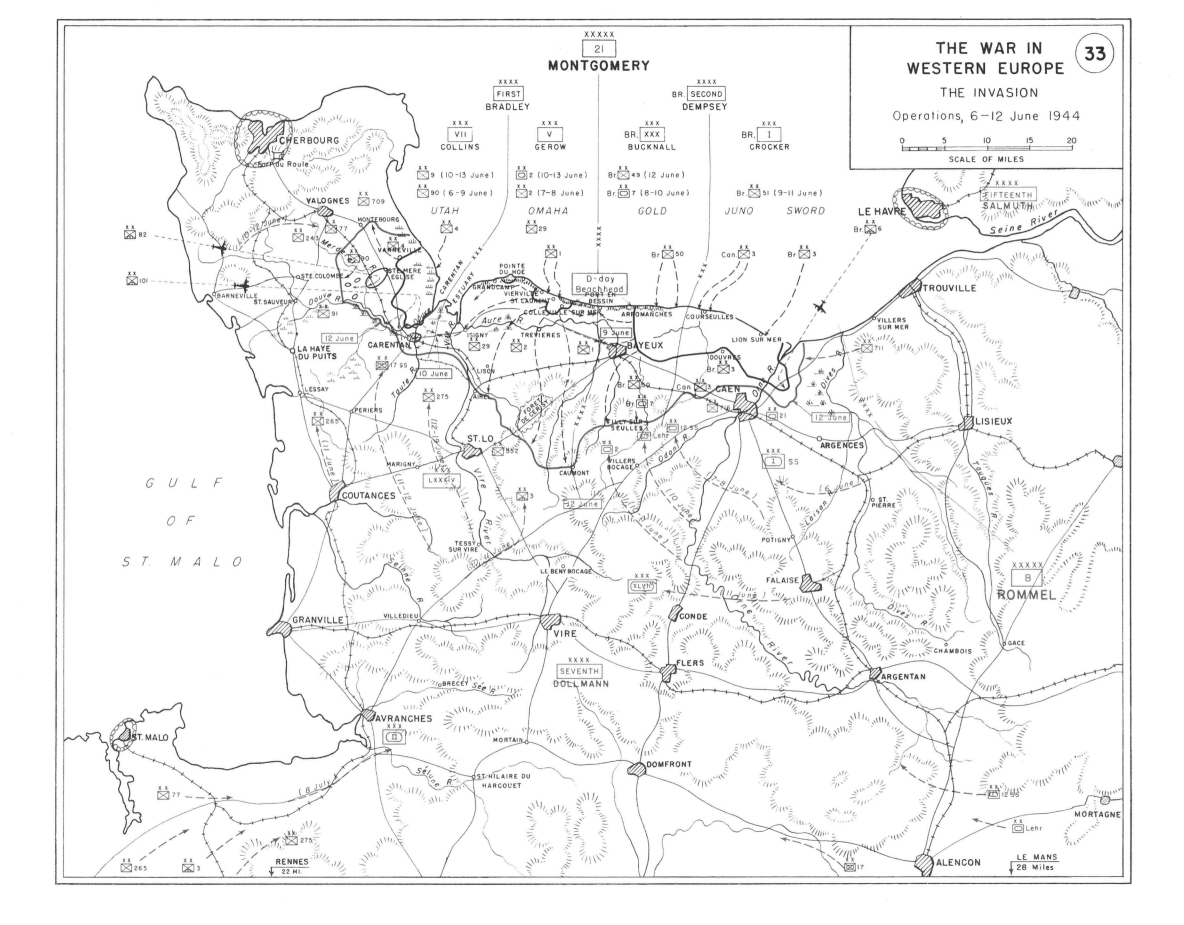

THE WAR IN
WESTERN EUROPE
THE INVASION
Operations, 6–12 June 1944

33

SCALE OF MILES
0   5   10   15   20

MONTGOMERY
XXXXX
21

FIRST
BRADLEY
XXXX

BR. SECOND
DEMPSEY
XXXX

VII
COLLINS
XXX

V
GEROW
XXX

BR. XXX
BUCKNALL
XXX

BR. I
CROCKER
XXX

9 (10–13 June)
90 (6–9 June)

2 (10–13 June)
2 (7–8 June)

Br. 49 (12 June)
Br. 7 (8–10 June)

Br. 51 (9–11 June)

FIFTEENTH
SALMUTH
XXXXX

CHERBOURG
Fort du Roule

VALOGNES   709
MONTEBOURG
77
243
VARREVILLE
90
STE. MERE EGLISE
STE. COLOMBE
BARNEVILLE
ST. SAUVEUR
91
LA HAYE DU PUITS
12 June
CARENTAN
10 June
17 SS
LESSAY
Taute R.
275
PERIERS
265
COUTANCES

UTAH
4

OMAHA
29
1

POINTE DU HOE
GRANDCAMP
VIERVILLE
ST. LAURENT
COLLEVILLE SUR MER
ISIGNY
TREVIERES
29
2
St. LO
352
MARIGNY
LXXXIV

D-day Beachhead
PORT EN BESSIN
ARROMANCHES
9 June
BAYEUX
1
LISON
AIRE
275
FORET DE CERISY
Lehr
VILLERS BOCAGE
2
CAUMONT
3
12 June

GOLD
Br. 50

COURSEULLES
DOUVRES
Br. 3
Can. 3
12 SS
Lehr
TILLY SUR SEULLES
I SS

JUNO   SWORD
Can. 3   Br. 3

LE HAVRE
Br. 6
Seine River

TROUVILLE
VILLERS SUR MER
711
LION SUR MER
Orne R.
CAEN
21
12 June
Odon R.
Loison R.
ST. PIERRE
POTIGNY
FALAISE

LISIEUX
ARGENCES
Touques R.
Dives R.
GACE
CHAMBOIS

B
ROMMEL
XXXXX

GULF
OF
ST. MALO

Vire R.
TESSY SUR VIRE
Seine R.
GRANVILLE
VILLEDIEU
LE BENY BOCAGE
XLVII
VIRE
CONDE
Orne River
FLERS
SEVENTH
DOLLMANN
BRECEY   See R.
ARGENTAN

ST. MALO
77
AVRANCHES
II
MORTAIN
Selune R.
ST. HILAIRE DU HARCOUET
DOMFRONT
12 SS
Lehr
MORTAGNE

265   3
RENNES
22 MI.
275

ALENCON
17
LE MANS
28 Miles

VII CORPS D-DAY OPERATIONS

★

The terrain behind Utah beach reveals why Eisenhower wanted two airborne divisions. The marshy bottom land along the Douve and Merderet rivers formed an easily defended barrier across the base of the Cotentin peninsula. Furthermore, there were flooded areas two miles wide directly behind the beach, crossed by only four narrow causeways. Thus, the prime mission of both American airborne divisions was to ensure the rapid expansion of the Utah beachhead across those flooded areas in preparation for a quick drive up the peninsula to Cherbourg.

Between 0100 and 0200, 6 June, the leading elements of six parachute regiments of the 82nd and 101st Airborne Divisions jumped over Normandy. A careful study of the map below indicates that, in general, the airborne drops were poorly executed and resulted in the wide dispersal of troops. Nevertheless, the 101st succeeded in capturing the important exits behind Utah Beach, but German resistance prevented them seizing the bridges northeast of Carentan and the destruction of those northwest of the city. By the end of D-Day, the division had taken 1,240 casualties and had assembled only about 2,500 of the 6,000 men who had jumped earlier that morning.

Had the Germans made a coordinated attack during the day against the weak positions north of Carentan, they might have seriously interfered with the landing at Utah; but instead, that night, they merely dispatched the 6th Parachute Regiment to set up a defensive position at St. Côme-du-Mont, northwest of Carentan.

Farther north, the 82nd Division, less scattered than the 101st, landed in a more heavily defended area. It did succeed in capturing the key communications center of Ste. Mère-Eglise and holding it against German attacks from the south. But the two regiments west of the Merderet River landed dispersed and were soon heavily engaged with elements of the German 91st Division. The paratroopers were hard-pressed and unable to secure the bridges over the Merderet and link up with the regiment east of the river. In the afternoon, the division's seaborne tail (tanks and infantry) came ashore over Utah Beach. It was unable to penetrate the German position south of Ste. Mère-Eglise and reach the division; worse still, it could not secure the glider zone, and as a result, the Germans took a heavy toll of the gliders landing at 2100. By the end of D-Day, the 82nd, like the 101st, had assembled only a fraction of its paratroopers and had suffered 1,259 casualties. It had no contact with either the 101st or 4th Divisions and faced a stiff two-day fight before the crossings over the Merderet were seized.

Meanwhile, about 0700, the 4th Infantry Division had landed a mile south of its planned destination, against minor opposition. Pre-assault air and naval bombardments had softened up the defenses, and the operations of the airborne divisions had put the Germans on the defensive. By the end of the day, the 4th Division, having suffered fewer than 200 casualties, was ashore and organized for offensive action.

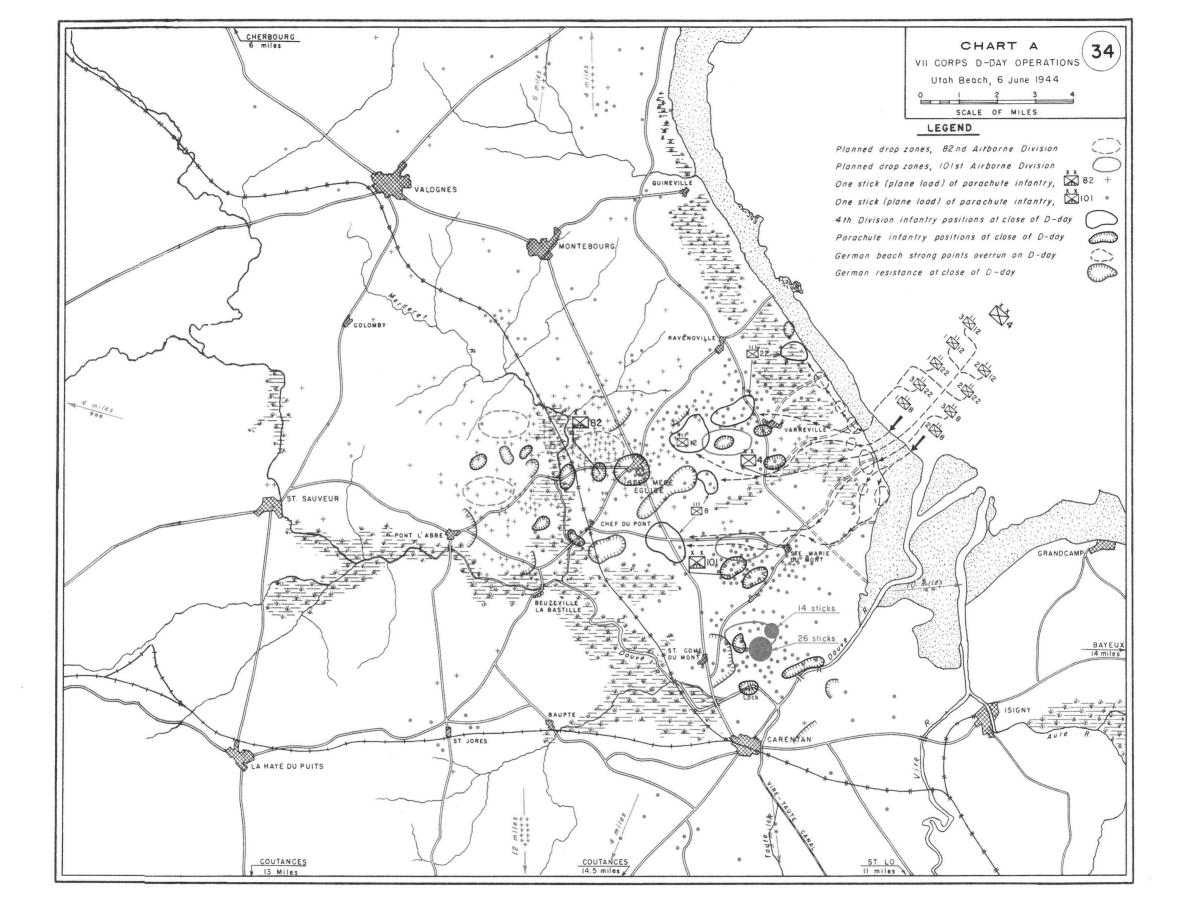

CHART A

VII CORPS D-DAY OPERATIONS

Utah Beach, 6 June 1944

34

SCALE OF MILES
0 1 2 3 4

LEGEND

Planned drop zones, 82nd Airborne Division
Planned drop zones, 101st Airborne Division
One stick (plane load) of parachute infantry, 82
One stick (plane load) of parachute infantry, 101
4th Division infantry positions at close of D-day
Parachute infantry positions at close of D-day
German beach strong points overrun on D-day
German resistance at close of D-day

CHERBOURG
6 miles

VALOGNES

QUINEVILLE

MONTEBOURG

COLOMBY

RAVENOVILLE

VARREVILLE

ST. SAUVEUR

STE MERE EGLISE

PONT L'ABBE

CHEF DU PONT

STE MARIE DU MONT

GRANDCAMP

BEUZEVILLE LA BASTILLE

BAYEUX
14 miles

ST. COME DU MONT

14 sticks

26 sticks

Lock

BAUPTE

ISIGNY

ST. JORES

CARENTAN

LA HAYE DU PUITS

COUTANCES
13 Miles

COUTANCES
14.5 miles

ST. LO
11 miles

V CORPS D-DAY OPERATIONS

★

While operations at Utah Beach and in the British sector were progressing favorably, elements of the U.S. 1st and 29th Divisions were struggling to secure a foothold on Omaha Beach against the strongest resistance of the day.

A typical cross-section of Omaha Beach is shown below. There was an imposing array of beach obstacles (covered at high tide, exposed at low), the shingle, (impassable to vehicles), and the steep cliffs. Combined, they presented formidable obstructions to a landing. The German strong points here were placed to defend the beach exits, and within those defenses were more than sixty light artillery pieces and many machine guns, sited to enfilade the beaches and their offshore approaches. Because many of the weapons were invisible from the sea, the preparatory naval bombardment was largely ineffective.

The intensive German resistance was largely due to the presence of the 352nd Infantry Division, a first line unit which surprisingly had gone undetected by Allied intelligence. So, instead of assaulting a four-battalion defensive front as expected, V Corps encountered eight battalions positioned in depth.

V Corps' plan specified that each of the assault regiments (16th and 116th) would land two battalions abreast—a total of eight infantry companies in the first assault wave whose task it was to reduce the enemy strong points protecting the exit roads from the beach. Immediately following them would come the special demolition teams to blow gaps in the obstacle zone; then the remainder of the assault regiment would land, to be followed by the divisional support units. Tanks adapted to be able to "swim" ashore were to provide the vital support for the assault waves. All personnel had been thoroughly trained to deal with their specific sectors, but herein lay a weakness; if a unit landed in anything other than its designated area, confusion might—and did—reign.

As the initial waves landed at 0630 they found an enemy relatively unscathed by air and naval bombardment. Furthermore, strong lateral currents and poor navigation brought the assault waves onto the beaches in unplanned positions. As a result, there was much intermingling and, under withering German fire, the right wing almost disintegrated. The tanks were dropped off too far out to sea and many sank, as did a large number of the amphibious trucks loaded with 105mm howitzers. The demolition teams, laboring heroically, took 40 percent casualties, but did manage to blast six gaps through the obstacles. The U.S. infantry who had survived the initial assault were huddled behind the shingle, demoralized, confused, and often leaderless. But there were some exceptional leaders who managed to get small groups working their way inland, generally up through the draws in the cliffs. Naval gunfire took over the direct support mission; engineers began clearing the mine fields; and by noon, the follow-up regiments (115th, 18th, and 26th) were landing. By the end of D-Day V Corps, having suffered about 2,000 casualties, had forward elements in position. The beachhead, nowhere more than a mile-and-a-half deep, was far from secure, but the build up was proceeding. There were still isolated German elements on the coast; only 100 tons of supplies out of a scheduled 2,400 had been unloaded; and many obstacles had yet to be cleared.

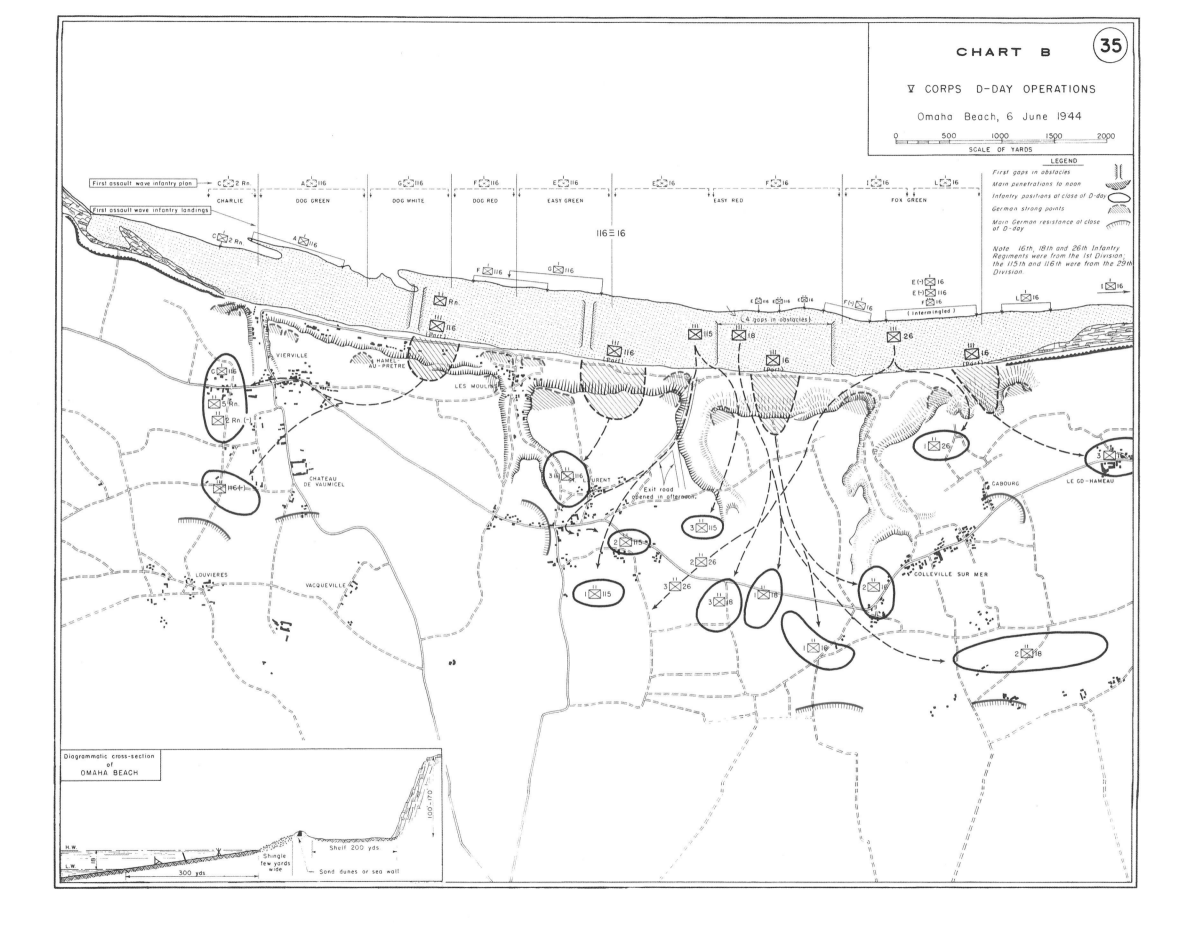

CHART B 35

V CORPS D-DAY OPERATIONS

Omaha Beach, 6 June 1944

0   500   1000   1500   2000
SCALE OF YARDS

LEGEND

First gaps in obstacles

Main penetrations to noon

Infantry positions at close of D-day

German strong points

Main German resistance at close of D-day

Note 16th, 18th and 26th Infantry Regiments were from the 1st Division; the 115th and 116th were from the 29th Division.

First assault wave infantry plan — C 2 Rn.   A 116   G 116   F 116   E 116   E 16   F 16   I 16   L 16

CHARLIE   DOG GREEN   DOG WHITE   DOG RED   EASY GREEN   EASY RED   FOX GREEN

First assault wave infantry landings

C 2 Rn.   A 116

F 116   G 116

116 ≡ 16

E 116 E 116 E 16   E(-) 16
E(+) 16
F(-) 16   L 16

1 16

Rn.

III 116 (Part)

E 116 E 116 E 16   F(-) 16   I 16
(Intermingled)   (Intermingled)

III 115   III 18   III 26

III 116 (Part)   III 16 (Part)

4 gaps in obstacles

VIERVILLE

HAMEL AU-PRETRE

LES MOULINS

III 116 (Part)

III 16 (Part)

C 116

5 Rn.

2 Rn. (-)

CHATEAU DE VAUMICEL

116 (-)

1 26

3 16

GABOURG   LE GD-HAMEAU

3 116
St LAURENT

Exit road opened in afternoon.

3 115

COLLEVILLE SUR MER

LOUVIERES

VACQUEVILLE

2 115

2 26

3 26   1 18

3 18   1 16   2 16

1 115

1 16

2 18

Diagrammatic cross-section of OMAHA BEACH

H.W.

L.W.

Shelf 200 yds

100-170'

300 yds   Shingle few yards wide   Sand dunes or sea wall

THE CAPTURE OF CHERBOURG

★

Initial logistical support of the invasion was to be over the beaches. But the beach capacity was limited, and unloading operations were subject to disruption by storms. It was essential, therefore, that Cherbourg be captured as soon as possible in order to serve as a major supply port. To supplement beach unloading during the critical period before ports were operational, the British designed two ingenious, artificial "Mulberry" harbors, but on 19 June, three days after the first Mulberry had been sited, a severe four-day long storm struck the Normandy coast, and halted all unloading.

Operations around Caen and on the Cotentin peninsula were very closely related. In Montgomery's view, "Caen was the key to Cherbourg," since its capture would reduce German lateral movement and free British forces for a shift westward, thus allowing more American troops to move against Cherbourg. Consequently, beginning on 13 June, Montgomery drove the British hard toward Caen and directed Bradley to speed the capture of Cherbourg. But when the German armor put up a stiff resistance at Villers-Bocage, Montgomery settled for the idea of drawing German strength on to Second Army, but he was under extreme pressure to show that he could be as aggressive as the Americans on the Cotentin. So, on the 18th he ordered the renewal of the attack on Caen by XXX and VIII Corps, but it soon bogged down in the face of fierce panzer counterattacks. Despite the criticism (then and subsequently) Montgomery's plan was effective. On 30 June, the British (on a 33-mile front) were opposed by seven panzer and two infantry divisions; the Americans (on a 55-mile front) were opposed by the equivalent of seven infantry divisions.

Meanwhile, Bradley's V and XIX Corps took up defensive positions on the shoulder of the Cotentin peninsula, protecting VII Corps as it drove toward the west coast of the Cotentin to cut off the Germans at Cherbourg. The going was costly as the Americans dealt with the *bocage* (small fields separated by hedges, high banks, and sunken roads), but their commander, Maj. Gen. J. Lawton Collins, had experience in the somewhat similar terrain of Guadalcanal, and pushed his troops forward on narrow fronts with reserves in depth. His sharp wedges hit the disintegrating Germans with great effect, and he reached the coast on the 18 June. Collis then turned north and attacked the outer defenses of Cherbourg. The Germans in Cherbourg refused a surrender ultimatum, and it took five days of hard fighting before the city capitulated.

The period 13–30 June destroyed all German hopes collapse. From the 16th on, Rundstedt, at Hitler's insistence, massed armor at Caen, not only to check the British, but reverse everything and drive on to the coast. It was completely unrealistic, but Hitler insisted on counterattack. By 30 June, German commanders had conceded defeat (although the Fifteenth Army, north of the Seine, was at full strength, yet uncommitted to the great battle in Normandy). On 3 July, Rundstedt was dismissed, and replaced by Kluge.

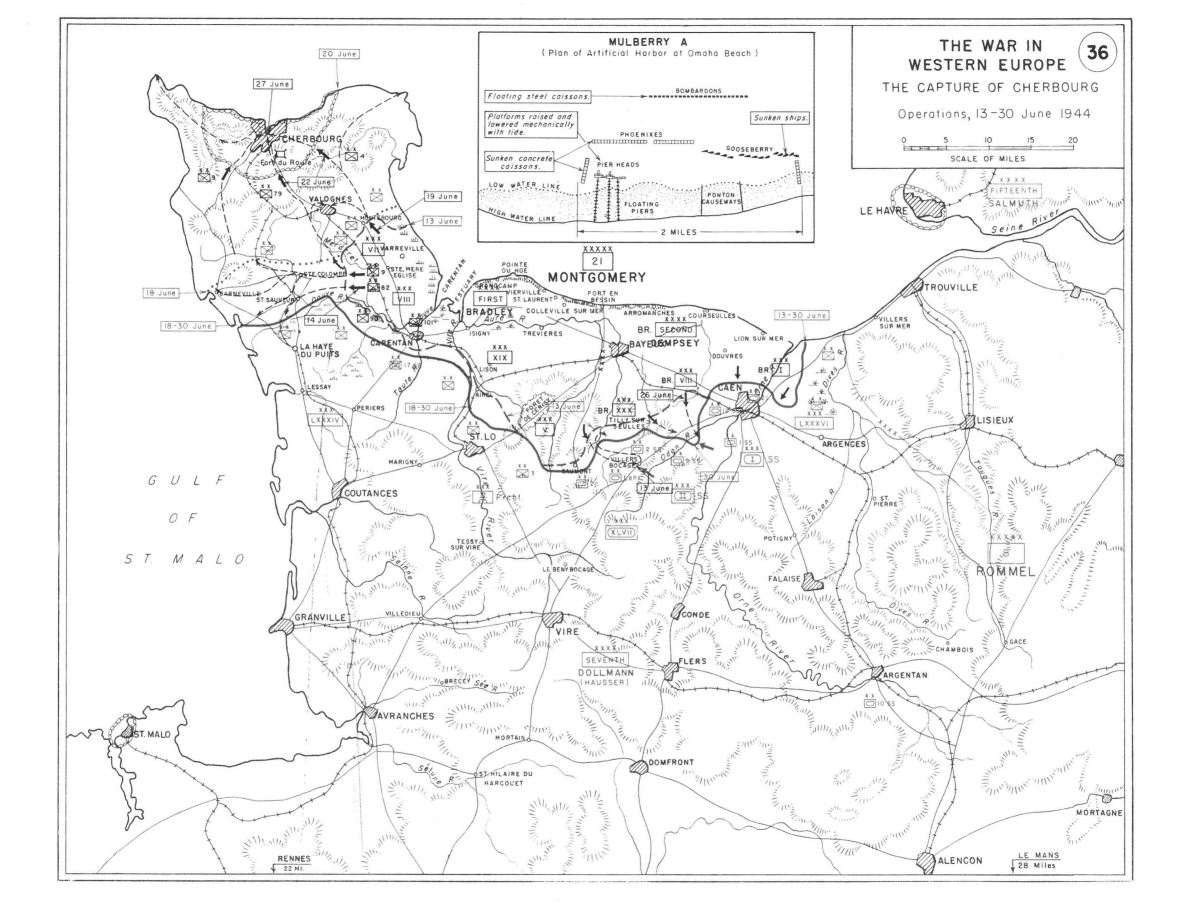

MULBERRY A
(Plan of Artificial Harbor at Omaha Beach)

Floating steel caissons. ——————→ BOMBARDONS

Platforms raised and lowered mechanically with tide. PHOENIXES

Sunken concrete caissons. PIER HEADS GOOSEBERRY Sunken ships.

LOW WATER LINE PONTON CAUSEWAYS

FLOATING PIERS

HIGH WATER LINE

2 MILES

THE WAR IN WESTERN EUROPE
36
THE CAPTURE OF CHERBOURG
Operations, 13-30 June 1944

0   5   10   15   20
SCALE OF MILES

GULF OF ST. MALO

CHERBOURG
Fort du Roule
20 June
27 June
22 June
VALOGNES
MONTEBOURG
19 June
13 June
VARREVILLE
STE. MERE EGLISE
STE COLOMBE
18 June
BARNEVILLE
ST. SAUVEUR
14 June
LA HAYE DU PUITS
CARENTAN
LESSAY
PERIERS
18-30 June
ST. LO
MARIGNY
COUTANCES
VILLEDIEU
GRANVILLE
TESSY SUR VIRE
LE BENY BOCAGE
VIRE
FLERS
SEVENTH
DOLLMANN
(HAUSSER)
BRECEY
See R.
AVRANCHES
MORTAIN
Sélune R.
ST. HILAIRE DU HARCOUET
DOMFRONT
ST. MALO
RENNES 22 MI.

MONTGOMERY
21
FIRST
BRADLEY
POINTE DU HOE
GRANDCAMP
VIERVILLE
ST. LAURENT
ISIGNY
COLLEVILLE SUR MER
PORT EN BESSIN
ARROMANCHES
COURSEULLES
LION SUR MER
DOUVRES
BAYEUX
BR. SECOND
DEMPSEY
TREVIERES
LISON
AIREL
FORET DE CERISY
13 June
TILLY SUR SEULLES
26 June
CAEN
VILLERS BOCAGE
CAUMONT
13 June
II SS
XLVII
POTIGNY
ST. PIERRE
FALAISE
CONDE
CHAMBOIS
GACE
ARGENTAN
10 SS
13-30 June
VILLERS SUR MER
TROUVILLE
LE HAVRE
FIFTEENTH
SALMUTH
Seine River
LISIEUX
ARGENCES
I SS
Laison R.
ROMMEL
B
Orne River
Dives R.
Touques R.

LE MANS 28 Miles
ALENCON
MORTAGNE

EXPANDING THE BEACHHEAD

★

On 1 July only one-fifth of the area projected in the OVERLORD plan had been seized, and Caen, a D-Day objective, was still in German hands. About one million men, 500,000 tons of supplies, and 150,000 vehicles had come ashore, but desired airfield sites had not been secured, and lateral communications were poor and subject to periodic German shelling. Nor was the terrain in the First Army sector favorable for offensive operations. The marshy Carentan plain was unsuitable for mechanized warfare; to the west, from La Haye-du-Puits to the coast, the ground was firmer and hillier, but throughout the area the *bocage* created perfect ambush conditions for the German defenders.

On 30 June, Montgomery directed Bradley's First Army to drive south, pivoting on Caumont. Elements of eleven German divisions (35,000 men with surprisingly high morale) prepared for the defense. They lacked supplies, but had excellent terrain to defend. Now convinced of the impracticability of an offensive thrust, Hitler planned to fight defensively, replace his panzers with infantry, and form a mobile reserve.

Bradley designated the St. Lô–Coutances–Caumont line as the first phase objective. First Army attacked on the dates shown on the map below and everywhere met stern, unexpected resistance, and all divisions took heavy, demoralizing casualties. La Haye-du-Puits fell on 7 July, but by the 8th, Bradley, disappointed with his slight gains, began to think he would have to accept the Lessay–St. Lô line as an intermediate objective where he could

mass—instead of attacking all along the line—for an attack on Coutances. By 13 July this idea was enthusiastically supported by Eisenhower and Montgomery, and eventually became Operation COBRA: the breakout. In the interim, however, First Army slogged forward, beginning to meet panzer reinforcements from Caen, but on 18 July finally took St. Lô. Six days later the attack halted. The five divisions attacking St. Lô had suffered 11,000 casualties in twelve days, but the Germans had also paid heavily and were stretched thin.

Meanwhile, to the east Montgomery, following his basic concept of holding German strength near Caen—but now also interesting in seizing the city—had ordered Second Army to attack on 8 July. The attack by I Corps, preceded by a 2,300-ton carpet air bombardment (4,000 by 1,500 yards, laid down by 470 strategic bombers) took that part of Caen west of the Orne, soaked up German strength, and then bogged down. On the 13th Montgomery ordered another attack, this time by the British VIII Corps (three armored divisions) and the Canadian II Corps, for 17 July. He appears to have considered these operations merely diversions to help relieve some of the pressure on COBRA, but Eisenhower seems to have considered them nothing less than the Allies' major bid to break out. Thus, there was considerable disappointment when the attack was halted south of Caen by Montgomery on 20 July.

The COBRA attack was to start on 25 July and at first was not seen as the major breakout that later, under Bradley and Collins' imaginative leadership, it would become.

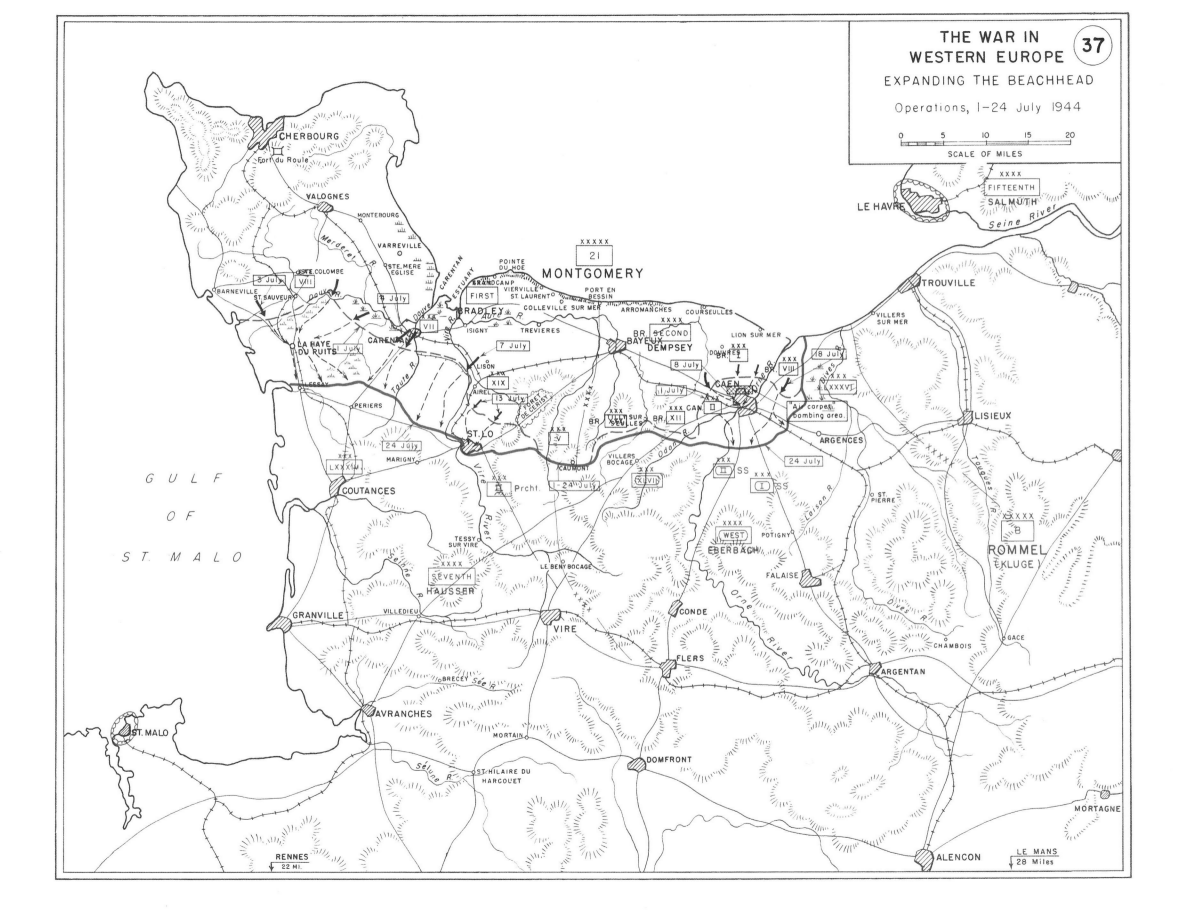

THE WAR IN
WESTERN EUROPE

37

EXPANDING THE BEACHHEAD

Operations, 1–24 July 1944

0 5 10 15 20
SCALE OF MILES

THE ST. LÔ BREAKTHROUGH

★

COBRA was led by Collins' VII Corps (three infantry, two armored, and one motorized infantry divisions). It would make the main effort, supported by extra artillery and another carpet bombing (2,500 by 6,000 yards, to be saturated by over 4,200 tons of bombs). The infantry divisions, attacking right behind the carpet, would break through the defensive crust, and the motorized infantry division would pass through the gap and seize Coutances. One armored division would envelop the town from the south, and the other armored division would drive southeast and establish blocking positions from Tessy-sur-Vire south to the Seinne River. To Collins' right, the VIII Corps, attacking after Coutances was captured, would move south to complete the encirclement of the German LXXXIV Corps; to his left, XIX and V Corps would exert pressure to prevent a shift of German forces to the west.

German defenses west of St. Lô on 25 July lacked depth. Kluge, concerned with creating a mobile reserve near Caen, virtually ignored the Seventh Army front. On the eve of the attack there were about 30,000 troops (including administrative and reserve echelons) opposite VII Corps, but in or near the front line there were only about 5,000, mostly from the Panzer Lehr division.

The carpet bombing, although causing 558 "friendly" casualties due to inaccurate delivery, practically wiped out Panzer Lehr and created such shock and confusion that it must be considered the major factor in the breakout. But still there was resistance (VII Corps suffered 1,060 casualties on the first day) and Collins, appreciating the need for rapid

exploitation and gambling that the German defenses were almost ruptured, committed two of his mobile columns the following day (26th). The first, advancing east of Marigny, met little resistance and by the 27th had reached Tessy-sur-Vire; then XIX Corps assumed control of the column and for the next three days fought of counterattacks reinforced with two panzer divisions. The second column moved toward Coutances, encountered fierce resistance and saw its objective assigned to VIII Corps on the 27th.

The German LXXXIV Corps of Hausser's Seventh Army, holding open a coastal escape corridor, evaded the planned Coutances trap, but instead of pulling back due south, moved eastward toward Tessy-sur-Vire, much to Kluge's dismay. It ran smack into Collins' armor and was chopped to bits. With the German line to the coast unhinged, Bradley ordered full exploitation on the 28th, and elements of VII and VIII Corps rapidly drove south. Coutances fell on 28 July; Granville and Avranches on the 30th.

In the British sector, the Canadian II Corps had made a diversionary attack on the 25th, which drew to them a vicious counterattack. The Montgomery moved the British VIII Corps to Caumont, where it attacked on the 30th to protect Bradley's left, but it came too late to prevent Kluge's movement of armor to the Tessy-sur-Vire area.

By 31 July, the Allies were in good positions. Two new headquarters had arrived: Lt. Gen. Henry D.G. Crerar's Canadian First Army (now controlling the British I Corps), and Lt. Gen. George S. Patton's Third Army (prepared to assume control of Bradley's westernmost divisions).

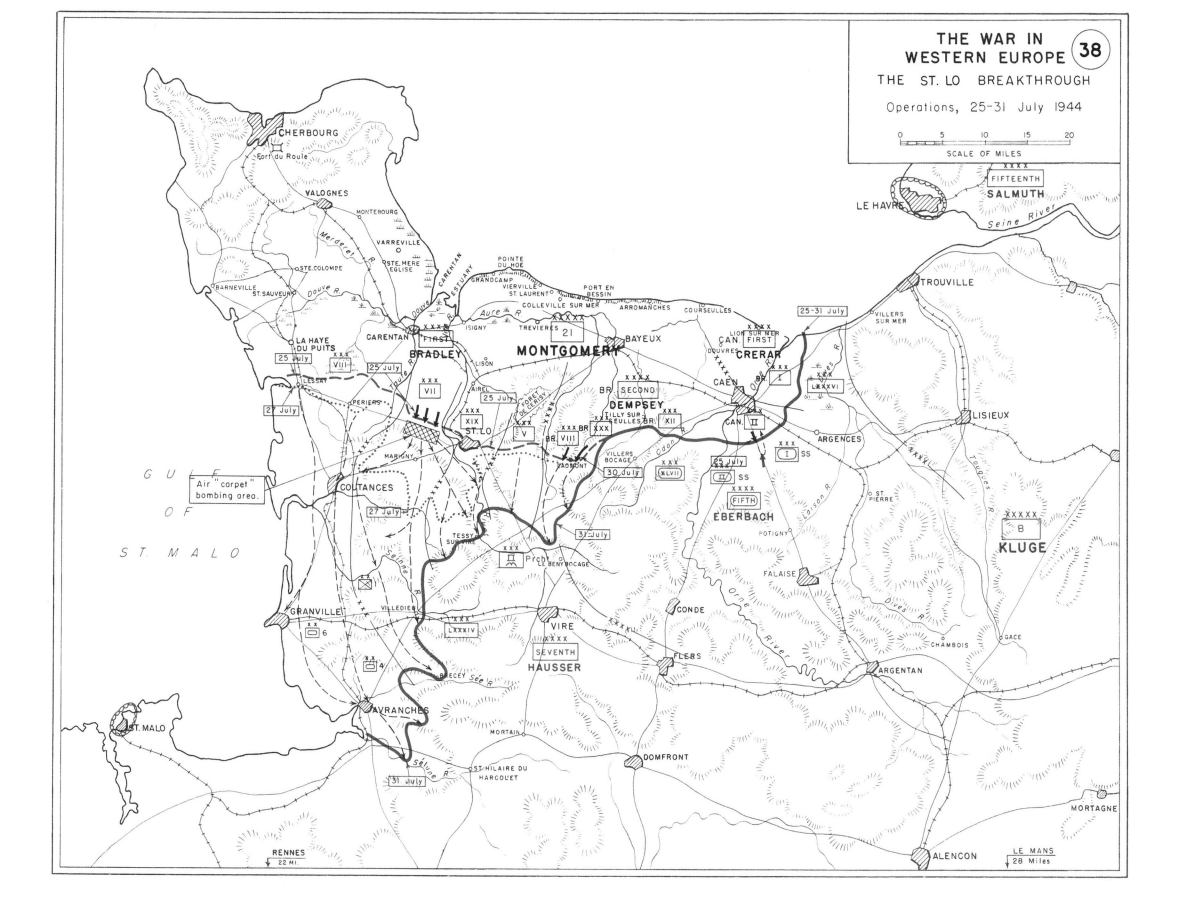

SCALE OF MILES
0   5   10   15   20

XXXX
FIFTEENTH
SALMUTH

CHERBOURG
Fort du Roule

LE HAVRE

Seine River

VALOGNES

MONTEBOURG

TROUVILLE

VARREVILLE

STE. COLOMBE

STE. MERE
EGLISE

POINTE
DU HOE

VILLERS
SUR MER

BARNEVILLE
ST. SAUVEUR

Douve R.

GRANDCAMP
VIERVILLE
ST. LAURENT

PORT EN
BESSIN

COLLEVILLE SUR MER
ARROMANCHES
COURSEULLES

25-31 July

Merderet R.

Douve R. ESTUARY

Aure R.

LION SUR MER

LA HAYE
DU PUITS

CARENTAN

XXXX
FIRST

ISIGNY

TREVIERES

XXXX
21

BAYEUX

CAN. FIRST
CRERAR

LISIEUX

25 July

XXX
VIII

25 July

BRADLEY

LISON

MONTGOMERY

DOUVRES

BR. I

CAEN

XXX
LXXXVI

Toques R.

27 July

XXX
VII

PERIERS

AIREL

25 July

FORET
DE CERISY

BR. SECOND

XXXX

DEMPSEY

TILLY SUR
SEULLES BR.

XXX
XII

ARGENCES

GULF

LESSAY

Taute R.

XXX
XIX

ST. LO

XXX
V

XXX
BR.

XXX

BR.
VIII

VILLERS
BOCAGE

Odon R.

CAN. II

XXX

25 July

I
SS

MARIGNY

30 July

XXXX
XLVII

II
SS

Laison R.

ST.
PIERRE

Air "carpet"
bombing area.

COUTANCES

27 July

XXXX
FIFTH
EBERBACH

POTIGNY

XXXXX
B
KLUGE

OF

31 July

Orne River

Dives R.

FALAISE

ST. MALO

Seine R.

TESSY
SUR VIRE

II
Prcb

LE BENY BOCAGE

CONDE

GRANVILLE

6

VILLEDIEU

XXX
LXXXIV

VIRE

GACE

CHAMBOIS

FLERS

4

SEVENTH
HAUSSER

See R.

AVRANCHES

MORTAIN

ARGENTAN

ST. MALO

Selune R.

31 July

ST. HILAIRE DU
HARCOUET

DOMFRONT

MORTAGNE

RENNES
22 MI.

ALENCON

LE MANS
28 Miles

THE BREAKOUT

★

It was part of the Allied plan that when First Army broke out of the Cotentin peninsula, a corps (controlled by Third Army) would be sent to secure the Brittany ports. Accordingly, when VIII Corps broke into the open south of Avranches on 1 August, Third Army became operational, and the Twelfth Army Group was formed, with Bradley in command. Lt. Gen. Courtney Hodges took over First Army.

While engineers labored on the restricted road network at the Avranches bottleneck, Patton drove VIII Corps westward into Brittany. He moved his other corps through the gap straight south of Avranches. Brittany was quickly overrun, except for the major ports. During these operations Allied close air support was superb. Tank columns had direct communications with their support aircraft, and so effectively were bridges, roads, and railroads destroyed that the Germans, whose lack of supplies was acute, were reduced to moving troops by night.

Near the end of July, Eisenhower, anticipating a great opportunity, had urged Montgomery to take bold action. Montgomery's response was his 4 August directive ordering Crerar to attack southeast not later than the 8th, Dempsey to continue attacking toward Argentan, Hodges to continue his swing eastward, and Patton (leaving VIII to guard Brittany) to advance toward Le Mans. Montgomery's intention was to force Kluge back against the bridgeless Seine and destroy him.

The Allied armies quickly implemented the plan, but late on 6 August a powerful German armored counterattack at Mortain, with a view to reach Avranches, isolate Third Army, and ultimately push north to crush the Allied beachhead, forced a reconsideration. The 30th Division (VII Corps) caught the full force of the onslaught and reeled backward, but Bradley was quick to reinforce it; air support in the shape of British rocket-firing Typhoons, together with Crerar's attack to the east which forced Kluge to divert some of his panzers, forced Kluge to halt his attack on the 8 August. Although under pressure from Hitler to continue, Kluge disengaged to meet what he saw as the greater threat from Patton coming up from the south.

On 8 August, in bold disregard of the German threat at Mortain, Montgomery and Bradley had turned Patton's XV Corps north toward Argentan. By the 13th, against increasing resistance, it had reached the army group boundary just south of Argentan. Here, much to Patton's disgruntlement, Bradley, fearing an Allied mix-up, ordered a halt. Meanwhile, Crerar's attack had been blunted by a skillful defense, and Kluge still had an escape route—if he moved fast.

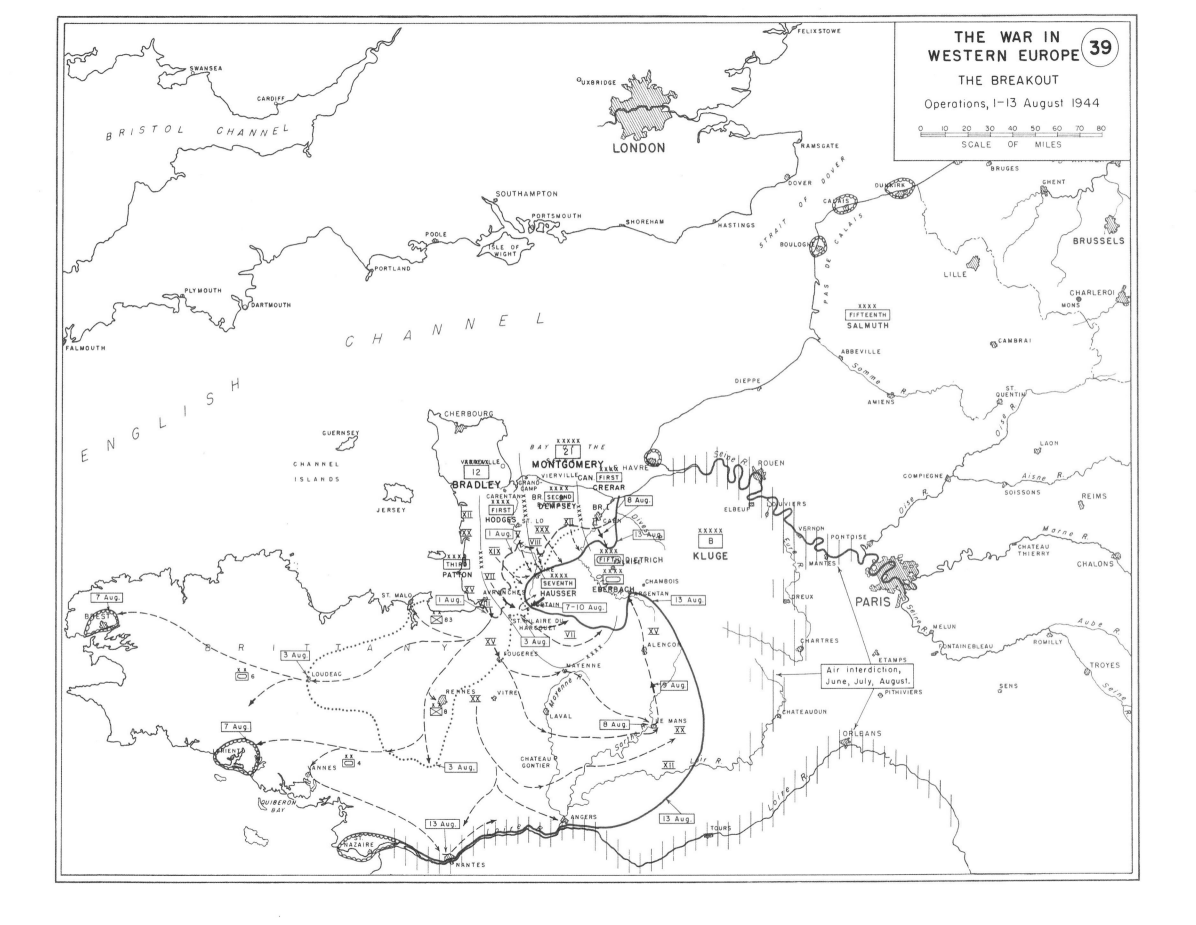

SCALE OF MILES
0 10 20 30 40 50 60 70 80

BRISTOL CHANNEL

SWANSEA
CARDIFF

LONDON

UXBRIDGE

FELIXSTOWE

RAMSGATE

DOVER

STRAIT OF DOVER

BRUGES
GHENT

DUNKIRK

BOULOGNE

PAS DE CALAIS

BRUSSELS

LILLE

CHARLEROI
MONS

XXXX
FIFTEENTH
SALMUTH

SOUTHAMPTON

PORTSMOUTH
SHOREHAM
HASTINGS

POOLE

ISLE OF WIGHT

PORTLAND

ENGLISH CHANNEL

PLYMOUTH
DARTMOUTH

FALMOUTH

CAMBRAI

ABBEVILLE

Somme R.

ST. QUENTIN

DIEPPE

AMIENS

Oise R.

LAON

SOISSONS

REIMS

GUERNSEY

CHANNEL ISLANDS

JERSEY

CHERBOURG

BAY

XXXXX
THE
21
MONTGOMERY

VARREVILLE
XXXX
12
BRADLEY

VIERVILLE

GRAND CAMP
CARENTAN
XXXX
FIRST
HODGES

ST. LO
1 Aug.

CAN. FIRST
CRERAR

BR. SECOND
DEMPSEY

BR. I
CAEN

8 Aug.

HAVRE

Seine R.

ROUEN

COMPIEGNE

Aisne R.

ELBEUF

LOUVIERS

VERNON

PONTOISE

Oise R.

Marne R.

CHATEAU THIERRY

CHALONS

XX V

XII

XIX

VIII

XXXXX
B
KLUGE

13 Aug.

XXXX
FIFTH
DIETRICH

MANTES

DREUX

Eure R.

PARIS

Seine R.

MELUN

FONTAINEBLEAU

ROMILLY

Aube R.

XXXX
THIRD
PATTON

XII

XX

XV

ST. MALO

7 Aug.

BREST

7 Aug.

B R I T T A N Y

LOUDEAC

XX
6

VII

AVRANCHES

1 Aug.

XX
83

ST. HILAIRE DU HARCOUET

3 Aug.

VII

FOUGERES

RENNES
XX
8

VITRE

LAVAL

Mayenne R.

MAYENNE

ALENCON

XV

XXXX

8 Aug.

CHATEAU GONTIER

Sarthe R.

LE MANS
XX

8 Aug.

XII

CHARTRES

CHATEAUDUN

ETAMPS

PITHIVIERS

SENS

ORLEANS

Loire R.

TROYES

Seine R.

Air interdiction,
June, July, August.

EBERBACH

7-10 Aug.

MORTAIN

SEVENTH
HAUSSER

LISE

ARGENTAN
CHAMBOIS

13 Aug.

3 Aug.

ANNES

XX
4

3 Aug.

LORIENT

7 Aug.

QUIBERON BAY

ST. NAZAIRE

13 Aug.

ANGERS

Loire R.

NANTES

13 Aug.

TOURS

MONTGOMERY

XXX

XXX

XXX

XXXXX

XII

THE EXPLOITATION

★

Bradley's decision to halt the northward drive of XV Corps on 13 August has since become controversial. On 14 August, he authorized Patton to send XV Corps with two of its divisions eastward toward Dreux, which was in keeping with Montgomery's instructions that if the Falaise–Argentan enclosure failed, a wider envelopment toward the Seine would be made. Several indications led Bradley to believe the encirclement had failed (it seemed to him, for example, that the slowness of Crerar's advance had allowed Kluge to withdraw, and Hodges and Dempsey seemed to be moving eastward with relative ease, suggesting the Germans had pulled out).

It was now clear to Kluge that immediate retreat was his only salvation, and Hitler was bluntly so informed. Hitler gave his approval on the 16th, and on the next day Kluge was replaced by Model. In preparation for the withdrawal, the Germans moved considerable strength to Falaise and Argentan to hold open the shoulders of the gap. Whereas, on the 13th (with the bulk of the Germans in the pocket west of Argentan) a continuation of the northward advance might have succeeded in closing the gap, the attempt of V Corps to do so met with stiff resistance.

The Germans conducted an orderly withdrawal against overwhelming air and ground attacks from three directions, and when the American and Polish pincers met near Chambois on the 19th, many of the panzer forces had escaped. The remaining Germans made one last attack and then surrendered. Hitler lost 50,000 prisoners, and 10,000 killed.

When Patton moved toward Dreux with XV Corps on 14 August, he ordered his XII and XX Corps to drive east also. XIX Corps moved toward the Seine on the 20th to aid Patton. Opposition was minor, and Dreux fell on the 16th; Chartres on the 18th. Bradley now removed restrictions on any advance, and Patton's corps, aided by emergency air supply, continued pounding eastward.

On 19 August, Eisenhower modified his pre-invasion plans and, taking a calculated risk on the adequacy of logistical support, he ordered exploitation beyond the Seine. Montgomery now urged the encirclement of the remnants of Army Group B south of the Seine, and the pincers closed at Elbeuf on the 26th, but most of the German infantry was in the bridgehead west of Rouen. During the next two days, many of them crossed to the north of the Seine, but the Seventh and Fifth Panzer Armies had been shattered (the latter could report only 1,300 men, 24 tanks, and 60 pieces of artillery).

On the 19th, XV Corps had seized the bridgehead at Mantes; by the 25th, three others had been established south of Paris, and V Corps took the city on the 25th, the honor of the triumphal entry being given to the French 2nd Armored Division.

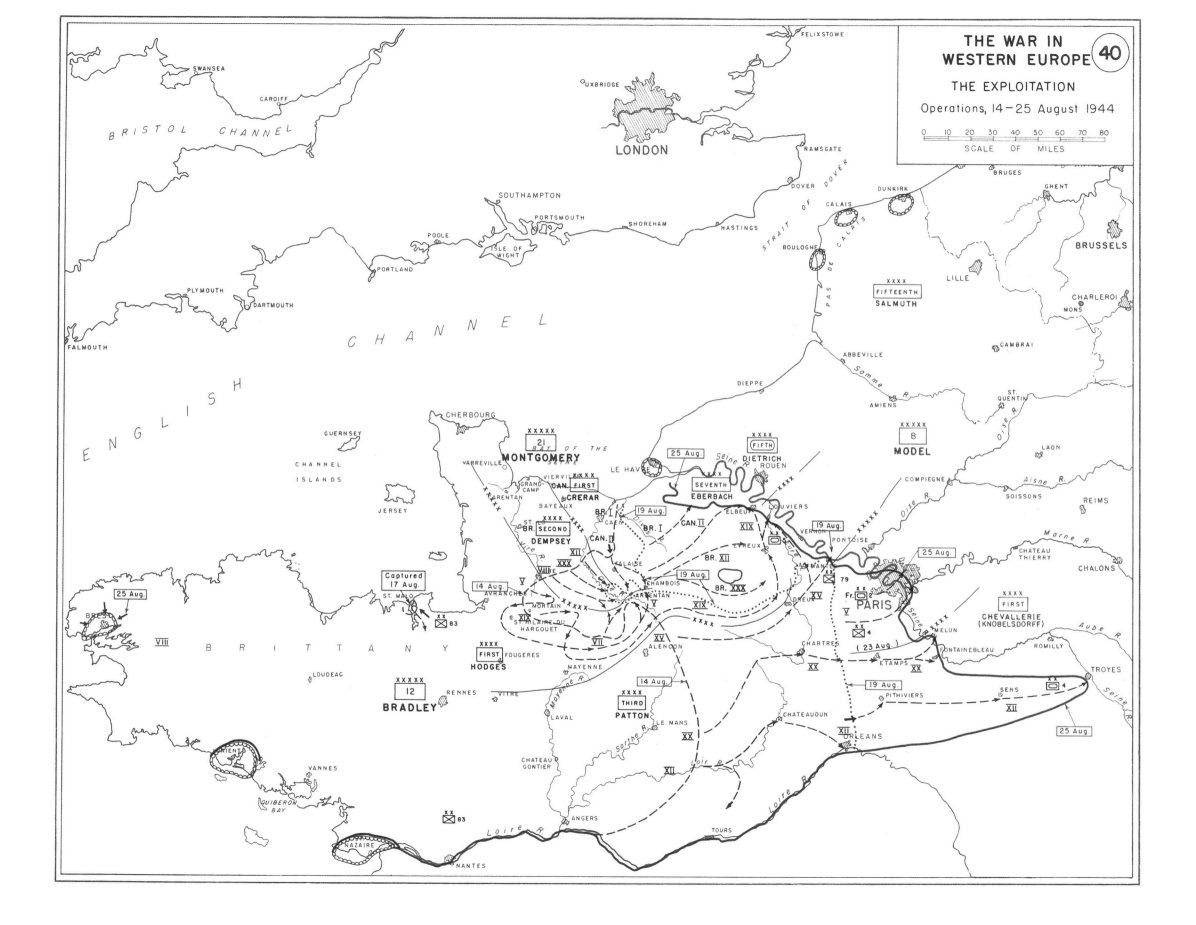

THE WAR IN
WESTERN EUROPE
40

THE EXPLOITATION

Operations, 14–25 August 1944

SCALE OF MILES
0 10 20 30 40 50 60 70 80

THE PURSUIT TO THE WEST WALL

★

German losses in Normandy had totaled 530,000 (and another 700,000 had been lost in Russia); only about 120 panzers had re-crossed the Seine, and Fifth Panzer and Seventh Armies had virtually ceased to exist. As the Allies raced from the Seine to the German stronghold of the West Wall, American and French forces landed in southern France (Operation ANVIL) and sped northward. The Germans withdrew more than half of their forces from southern and southwestern France before the northern and southern Allied forces liked up at Sombernon on 11 September 1944.

In northern France, Eisenhower's victory flushed armies drove into the Low Countries and to the German border, while Lt. Gen. William H. Simpson's Ninth Army protected the Allied flank along the Loire River.

The Ruhr had been targeted as the Allies' main initial objective in Germany, and it had been concluded that the advance would be made along the Ameins–Liège–Ruhr axis, supported by a secondary push in the direction of Verdun–Metz. Eisenhower directed Bradley to support Montgomery's advance with the American First Army, while Patton (much to his dismay) was to advance only if supplies would permit it after Hodges' needs were met.

Patton's forces debouched from their Seine bridgeheads on 26 August and, against spotty resistance, raced toward the Meuse, crossing it on the 30th, but ground to a halt for lack of fuel. Hodges attacked northeast on the 27th and, by 3 September, had pocketed 25,000 prisoners at Mons. Montgomery's armies attacked on 29 August. Dempsey's XXX Corps captured Amiens (and General Eberbach), and went on to take Brussels by the 3 September.

The 4th September was a critical date for the Germans. That day, Dempsey entered Antwerp, probably the most important port for the Allies, and seized all its facilities intact. Meanwhile, Eisenhower had assumed control of Allied ground forces on 1 September, and ordered Patton to continue his advance. Hodges shifted his advance to the east and, by the 14th, had reached the German border, whereas Patton was held up by stiffer resistance.

During the period 4–10 September, Montgomery argued that if 21st Army Group were to be given unequivocal support, it could reach the Ruhr. Eisenhower, however, refused to halt Bradley's diverging attacks but gave Montgomery supply priority, with the instruction to get Antwerp up and running again as a port because the Allied advance had created severe supply problems.

On the German side, Rundstedt (who had been recalled on 5 September) surveyed the sad state of the West Wall. He had only 63 divisions in the line, and they were only 50 percent effective.

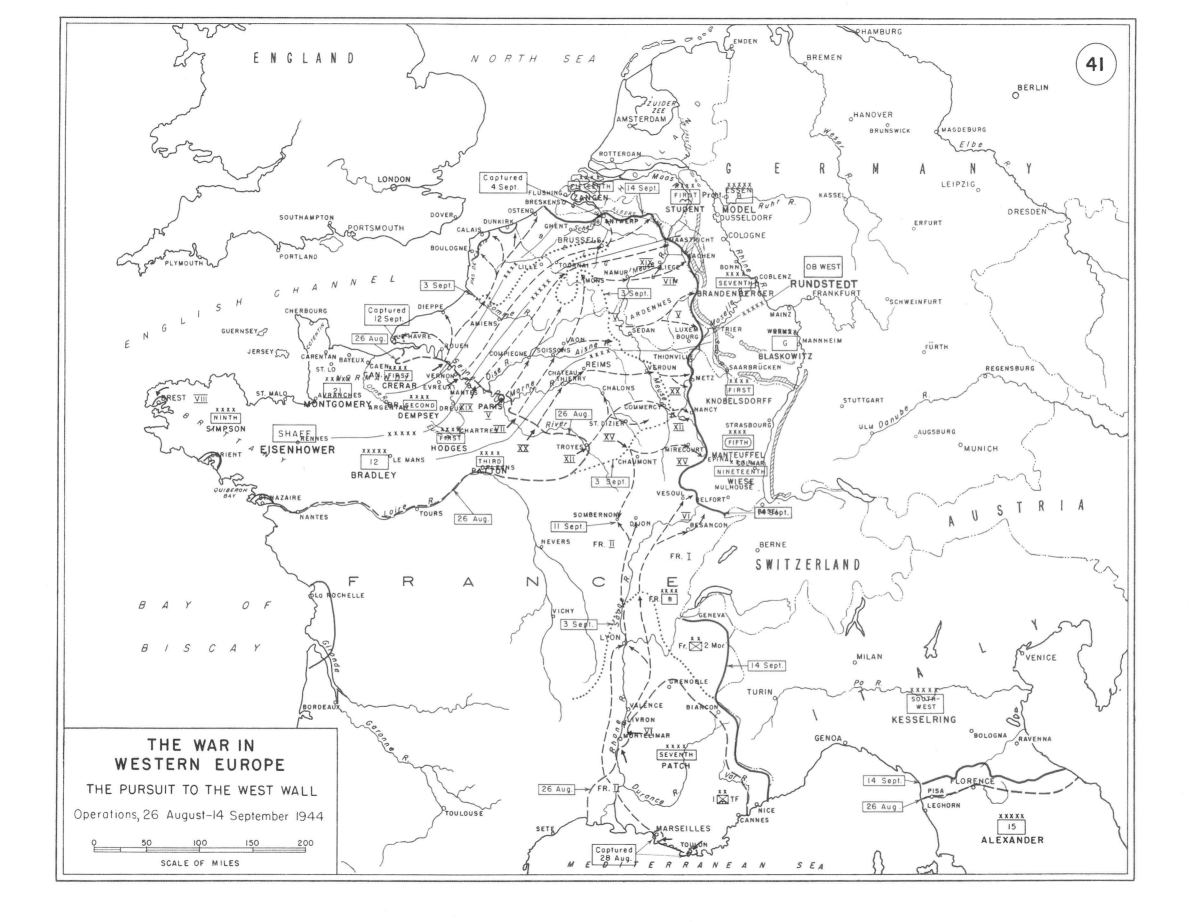

THE WAR IN
WESTERN EUROPE

THE PURSUIT TO THE WEST WALL

Operations, 26 August–14 September 1944

SCALE OF MILES
0   50   100   150   200

GENERAL SITUATION, SEPTEMBER 15, 1944

★

As the Allies fought the logistical battle, Rundstedt drew his armies together and stabilized a defensive line. He decided to hold the advanced position along the Scheldte and the Meuse–Escaut Canal as long as possible. A key element of the defense was the West Wall that had been feverishly refurbished since the Allied breakout from Normandy.

While the 6th and 12th Army Groups struggled to reach and penetrate the West Wall, Montgomery, contending with an intricate maze of waterways in Belgium and Holland, sought to turn the Wall's north flank. In early September, hopeful of securing a Rhine bridgehead and willing to postpone operations to open Antwerp, Eisenhower authorized Montgomery to mount an attack toward Arnhem. Montgomery planned to drop the three airborne divisions allotted to him (Operation MARKET) and make a ground attack with Second Army (Operation GARDEN) to link up the airborne spearheads and cross the Lek River. Extremely bold in its conception, the plan envisioned a single corps' advance along a narrow corridor, 64 miles to Arnhem, over seven major bridges to be secured by paratroopers, all to take place during the worst season for weather in northern Europe.

At 1400 on 17 September, the airborne divisions began landing, and at 1430 XXX Corps attacked toward Eindhoven. The 101st Airborne captured several of it assigned bridges, but the 82nd Airborne was unable to seize the vital Nijmegan bridges until the 20th. The British 1st Airborne Division, landing seven miles west of Arnhem, could only secure the north end of Arnhem bridge. German reaction was prompt (Student and Model happened to be in the area, and organized a vigorous response). Poor weather during the next five days upset plans for air reinforcement and supply, while German attacks on the airborne spearheads and the corridor slowed the link-up.

On the 21st, those elements of the 1st Airborne at Arnhem were forced to surrender, and on the 25th, the remnants of that division had to withdraw across the Lek, where a XXX Corps spearhead waited to receive them. The two American divisions continued to fight with heavy losses until relieved on 6 November, but MARKET GARDEN had failed. Poor weather, the inability of the Second Army to move north rapidly or widen the corridor, Allied failure to concentrate enough strength at Arnhem, and the rapid German reaction, had spelled its doom.

Montgomery now focused on widening the corridor, and used the Canadian First Army to reduce the Schelde area, at heavy cost as the German Fifteenth Army defended skillfully.

With Montgomery concentrating on the Schelde estuary and too weak to make a strong attack toward the Rhine, Eisenhower had assigned Bradley the main effort to crack the West Wall in October. To support Bradley, Montgomery attacked on 14 November and cleared the area west of the Maas.

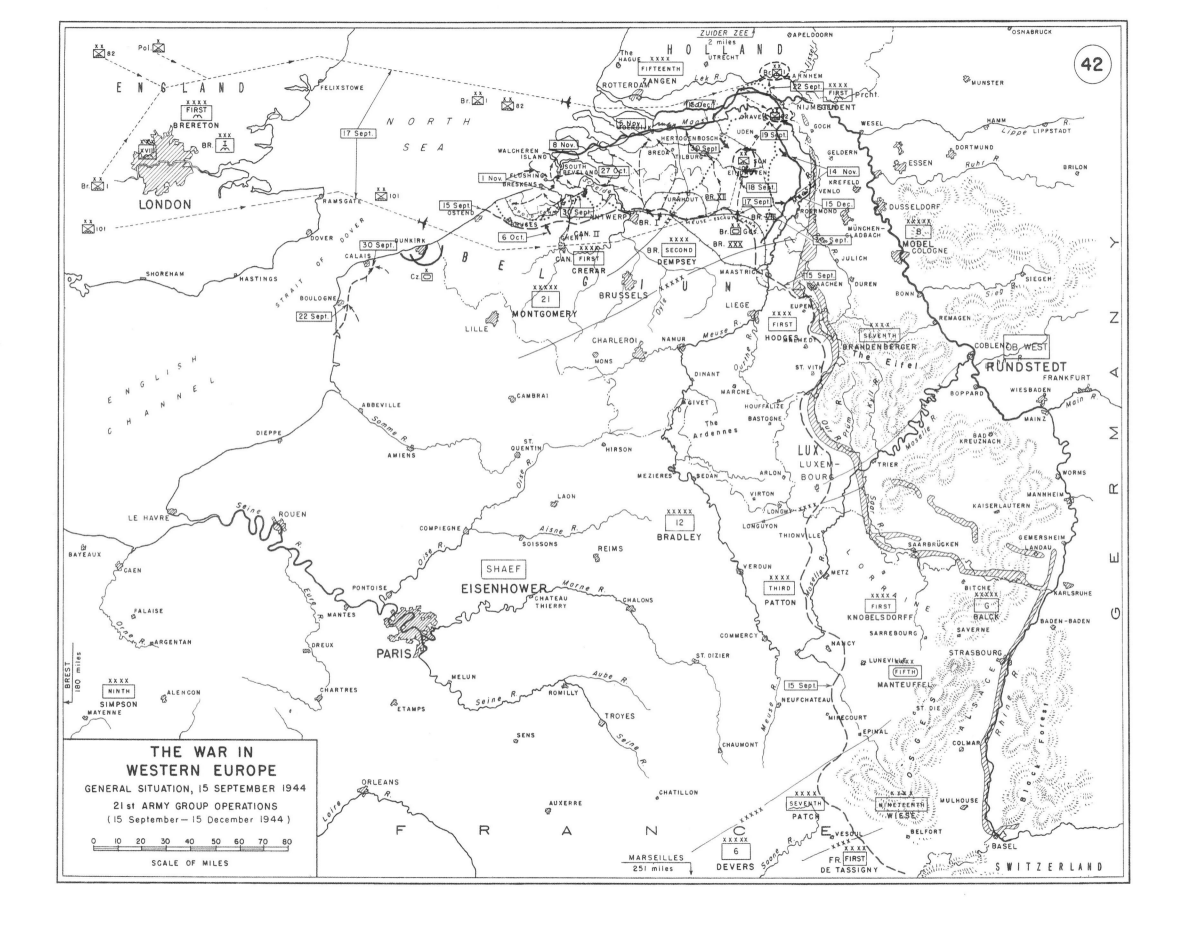

THE WAR IN
WESTERN EUROPE

GENERAL SITUATION, 15 SEPTEMBER 1944

21st ARMY GROUP OPERATIONS
(15 SEPTEMBER – 15 DECEMBER 1944)

0 10 20 30 40 50 60 70 80

SCALE OF MILES

6TH AND 12TH ARMY GROUP OPERATIONS

★

During Montgomery's operations in the north, Bradley's 12th Army Group and Lt. Gen. Jacob L. Devers' 6th Army Group slowly advanced to the east. On 22 September, Eisenhower had directed Bradley to support Montgomery's thrust toward the Rhine with a First Army drive toward Cologne; Patton was to operate within the limits of his supply quota; and Devers would drive toward Mulhouse and Strasbourg.

In some of October's most vicious fighting, Hodges' VII and XIX Corps moved through the West Wall at Aachen, entered the city on 13 October and, after severe house-to-house fighting, captured it on the 21st.

Patton's efforts were forestalled by a German attack on 18 September. Hitler, aiming to drive a wedge between Patch and Patton and force the latter back on Reims, ordered Fifth Panzer to attack, but it was roughly handled by XII and XV Corps, and even Hitler recognized the futility of these assaults and stopped them. Now Patton took the offensive. Farther south, Devers' troops, fighting in mountainous terrain and increasingly bad weather, forced the Germans back into the Vosges.

By the middle of October, Eisenhower appreciated that Montgomery, burdened with the Schelde operation, was too weak to make the main attack toward the Rhine simultaneously, and so he temporarily assigned Bradley's northern armies the main effort for the November offensive, with Montgomery, Patton, and Devers making secondary efforts.

The Ninth and First Armies launched the main attack on a narrow front on 16 November, preceded by one of the heaviest air bombardments yet used in the West. Nevertheless, the advanced troops moved through the West Wall against bitter opposition, particularly in the dense Hurtgen Forest, where V Corps had been attacking since 2 November. By 1 December, the advance had reached the Roer River against stiffening German defenses. Meanwhile, Third Army had encircled strategically located Metz by 18 November and the city capitulated on the 22nd. At the same time, XII and XX Corps forced the Germans back into the West Wall, took Sarreguemines on 6 December and, by the 15th, had several small bridgeheads across the Saar River. Patton, now fighting with adequate supplies but in abominable weather, was in a position to plunge into Germany.

The advances of November, though they brought the Allies closer to the Rhine, had not lived up to expectations. Considerable damage had been inflicted on the hard-pressed Germans (in November and December about 75,000 were taken prisoner) but there had also been hard knocks for the Allies. The logical outcome of this disappointment was a renewal of Montgomery's argument for a single, well-supported thrust in the north, something which Eisenhower steadfastly refused to accept.

Hitler met this situation with a counteroffensive that would attack through the Ardennes, repeating, he hoped, his 1940 triumph on a smaller scale. Its objective was the capture of Antwerp and the destruction of Allied forces north of the line Bastogne–Brussels–Antwerp. Sixth Panzer, flanked by Fifth Panzer, would make the main effort. The Fifteenth and Seventh Armies would form the defensive flanks for the panzers. Hitler counted on winning a decisive, quick victory in the West; then, shifting his reserves eastward, he would crush the next Russian offensive, and thereby gain either a negotiated peace or win time to put large numbers of his various new weapons into action.

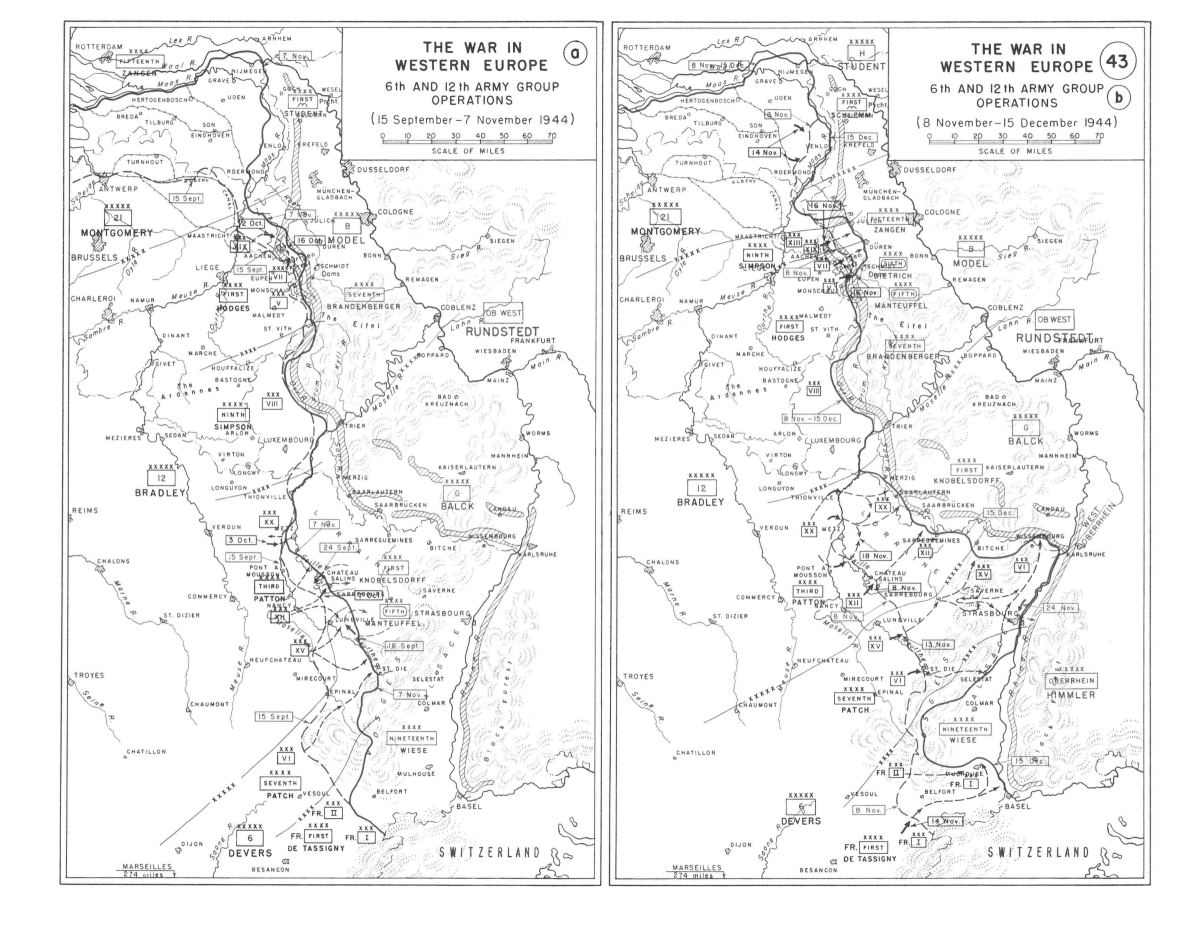

THE WAR IN WESTERN EUROPE

6th AND 12th ARMY GROUP OPERATIONS

(15 September – 7 November 1944)

a

SCALE OF MILES
0 10 20 30 40 50 60 70

THE WAR IN WESTERN EUROPE

43

6th AND 12th ARMY GROUP OPERATIONS

(8 November – 15 December 1944)

b

SCALE OF MILES
0 10 20 30 40 50 60 70

THE ARDENNES CAMPAIGN

★

The Germans had waited for a period of bad weather to minimize Allied air attacks, and at 0530 on 16 December 1944, their infantry struck the American front from Monschau to Echternach. Sixth Panzer under Obergruppenführer Sepp Dietrich led the main effort, but Dietrich was not experienced in handling large panzer forces; traffic jammed, and his force would be eventually checked and cut off by 30th Division at Stavelot. Fifth Panzer, better led and with more room, shattered 28th and 106th Divisions, while Seventh Army made slight gains. Generally, though, there was great confusion in the Allied lines.

Late on 17 December, 7th Armored Division occupied the important road junction of St. Vith, where it temporarily blocked Dietrich. Also on the 17th, Eisenhower committed 101st Airborne to the strategically critical town of Bastogne, while 82nd Airborne joined XVIII Corps on the northern flank of the salient. By 21 December, the 101st, together with parts of the 9th and 10th Armored Divisions, had been surrounded at Bastogne.

On 25 December, U.S. 2nd Armored Division crushed 2nd Panzer Division at the furthest point of the German penetration, Celles, and beat back German attempts at rescue. Late that same day, Patton punched a narrow corridor into Bastogne, and on the 26th, German supply convoys west of St. Vith were pounded by Allied tactical aviation.

The heaviest combat over the next two days was along the corridor into Bastogne. Savage fighting raged, with heavy losses on both sides, through 4 January 1945, without any great change of position. By the end of the 4th, it was obvious to Patton that only a coordinated attack with fresh troops could make appreciable headway, and so he ordered 90th Division northward and organized a major assault by II and VIII Corps, to be launched on 9 January.

On 3 January, Montgomery (under strict instruction from Eisenhower) began a counteroffensive, and driving through fierce German opposition combined with bitter winter weather, VII Corps cut the vital Laroche–Vielsalm road, which left the Germans only the road through Houffalize. Model demanded permission to withdraw, which Hitler granted on the 8th, directing that Sixth Panzer be withdrawn immediately for rehabilitation.

The Germans, by now hardened to winter warfare in the Russian school, waged a fighting retreat, taking their price in Allied casualties for every foot of ground. On 13 January, patrols of 87th Division and British 6th Airborne reached across the salient and established contact, as did, at 0905 16 January, 2nd and 11th Armored Divisions.

With the American front now stabilized, Bradley maintained pressure in the Ardennes where the Germans, although suffering from American artillery and air strikes, pulled back in good order. While Rundstedt made every effort to reestablish the run-down West Wall, Hitler was stripping the Ardennes front: Sixth Panzer was sent to Hungary, and other troops in the First Army were sent off to Alsace to take part in a second offensive. Nevertheless, the stubbornness of the German defense was only matched by the determination of the American attacks. The West Wall was finally pierced, west of Prüm and in the Gemünd area further north. On 7 February, Eisenhower ordered all attacks except for those by V Corps aimed at the Roer dams.

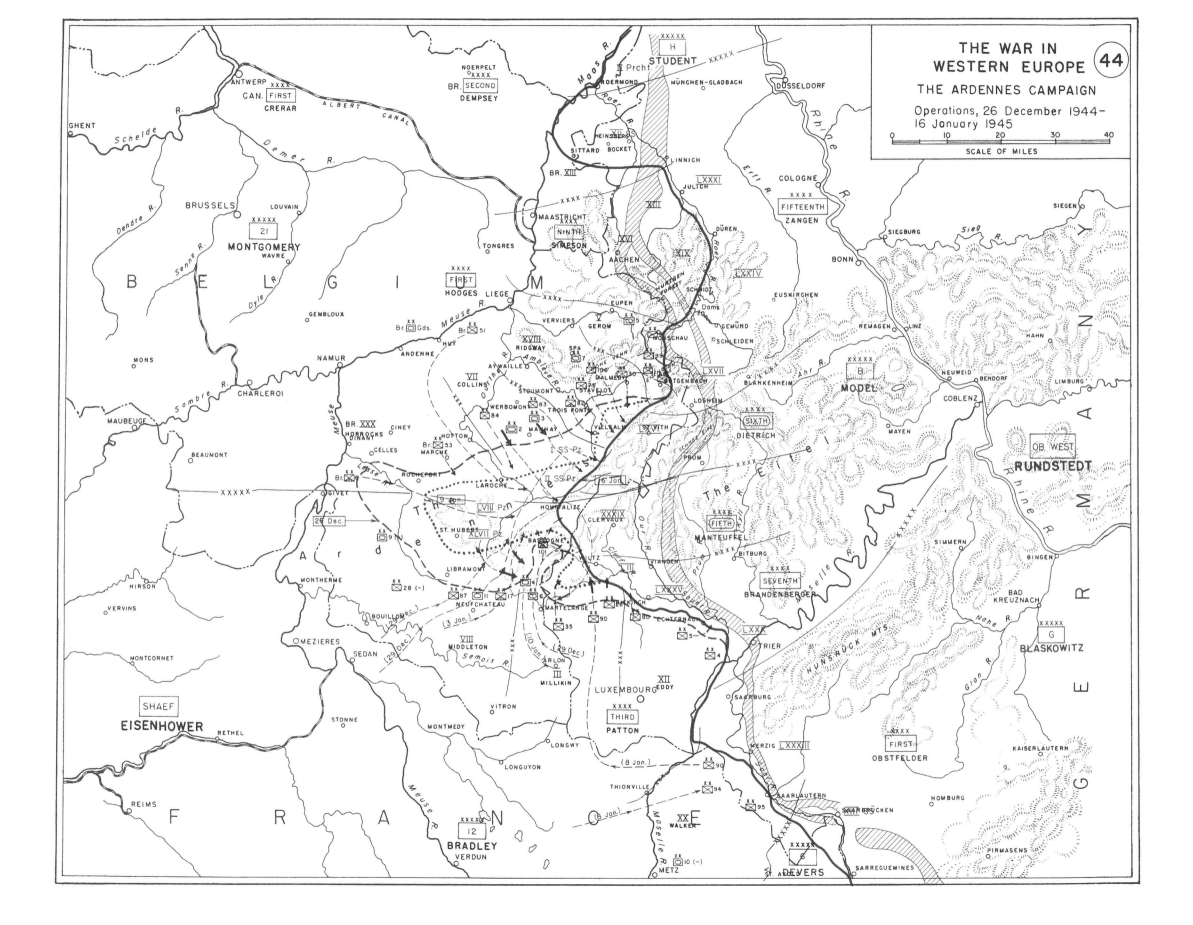

THE WAR IN
WESTERN EUROPE

44

THE ARDENNES CAMPAIGN

Operations, 26 December 1944–
16 January 1945

0   10   20   30   40
SCALE OF MILES

THE GERMAN OFFENSIVE IN ALSACE-LORRAINE

★

Hitler's second offensive was probably primarily based on a desire to try and gain an initiative in the West. If he could push troops through southward from Bitche, it would force Eisenhower to draw troops from the Ardennes to reinforce Devers' 6th Army Group. But there would be two problems for Hitler. First, his own divisions in this area were generally badly understrength and short of equipment. Second, having seen what had just happened in the Ardennes, where the Americans had been caught napping, 6th Army Group's intelligence arm was alert. In addition, Seventh Army organized a rear defensive position along the trace of the old Maginot Line, and a final lie along the eastern slope of the Vosges Mountains.

Early on 1 January, Blaskowitz attacked with his XIII SS Corps southward near Rohrbach, but was halted after a ten-mile advance. His XC Corps, however, broke into the American positions around Bitche, and forced VI Corps to withdraw during the night of 2 January. General de Gaulle, head of the French government in exile, was alarmed that Strasbourg might be abandoned and created such a political brouhaha that it forced Eisenhower to order Devers to hold the city at all costs. Early on 5 January, the Germans launched a surprise attack across the Rhine to hold a bridgehead in the Drusenheim–Gambsheim area, and on 7 January they struck north at Rheinau but were contained by the French. Other crossings created the "Colmar Pocket" which French and American forces pinched out between 20 January and 9 February, after heavy fighting. Hitler again delayed authorizing the evacuation of the pocket, which condemned the German Nineteenth Army to unnecessarily heavy losses.

With the major German bridgeheads eliminated, the Allies could prepare to close up to the Rhine from Switzerland to the North Sea. The campaign was visualized in three phases. First, Operation VERITABLE (an attack southeast by the Canadian First Army from its Nijmegan bridgehead) that would link up at Mörs with Operation GRENADE (a converging advance by Ninth Army). While these operations were progressing, Bradley was to seize the Roer dams and cover Montgomery's right flank. Second, would be Operation LUMBERJACK—and advance to the Rhine by Bradley's 12th Army Group, and third, in Operation UNDERTONE, an advance to the Rhine by 6th Army Group. These operations completed, Montgomery, reinforced by the U.S. Ninth Army, would launch Operation PLUNDER, the principal crossing of the Rhine that would envelop the Ruhr from the north. Initially, this drive was to go on to Berlin, but once it was realized that the Russians would get to Berlin first, the objective was switched to Hamburg.

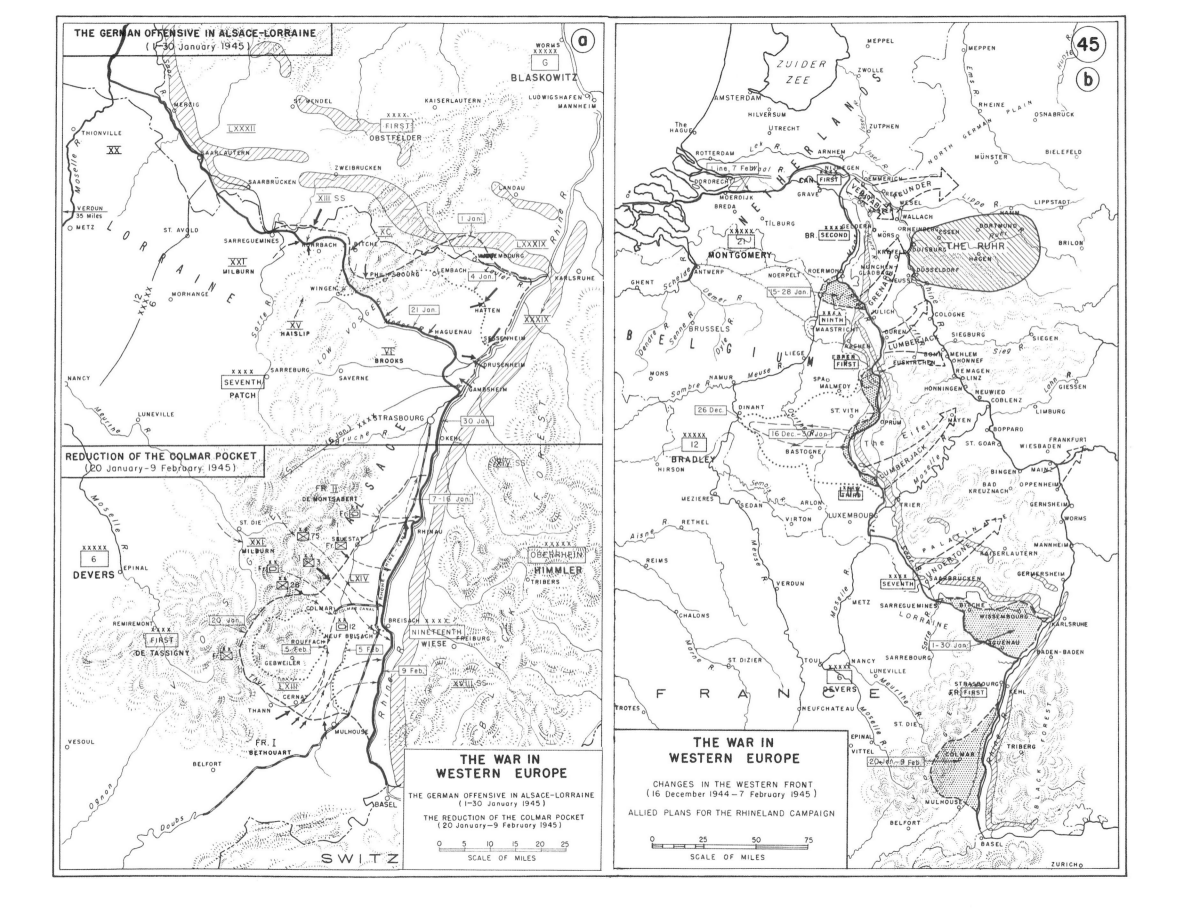

THE GERMAN OFFENSIVE IN ALSACE-LORRAINE
(1–30 January 1945)

REDUCTION OF THE COLMAR POCKET
(20 January–9 February 1945)

**THE WAR IN
WESTERN EUROPE**

THE GERMAN OFFENSIVE IN ALSACE-LORRAINE
(1–30 January 1945)

THE REDUCTION OF THE COLMAR POCKET
(20 January–9 February 1945)

0   5   10   15   20   25
SCALE OF MILES

**THE WAR IN
WESTERN EUROPE**

CHANGES IN THE WESTERN FRONT
(16 December 1944–7 February 1945)

ALLIED PLANS FOR THE RHINELAND CAMPAIGN

0   25   50   75
SCALE OF MILES

45

THE RHINELAND CAMPAIGN

★

Operation VERITABLE faced deep German defenses. The first was the Reichswald, which was thoroughly organized in depth and, in addition, the Germans had flooded the low ground along the rivers. Montgomery planned to launch VERITABLE on 8 February, and GRENADE on the 10th. The area around Cleves and Goch was pounded by bombers and artillery; so much so that when XXX Corps reached Cleves it confronted a wilderness of craters that halted all progress.

Bradley, meanwhile, had been battering toward the Roer dams and, after bitter fighting, V Corps won control on 10 February—only to discover that the discharge valves had been sabotaged the previous evening, thus creating a steady flooding that would halt Ninth Army for two weeks. This left Blaskowitz free to concentrate against the British attack. German parachute units, composed of fanatical young Nazis, fought literally to the last man. Continued rains and floods put most of the battlefield under water, and amphibious vehicles were needed to resupply the troops and evacuate the wounded; attacks struggled through waist-high water. But neither German courage nor foul weather stopped the British and Canadians. By 23 February, they had overrun the first two German positions and were regrouping to attack the third.

However, during the enforced pause, Ninth Army fine-tuned its preparations for crossing the Roer. Foregoing a long softening-up barrage, Ninth Army attacked even before the flood waters had subsided, and resolutely beat off German counterattacks. By the 28th it had broken out of its bridgeheads, while most of the Germans in the area were struggling vainly to check the British, who had resumed the offensive on the 26th. On 3 March, U.S. and British troops linked up at Geldern. Two days later, the Germans held only the Xantern–Wesel bridgehead, which Hitler insisted must be held. The Canadians, however, pushed them out on 10 March, and Montgomery began to concentrate on Operation PLUNDER.

Bradley, meanwhile, had carried out his pre-LUMBERJACK mission of covering Ninth Army's right flank. Attacking on 23 February, First Army scored considerable gains, and further south, Patton, assigned the temporary mission of "active defense" until LUMBERJACK began, gnawed his way through the West Wall. On 7 March, leading units of 9th Armored discovered the Rhine bridge at Remagen still standing and seized it in a daring rush. It would prove to be one of those fortuitous turns of fortune that changed the entire balance of the Allied offensive.

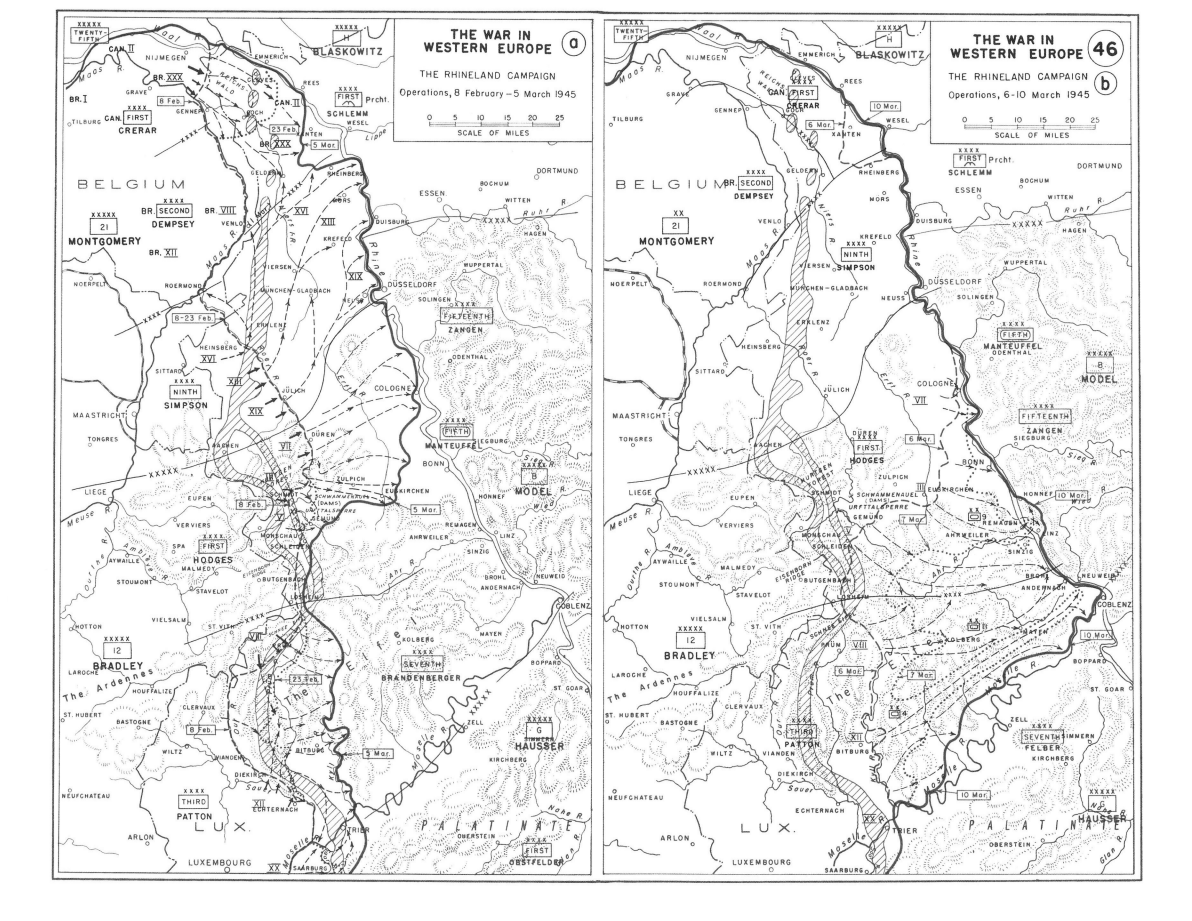

THE WAR IN
WESTERN EUROPE ⓐ

THE RHINELAND CAMPAIGN
Operations, 8 February – 5 March 1945

0 5 10 15 20 25
SCALE OF MILES

THE WAR IN
WESTERN EUROPE ㊼

THE RHINELAND CAMPAIGN
Operations, 6–10 March 1945 ⓑ

0 5 10 15 20 25
SCALE OF MILES

THE RHINELAND CAMPAIGN

★

The first German counterattacks against the Remagen bridgehead were piecemeal and futilely used up most of the available panzer units. American reinforcements poured across the shaky bridge, and once the bridgehead had been sufficiently enlarged, pontoon bridges were installed on 11 March. The Germans made determined efforts to wreck the bridge, but all were thwarted by the elaborate American defenses. By 21 March, the bridgehead was approximately twenty miles long and eight miles deep, with six bridges connecting it to the west bank.

Patton was now instructed to attack southward across the Moselle River to strike part of Seventh Army's north flank, while Devers hit its front. If successful, they would crush First and Seventh Armies and liquidate the last German foothold on the west bank of the Rhine. The German commanders involved were only too conscious of the weakness of their positions. A large part of their forces consisted of recently organized, poorly officered Volksgrenadier divisions. Fuel and ammunition were in short supply. They pleaded for permission to withdraw, but Hitler's answer was the usual one: defend to the last.

Devers concentrated his main effort toward Kaiserlautern. Patton, meanwhile, had begun his attack across the Moselle on 13 March, and swiftly moved through the demoralized German resistance. Seventh Army's advance was slower because it had to fight through some of the strongest sections of the West Wall, but by 21 March most of the German Seventh Army had been destroyed, and the German First Army was struggling for its life in a shrinking salient.

The Rhineland campaign had been one of the greatest defeats inflicted on Hitler. Exact figures are not available, but approximately a quarter of a million Germans were taken prisoner, with possibly another 60,000 killed or wounded. The outcome was nothing less than the destruction of the German army in the West. Militarily, Hitler's conduct appears to have been another piece of lunacy. He might have utilized the West Wall as a delaying position while withdrawing his heavy equipment east of the Rhine during January and February, when the prevalent bad weather would have offered protection against Allied air interdiction. The Rhine is a formidable barrier, behind which Hitler could have waged an effective defense for some time. Various reasons have been advanced for his decision to make his stand west of the Rhine: for example, the importance of the river and its tributaries as a communications network (more so because the German railroad system had been so badly damaged), or the need to protect the industrial Ruhr now that the Russians controlled most of the industry of Silesia. But perhaps something more sinister was involved; Hitler had decreed on 19 March that the battle should be conducted without regard to the civilian population, and that the Nazi Party leaders were to begin the destruction of everything in Germany that might be of use to the enemy.

Note: the numbers in parentheses under American and German units in the right-hand map below, represent those killed in action.

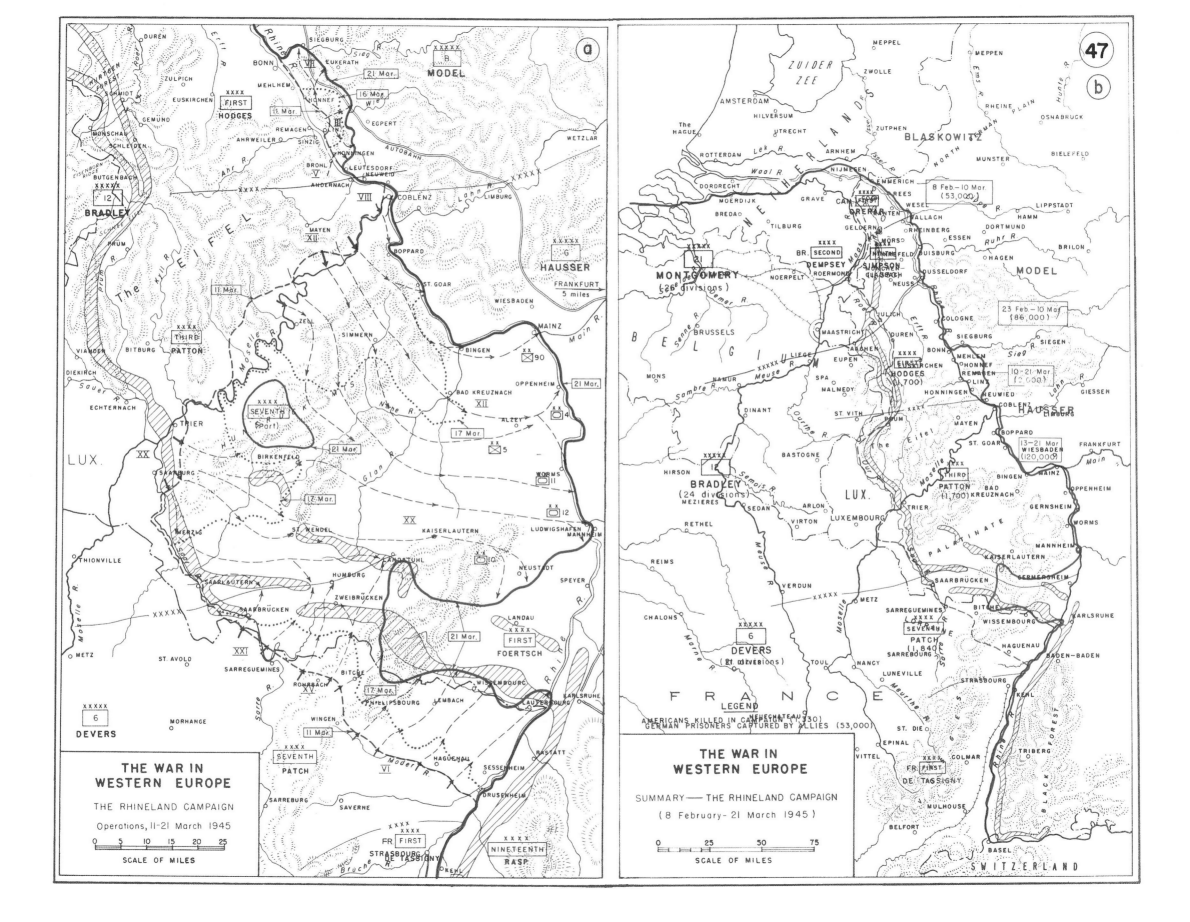

(a) THE WAR IN WESTERN EUROPE

THE RHINELAND CAMPAIGN
Operations, 11-21 March 1945

SCALE OF MILES
0 5 10 15 20 25

(b) THE WAR IN WESTERN EUROPE

SUMMARY — THE RHINELAND CAMPAIGN
(8 February - 21 March 1945)

LEGEND
AMERICANS KILLED IN CAMPAIGN (11,330)
GERMAN PRISONERS CAPTURED BY ALLIES (53,000)

SCALE OF MILES
0 25 50 75

47

CROSSING THE RHINE

★

On 22 March, one of Patton's divisions (5th) made an opportunistic assault across the Rhine at Oppenheim, and by the evening of 24 March, Patton had supported the crossing, and soon four of his divisions were on the east bank. Faced with only light opposition, three large bridgeheads were established on the central Rhine.

On paper, the Germans had more than sixty divisions east of the Rhine, but over twenty of these were mere fragments (four consisting of their staffs alone). Their total numerical strength may have been the equivalent of twenty-six divisions but their ranks were full of untrained and often unwilling recruits. Every kind of supply was lacking, and the Luftwaffe was also nowhere to be found. Against this shadow army, Eisenhower deployed eighty-five full-strength divisions, reinforced by dozens of additional artillery, antiaircraft, tank and tank-destroyer battalions; Allied air power had free range of the skies. The hopelessness of the German cause was starkly evident, but Hitler still managed to exert almost total control over his military hierarchy.

Montgomery's plans for crossing the Rhine were, characteristically, meticulous in accumulating enough supplies to thrust deep into Germany. The British Second Army launched its crossing against Wesel at 2100 on 23 March with massive artillery support. Later that morning, one American and one British airborne division began landing north of Wesel and, linking up with ground troops, soon overwhelmed the opposition (although some German paratroopers died hard, holding out for three days). Two days later, the Allies broke through the German lines near Haltern, opening the North German Plain.

Southward, Bradley's troops broke out of their bridgeheads on 25 March, completely surprising Model, who had expected an attack northward out against the Ruhr. The advance of the American First and Third Armies during the next few days was hindered more by the rough terrain than by German opposition. Bradley sent First Army due north toward Paderborn, where it became involved in furious fighting with SS panzer troops, and Seventh Army to Kassel. On the afternoon of 1 April, units of Ninth Army's 2nd Armored Division made contact with First Army's 3rd Army Division near Lippstadt, and the Ruhr pocket was enclosed.

In the north, the Canadian First Army turned northward to cut off the German forces in Holland, while the British Second Army drove eastward to the Elbe. The U.S. Fifteenth Army had been brought up to hold the west bank of the Rhine opposite the Ruhr pocket and was to prepare itself to take over control of the Rhineland provinces as the rest of 12th Army Group advanced eastward.

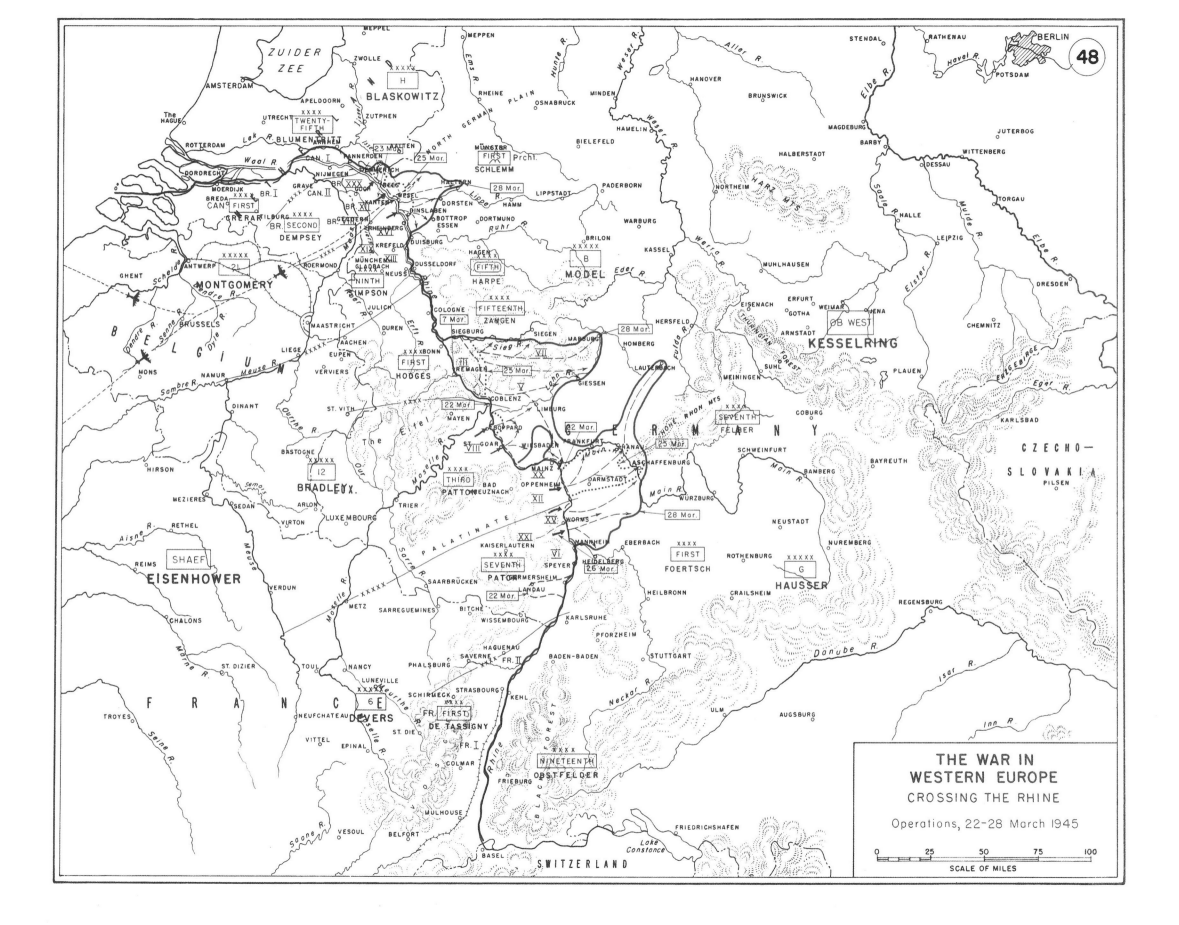

THE WAR IN
WESTERN EUROPE

CROSSING THE RHINE

Operations, 22-28 March 1945

SCALE OF MILES

0   25   50   75   100

THE REDUCTION OF THE RUHR POCKET & THE ADVANCE TO THE ELBE AND MAULDE

★

The German chain of command was now thoroughly shattered, but Hitler still bombarded his commanders with deluded orders for grand counterattacks and resistance to the last drop of blood. While the Allied front surged eastward, the Ruhr pocket was methodically reduced. While Fifteenth Army's XXII Corps attacked the northern front of the pocket, First Army's III and XVIII Corps moved against the east and southern fronts, respectively. Resistance ended on 18 April, and more than 317,000 prisoners were gathered in: the largest surrender of German troops during the war.

Other German forces were swept ahead of the Allied tide. Balskowitz took over the German troops in Holland, and prepared to stand siege behind the country's water barriers. A new Army Group Northwest was created to take over First Parachute Army and other remnants trying to halt Montgomery. Kesselring attempted to maintain control of Army Group C and other fragments to the south. The German Eleventh Army, a grab-bag collection of new units, hastily assembled with some vague idea of relieving Model, had been ordered to hold the Harz Mountain area, and the Nazi Party's efforts to organize a guerrilla force of "Werewolves" was an outstanding failure.

As the Allied armies plunged headlong toward the Elbe, the British urged an all-out advance on Berlin, but Eisenhower, not unaware of the political advantages of getting to Berlin before the Russians, nevertheless reflected the policy of the American Joint Chiefs of Staff, and intended to halt on the line of the Elbe and Mulde Rivers and concentrate on the destruction of the German forces on his flanks. Actually, the occupation zones had already been decided at the highest level at the Yalta Conference of February 1945.

On the whole, the advance during this period was delayed more by terrain and traffic jams than enemy opposition. The Canadians had some stiff fighting on the approaches to Emden and Williamshaven. Ninth Army reached to Elbe near Magdeburg on 11 April, and on 17 April, Patton was sending patrols across the Czech frontier. The 6th Army Group, meanwhile, was still meeting determined resistance at Nuremburg.

The danger of accidental clashes, as his forces came into contact with the Russians, now became one of Eisenhower's major concerns. Also he was anxious to destroy the German forces on his flanks, especially in the "redoubt" area to the south, where 100 German divisions were rumored to be concentrating. He therefore ordered Bradley to hold the Elbe River–Mulde River–Erzgebirge Mountains line with two armies, and to send Third Army through Nuremburg and Regensburg and down the Danube Valley. Montgomery, reinforced by the American XVIII, would advance northward across the Elbe to the Lübeck area, and Devers was ordered to move slightly westward to clean out the "redoubt."

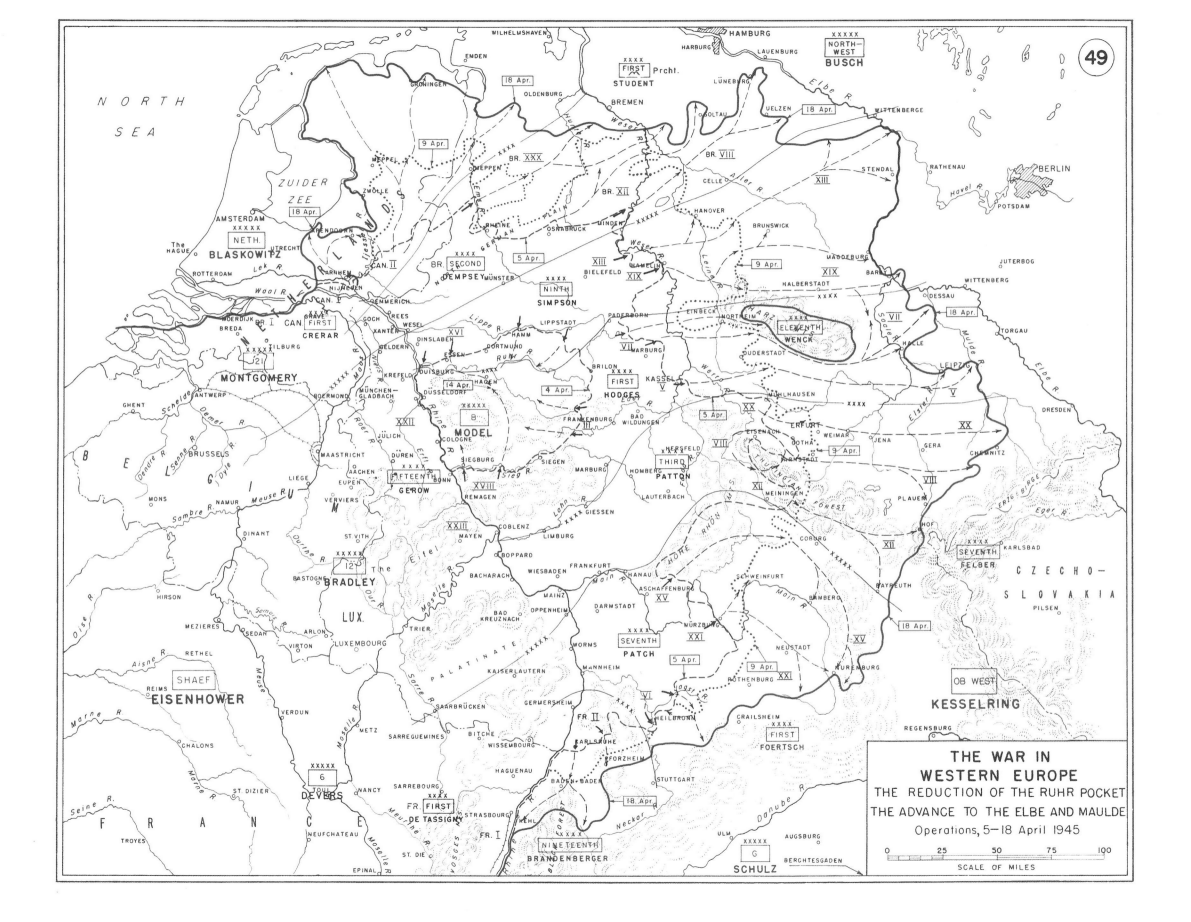

THE WAR IN
WESTERN EUROPE
THE REDUCTION OF THE RUHR POCKET
THE ADVANCE TO THE ELBE AND MAULDE
Operations, 5–18 April 1945

SCALE OF MILES
0   25   50   75   100

THE FINAL OPERATIONS

★

The British Second Army had cleared most of the west bank of the Elbe in its sector by 26 April, and on 1 May drove northward, seizing Lübeck and Wismar. On 3 May Hamburg surrendered. By 6 May, the Russians had closed up to the Elbe, and Ninth Army turned its bridgehead over to them. Meanwhile, First Army had cleared Leipzig on 19 April, liquidated the Harz Mountains pocket on 21 April, and closed to the Mulde River. On 25 April, its V Corps' patrols met Russian detachments near Torgau—the first contact between the Eastern and Western Fronts.

On 22 April, Patton renewed his advance, moving rapidly against scattered opposition, and on 4 May, Third Army took Linz, Austria, and was approaching Pilsen, Czechoslovakia with orders from Bradley to advance to the line Budejovice–Pilsen–Karlsbad. When Eisenhower suggested to the Russians that Patton go on to liberate Prague, he was met with such anguished protests that he had to back off.

The 6th Army Group had finally cleared Nuremburg on 20 April and Stuttgart on the 23rd. Munich surrendered on the 30th, Salzburg and Berchtesgaden on 4 May. Also on the 4th, Seventh Army troops advanced through the Brenner Pass to meet leading units of Fifth Army advancing northward from Italy.

German forces now began to surrender piecemeal. On 5 May, all German troops in Holland, Denmark, Schleswig-Holstein, and northwest Germany surrendered to Montgomery. Army Group G surrendered to Devers that same day. Thousands of individual German soldiers fled across the Elbe to escape the Russians, and at the same time Hitler's successor, Admiral Doenitz, began the negotiations that culminated in the final surrender of Germany on 7 May at Reims (hostilities in Europe ended officially at 2301, 8 May).

The Allied victory in Western Europe, like most of history's other great victories, was won by the greater force with the better means. The Allied forces were superior in numbers of men, weapons, and aircraft; they had almost unlimited resources behind them. Their leadership, if generally cautious and conservative, was also steady and unrelenting.

The Germans fought with their supply lines cut and their armament industries shattered by Allied air offensives. As in Russia, Hitler's insane demand that every position must be held trapped them repeatedly in untenable positions. Yet, they fought well.

Allied intelligence was poor. It overlooked, for example, the defensive potential of the Normandy *bocage*; it failed in the Ardennes; it bemused itself with the fable of the "National Redoubt" at the end of the war. Despite its many accomplishments, the Allied logistical system lacked flexibility to provide support for the pursuit after the Normandy breakout. On the highest levels, Allied psychological warfare was a dismal failure; instead of driving a wedge between the German people and Hitler, it drove them together by schemes such as the Morgenthau Plan to convert Germany to an agrarian state. Finally, Americans as a nation were only gradually awakening to the stark reality that cessation of armed conflict does not end war, but that war as an instrument of policy has many forms.

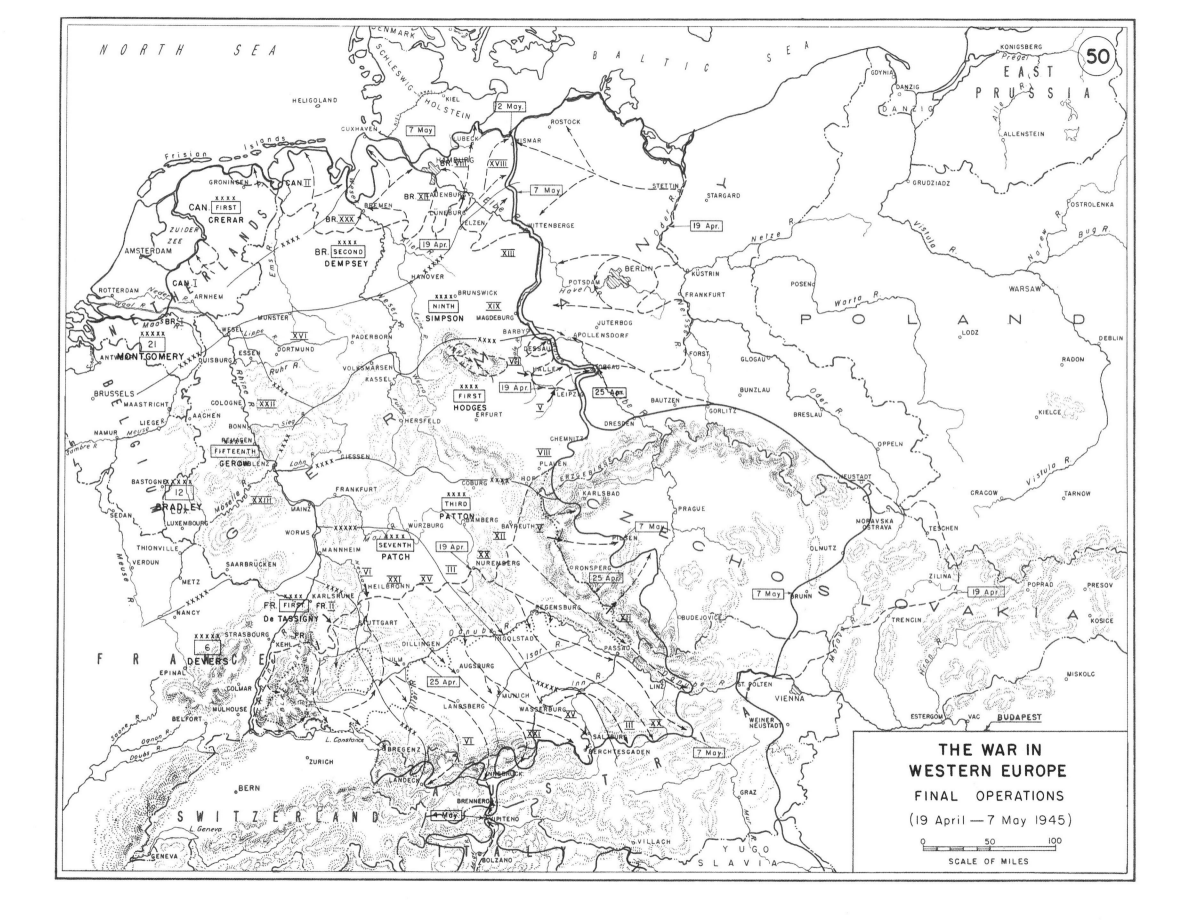

THE WAR IN
WESTERN EUROPE

FINAL OPERATIONS

(19 April — 7 May 1945)

0   50   100
SCALE OF MILES

THE WAR IN NORTH AFRICA: GENERAL MAP

★

North Africa played an important role in the war. It was the only area, other than the British Isles, from which the Western Allies could approach the German controlled Continent. Its possession was necessary for the control of the Mediterranean, the vital Suez Canal, and the Middle East with its oil.

After the fall of France in 1940, the disposition of the French fleet became of serious concern to Britain who was determined that it should not become available to the Axis navies. Consequently, it was either interned or destroyed, as at Oran and Dakar in July 1940.

In September 1940, the British supported an abortive attempt by De Gaulle to occupy Dakar and ring the French colonies in West and Equatorial Africa under the control of the embryonic Free French Forces, but the Dakar garrison remained loyal to Vichy France and defeated the landing force.

Egypt was the key to British success in the Middle East. Egypt, once a British protectorate, had signed a treaty with Britain in 1936 pledging aid in case of war and authorizing the stationing of British troops. With the fall of France, Vichy-controlled Syria and Algeria could well become the entryways for Axis troops which, together with Italian-controlled Libya, might strike at the Suez Canal, a main arterial route to India and the heart of the British Empire.

The Western Desert is, in the words of the German General von Ravenstein, "a tactician's paradise and a quartermaster's hell." It stretches 1,400 miles from Tripoli to Alexandria, with no major road except the coastal highway and only one major port—Benghazi—between the terminal ports of Tripoli and Alexandria. In the ensuing operations, the opposing forces, operating from the two major bases at the desert's extremities, seesawed back and forth. As one advanced and its supply line became tenuous, the other, falling back toward its base, became stronger and repelled the weakened aggressor. The terrain, ideal for the maneuver of armor (there is only one natural defensive position between El Agheila and El Alamein) is not the sandy waste the name implies. Except for the coastal strip, it is underlaid by limestone, while plateaus and escarpments rise further inland. But overall, the major characteristic of the region was that, forbiddingly, it offered very little by way of natural resources to support the armies.

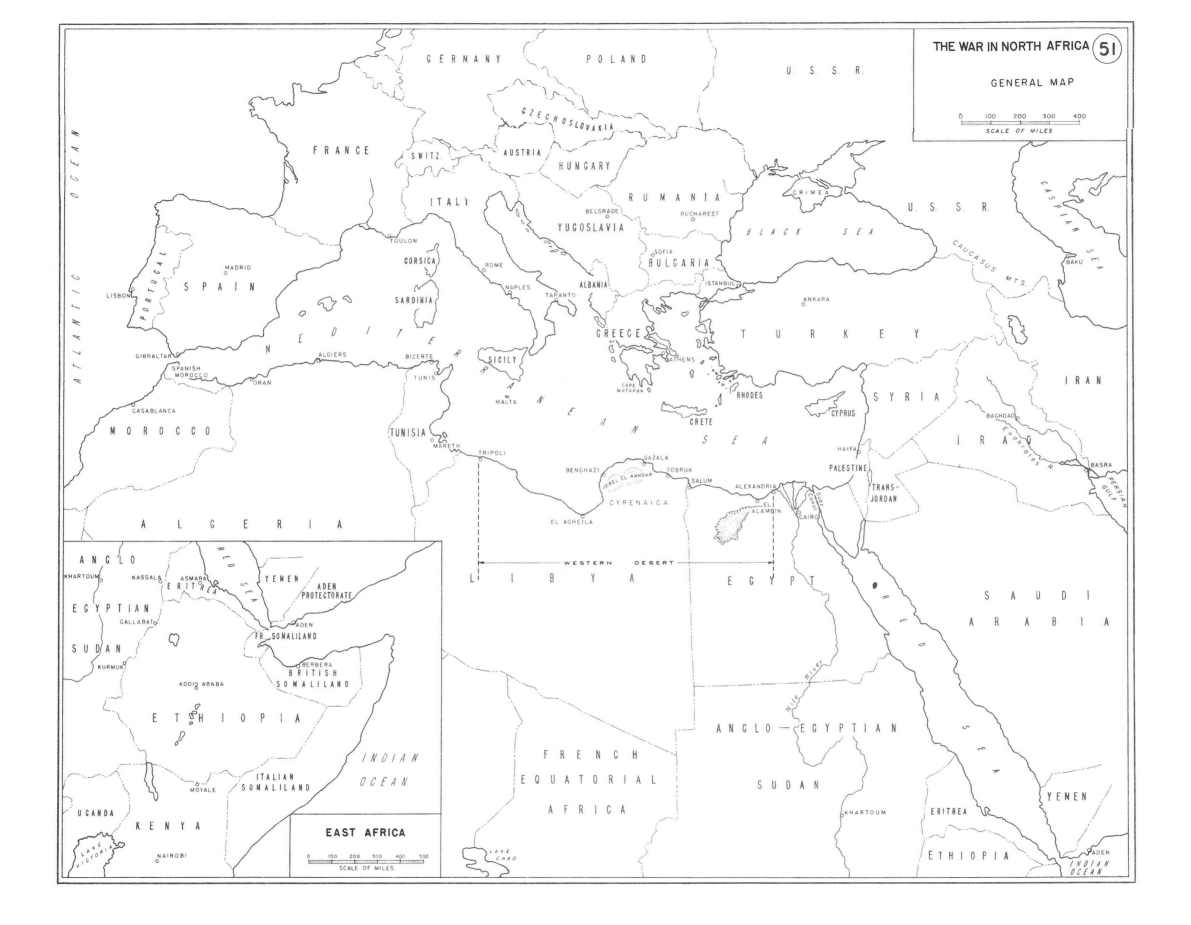

0 100 200 300 400
SCALE OF MILES

ATLANTIC OCEAN

GERMANY

POLAND

U. S. S. R.

CZECHOSLOVAKIA

SWITZ.   AUSTRIA

FRANCE

HUNGARY

RUMANIA

CRIMEA

U. S. S. R.

ITALY

YUGOSLAVIA

BELGRADE   BUCHAREST

BLACK   SEA

CAUCASUS MTS.

CASPIAN SEA

TOULON

PORTUGAL

SPAIN

MADRID

CORSICA

ROME

SOFIA

BULGARIA

BAKU

LISBON

SARDINIA

NAPLES

ALBANIA

ISTANBUL

ANKARA

GIBRALTAR

MEDITER

ALGIERS

BIZERTE

SICILY

TARANTO

GREECE

ATHENS

TURKEY

IRAN

SPANISH MOROCCO

ORAN

TUNIS

CAPE MATAPAN

RHODES

CYPRUS

SYRIA

BAGHDAD

CASABLANCA

MALTA

A   N   E   A   N

CRETE

HAIFA

IRAQ

BASRA

MOROCCO

TUNISIA

MARETH

TRIPOLI

BENGHAZI

JEBEL EL AKHDAR

GAZALA

TOBRUK

SALUM

ALEXANDRIA

PALESTINE

TRANS-JORDAN

Euphrates R.

PERSIAN GULF

S   E   A

SUEZ CANAL

ALGERIA

CYRENAICA

EL AGHEILA

EL ALAMEIN

CAIRO

L   I   B   Y   A

WESTERN   DESERT

E   G   Y   P   T

RED SEA

SAUDI

ARABIA

Nile River

ANGLO-EGYPTIAN

FRENCH

EQUATORIAL

SUDAN

KHARTOUM

ERITREA

YEMEN

AFRICA

LAKE CHAD

ETHIOPIA

ADEN

INDIAN OCEAN

Inset (East Africa)

ANGLO

KHARTOUM   KASSALA   ASMARA

ERITREA

RED SEA

YEMEN

ADEN PROTECTORATE

EGYPTIAN

GALLABAT

ADEN

SUDAN

KURMUK

FR. SOMALILAND

BERBERA

BRITISH SOMALILAND

ADDIS ABABA

E   T   H   I   O   P   I   A

UGANDA

MOYALE

ITALIAN SOMALILAND

INDIAN OCEAN

KENYA

LAKE VICTORIA

NAIROBI

EAST AFRICA

0 100 200 300 400 500
SCALE OF MILES

GRAZIANI'S ADVANCE & ROMMEL'S FIRST OFFENSIVE

★

In the summer of 1940, the commander of the British forces in the Middle East, General Sir Archibald P. Wavell, had only 100,000 men, whereas his Italian counterpart, Marshal Rodolfo Graziani, based around Bardia in Libya, mustered some 250,000, and an air force several times the size available to Wavell. Even so, it took some prodding by Mussolini to get Graziani up and running.

On 13 September, five Italian divisions moved across the border against a light British screening force. The bulk of Wavell's two available divisions were at Mersa Matruh, his elected defensive position. By the 16th, the Italians had occupied Sidi Barrani, but then Graziani decided to settle down into a series of defensive camps that stretched fifty miles from the coast inland to Sofafi. They had little mutual support or defense in depth and, in addition, there was an inviting gap of twenty miles separating the outer two. Wavell decided to seize the initiative.

The Western Desert Force, commanded by Lt. Gen. Richard O'Connor, attacked through the gap on 9 December, and one day later was in Sidi Barrani. Surprised, cut off, and thoroughly demoralized, some 38,000 Italians surrendered and, by 16 December, Graziani had been driven from Egypt. Pausing to reorganize and resupply his forces, O'Connor moved westward and, maintaining relentless pressure, struck the remaining Italians at Mekili and Derna and boldly sent his armor across the unreconnoitered desert to block their retreat at Beda Fomm. Graziani's troops, after trying to break out, surrendered on 7 February (1,928 were casualties, 130,000 were captured).

Wavell now wanted to drive on to Tripoli, but was ordered to hold near Benghazi using only minimum forces in order to be able send troops to Greece (see page 22). Mussolini, having failed in Libya and Albania (see page 22), now had no other option but to accept Hitler's offer of support in North Africa. In March 1941 General Irwin Rommel landed two divisions of the Deutches Afrika Corps (DAK) at Tripoli. It would have a dramatic impact on events.

On 24 March, Rommel launched a heavy raid against El Agheila and, discovering how weak the British were there, pushed on boldly until, by 11 April, he had driven the British, except for the Tobruk garrison, out of Libya, scooping up General O'Connor in the process, and destroying most of the British armored brigade. Wavell rushed reinforcements westward as Egypt's defense took priority over Greece. Meanwhile, Rommel launched a hasty and ill-prepared attack on Tobruk (19–14 April), and received a nasty rebuff, but managed to occupy Bardia and Salum.

Wavell, under pressure to strike back, made an abortive attack in May and another on 15 June, which was repulsed with heavy tank losses. For it was here that the British were first introduced to Rommel's skillful use of antitank gun screens, including the dreaded 88mm gun, perhaps the deadliest antitank weapon of the whole war.

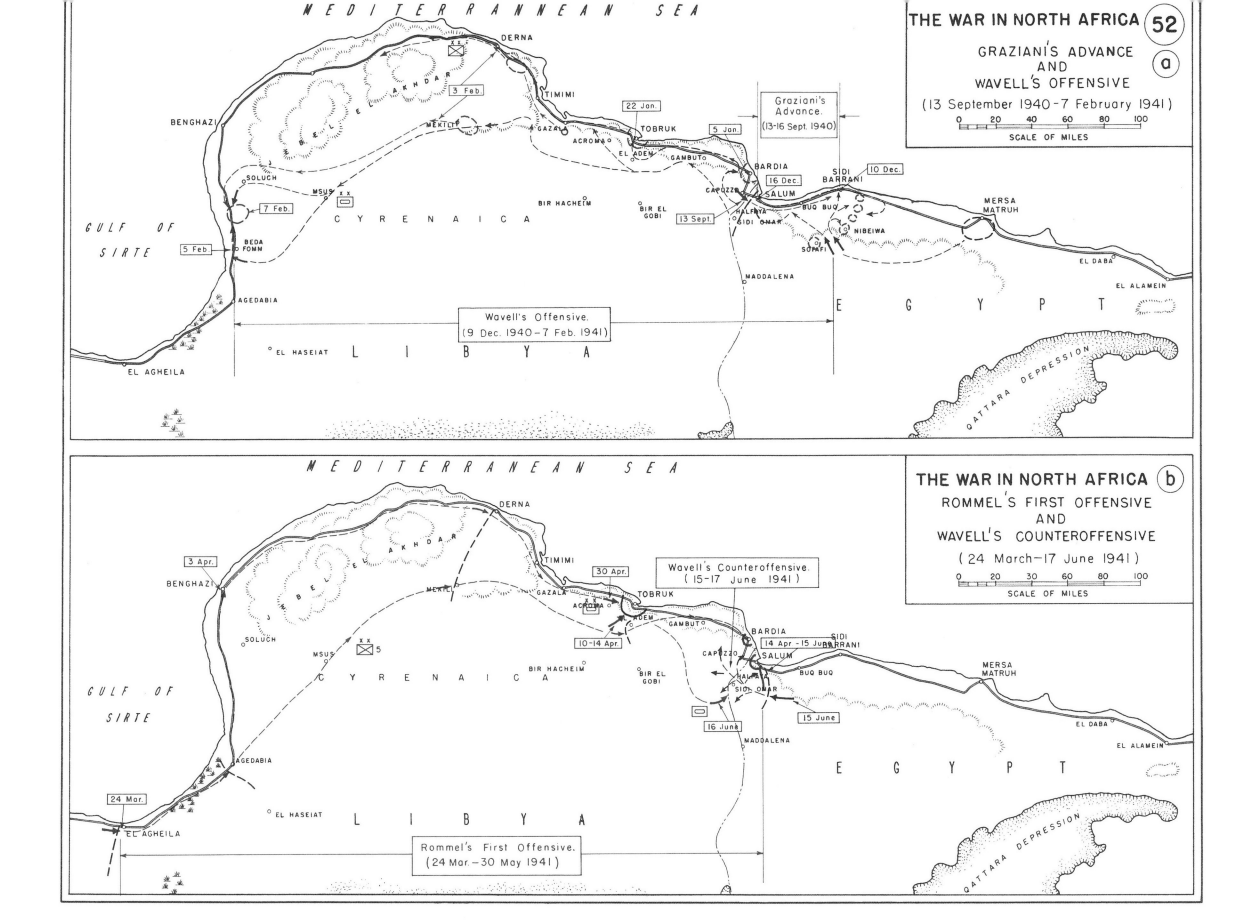

THE WAR IN NORTH AFRICA **52**

a

GRAZIANI'S ADVANCE
AND
WAVELL'S OFFENSIVE

(13 September 1940 – 7 February 1941)

SCALE OF MILES
0 20 40 60 80 100

MEDITERRANNEAN SEA

DERNA

BENGHAZI

J BEL EL AKHDAR

3 Feb.

MEKTILT

TIMIMI

22 Jan.

GAZALA

ACROMA

TOBRUK

EL ADEM

GAMBUTO

5 Jan.

Graziani's
Advance.
(13-16 Sept. 1940)

BARDIA

16 Dec.

SIDI
BARRANI

10 Dec.

SOLUCH

MSUS

CYRENAICA

BIR HACHEIM

BIR EL
GOBI

CAPUZZO

SALUM

HALFAYA

SIDI OMAR

BUQ BUQ

MERSA
MATRUH

13 Sept.

NIBEIWA

7 Feb.

GULF OF
SIRTE

5 Feb.

BEDA
FOMM

SOFAFI

MADDALENA

EL DABA

EL ALAMEIN

AGEDABIA

Wavell's Offensive.
(9 Dec. 1940 – 7 Feb. 1941)

E G Y P T

EL HASEIAT

L I B Y A

EL AGHEILA

QATTARA DEPRESSION

MEDITERRANEAN SEA

THE WAR IN NORTH AFRICA **b**

ROMMEL'S FIRST OFFENSIVE
AND
WAVELL'S COUNTEROFFENSIVE

(24 March – 17 June 1941)

SCALE OF MILES
0 20 30 60 80 100

DERNA

3 Apr.

BENGHAZI

J BEL EL AKHDAR

MEKILI

TIMIMI

30 Apr.

GAZALA

ACROMA

TOBRUK

Wavell's Counteroffensive.
(15-17 June 1941)

EL ADEM

10-14 Apr.

GAMBUT

BARDIA

SIDI
BARRANI

SOLUCH

MSUS

5

CYRENAICA

BIR HACHEIM

BIR EL
GOBI

CAPUZZO

14 Apr - 15 Ju

SALUM

HALFAYA

SIDI OMAR

BUQ BUQ

MERSA
MATRUH

16 June

15 June

GULF OF
SIRTE

MADDALENA

EL DABA

EL ALAMEIN

AGEDABIA

E G Y P T

24 Mar.

EL HASEIAT

L I B Y A

EL AGHEILA

Rommel's First Offensive.
(24 Mar. – 30 May 1941)

QATTARA DEPRESSION

AUCHINLECK'S OFFENSIVE & ROMMEL'S SECOND OFFENSIVE

★

Wavell's defeat led to his replacement by General Sir Claude Auchinleck in July 1941, but it was not until November 1941 that the new commander had overcome some of the problems with training and supply deficiencies. By then, the forces in North Africa (now reorganized by Auchinleck as Eighth Army under General Alan Cunningham) comprised seven divisions, some 700 tanks (mostly inferior to German models) and about 1,000 operational aircraft.

Auchinleck's plan visualized an advance through Maddalena by the armor-heavy XXX Corps, designed to draw Rommel's panzers south, while XIII Corps encircled the Salum and Bardia garrisons and then drove to the relief of Tobruk, after which the whole of Cyrenaica would be recovered. Rommel, meanwhile, appreciated his danger in the Bardia–Salum area and readied plans to capture Tobruk. But with Germany fully engaged in Russia, Rommel could not expect additional troops and supplies; and added to this was the increasingly effective grip on the Mediterranean by British air and naval forces. So, as November 1941 approached, the situation in Rommel's command (now called Panzer Group Afrika) steadily worsened. When Auchinleck attacked, Rommel had three German divisions, a two-division Italian motorized corps (Ariete and Trieste), and four Italian infantry divisions. He had 414 tanks (154 of which were Italian) and 320 aircraft (200 of which were Italian).

The British attack achieved surprise, but Rommel threw most of his troops against XXX Corps, and the battle raged for two weeks south of Tobruk. The Tobruk garrison tried to break out but were sealed off by the Germans. Cunningham's armor was badly mauled, and he asked to be allowed to retreat. Auchinleck replaced him with Maj. Gen. Neil Ritchie.

On the 27 November, the New Zealand Division linked up with the Tobruk garrison, which had again broken out, but now Rommel tightened his grip; by 1 December the New Zealanders had been chopped to pieces, and the encirclement of the port reestablished. XXX Corps, however, was pressurizing the Italians at Bir El Gobi, which forced Rommel to drop his support of the Bardia/Salum enclave (the defenders would surrender on 17 January) and pull back his panzers to the line north of Bir El Gobi, and from there all the way back to the Gazala line, and from there right back to El Agheila on the 31st.

Ironically, Rommel, being closer to his base, now had the tactical advantage, despite his retreat. He counterattacked on the 21 January 1942 and caught Eighth Army off balance, which was forced to retreat eastward to the Gazala–Bir Hacheim line, in the process abandoning supplies that Rommel badly needed.

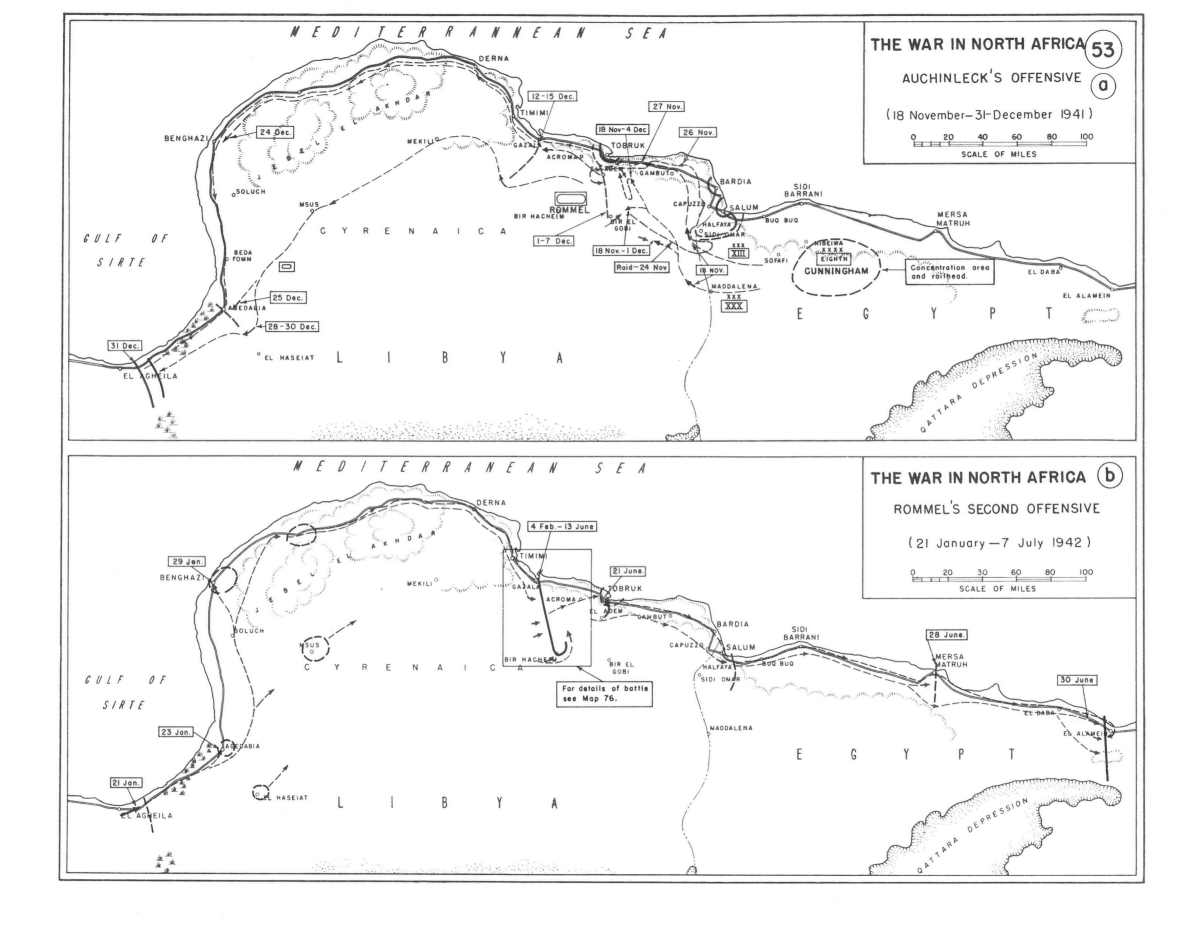

THE WAR IN NORTH AFRICA (53) (a)

AUCHINLECK'S OFFENSIVE

(18 November–31 December 1941)

0 20 40 60 80 100
SCALE OF MILES

Map a labels:

MEDITERRANEAN SEA

DERNA
JEBEL EL AKHDAR
TIMIMI
12-15 Dec.
24 Dec.
BENGHAZI
MEKILIO
18 Nov-4 Dec.
TOBRUK
27 Nov.
GAZALA
ACROMA
26 Nov.
EL ADEM
GAMBUTO
SOLUCH
BARDIA
BIR HACHEIM
ROMMEL
SIDI BARRANI
CAPUZZO
SALUM
CYRENAICA
MSUS
BIR EL GOBI
HALFAYA
BUQ BUQ
MERSA MATRUH
GULF OF SIRTE
BEDA FOMM
1-7 Dec.
SIDI OMAR
XXX XIII
NIBEIWA XXXX
EIGHTH
EL DABA
18 Nov.-1 Dec.
SOFAFI
CUNNINGHAM
Concentration area and railhead.
Raid-24 Nov.
18 NOV.
25 Dec.
AGEDABIA
28-30 Dec.
MADDALENA
XXX XXX
EL ALAMEIN
31 Dec.
EL HASEIAT
L I B Y A
E G Y P T
EL AGHEILA
QATTARA DEPRESSION

THE WAR IN NORTH AFRICA (b)

ROMMEL'S SECOND OFFENSIVE

(21 January–7 July 1942)

0 20 30 60 80 100
SCALE OF MILES

Map b labels:

MEDITERRANEAN SEA

DERNA
JEBEL EL AKHDAR
4 Feb.-13 June
TIMIMI
29 Jan.
BENGHAZI
MEKILI
21 June.
GAZALA
TOBRUK
ACROMA
EL ADEM
GAMBUTO
SOLUCH
BARDIA
BIR HACHEIM
CAPUZZO
SALUM
SIDI BARRANI
MSUS
BIR EL GOBI
HALFAYA
BUQ BUQ
28 June.
MERSA MATRUH
CYRENAICA
For details of battle see Map 76.
SIDI OMAR
GULF OF SIRTE
23 Jan.
AGEDABIA
MADDALENA
30 June
EL DABA
21 Jan.
EL HASEIAT
EL ALAMEIN
L I B Y A
E G Y P T
EL AGHEILA
QATTARA DEPRESSION

BATTLE AT THE GAZALA-BIR HACHEIM LINE

★

The Axis forces entered the battle of Gazala–Bir Hacheim with 560 tanks, while the British committed about 700 by the battle's end. The 200 American-made Grant tanks employed by the British outgunned the German armor (Italian tanks were virtually useless in battle), but Rommel's ace card would be the 88mm antitank gun, of which he had fifty.

Ritchie had fallen back into a series of strong points ("boxes"), anchored on the south by the Bir Hacheim fortress. The whole line was interwoven with extensive minefields (approximately 500,000 mines) and was backed by armored elements concentrated behind the open southern flank.

Rommel started his offensive on 26 May with a feint toward Gazala by the Italian X and XXI Corps supported by panzer corps that Rommel then pulled back and had swing around in a southern loop to attack the British southern flank. By the morning of the 27th they had attacked the Bir Hacheim fortress and pushed back 3rd Indian Brigade. They now swung north toward Acroma and the coast, with the 90th Division protecting the right flank by seizing El Adem, while the panzers of the DAK and a portion of the Ariete Division were to disperse the British 7th Armoured and isolate the infantry divisions.

By noon, the 90th Division was in El Adem but the Afrika Corps was still struggling with British 7th Armoured, with both sides taking heavy losses. By nightfall, the panzers had worked their way to the Knightsbridge–El Adem road against the two British armored divisions. By now, German tank losses had become serious, and Rommel's extended supply line was being harried by the RAF and parts of 7th Armoured. Rommel now decided to bring his armor back into an enclave (the "Cauldron") where it could be resupplied. The withdrawal was begun on the 30th, but heavy tank fighting continued for two days around Knightsbridge.

After ten days of the hardest fighting, with Ritchie frittering away his armor on piecemeal attacks against the Cauldron, Rommel, now resupplied, broke out on the 11 June and forced Ritchie back just south of the Knightsbridge–El Adem road. For the next two days Ritchie held off the Axis attacks while the 1st South African and 50th Divisions withdrew. British tank losses rose (by the 16th there were only sixty-five left) but most of the infantry got away. On 13 June the panzers reached the coast, and the battle ended with Eighth Army streaming eastward and Rommel bearing down on Tobruk.

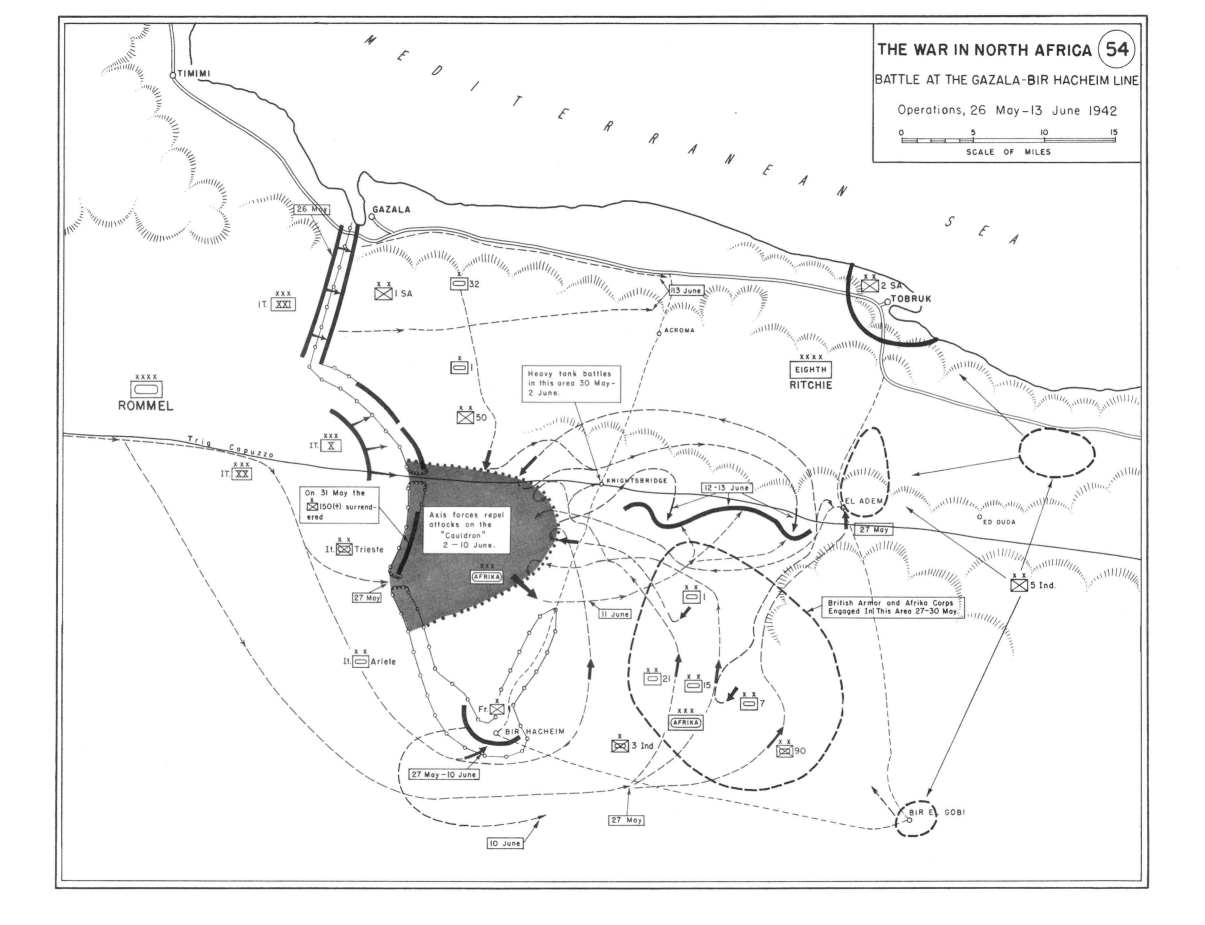

0   5   10   15

SCALE OF MILES

M E D I T E R R A N E A N   S E A

TIMIMI

26 May

GAZALA

IT. XXX XXI

XX 1 SA

X 32

XX 2 SA

TOBRUK

1 13 June

ACROMA

X 1

XXXX EIGHTH RITCHIE

ROMMEL

Trig Capuzzo

IT. XXX X

IT. XXX XX

XX 50

Heavy tank battles in this area 30 May–2 June.

KNIGHTSBRIDGE

12-13 June

EL ADEM

27 May

ED DUDA

On 31 May the X 150(†) surrendered

Axis forces repel attacks on the "Cauldron" 2 — 10 June.

XXX AFRIKA

It. XX Trieste

27 May

11 June

XX 1

British Armor and Afrika Corps Engaged In This Area 27-30 May.

XX 5 Ind.

It. XX Ariete

XX 21

XX 15

XXX AFRIKA

X 7

Fr. X

BIR HACHEIM

X 3 Ind

XX 90

27 May–10 June

27 May

BIR EL GOBI

10 June

BATTLE OF ALAM HALFA

★

Auchinleck admitted that he was at an impasse at Tobruk, and even when reinforced, declined to attack. So, on 13 August, he was replaced with the dynamic duo of General Harold R.L.G. Alexander and Lt. Gen Bernard L. Montgomery, taking over Middle East Command and Eighth Army respectively.

While Axis and Allies faced off at Tobruk, Rommel was driven to despair by his worsening logistical situation. Hitler, ignorant of the true situation, forbade any thought of withdrawal and, in fact, urged him to attack. This Rommel reluctantly agreed to do if he were to be guaranteed 6,000 tons of fuel. This was promised but, of course, only a fraction ever arrived.

Facing Rommel's 440 tanks (of which 240 were Italian), Montgomery could field 480, with more available at Alexandria. His infantry occupied well fortified positions, except in the south around the Ragil Depression, although he had heavily mined the area. Expecting Rommel to seek a penetration up through the soft southern underbelly, Montgomery defended Alam Halfa Ridge in great strength to prevent any encirclement toward the coast. On the ridge, he dug in two tank brigades that he considered too green for mobile warfare, and a third was placed further north.

Rommel's plan was strikingly similar to that used at Bir Hacheim, and as Montgomery had predicted, he swung his main attack up through the south at midnight on 30 August. He expected to breach the minefields quickly and to have his armor east of Gabala at dawn; it would then turn north, bypass most of Alam Halfa Ridge to the east, and strike for the coast. The minefields, however, proved to be unexpectedly difficult, and it was not until 0930 that the DAK was ready to drive east, by which time it was under heavy air attack. Having lost his chance for surprise, Rommel considered calling off the whole operation, but finally decided to make a shallower envelopment. Fighting the withdrawing 7th Division and harassed from the air, the panzers did not reach Alam Halfa Ridge until late afternoon. Here, they were stopped by the 22nd Tank Brigade. Rommel, running short of fuel, ordered only local attacks for 1 September, and these, made by 15th Panzer Division, were easily stopped as Montgomery brought in 23rd Armoured Division from its position north of the ridge. On 2 September DAK began to withdraw, and Montgomery had the New Zealand 2nd Division attack on the 3 September, but it was a costly failure.

Rommel's withdrawal came to a halt on the 7th, but Montgomery, feeling that Eighth Army was not yet ready for a decisive showdown, was content to let the Desert Fox lick his wounds.

After Alam Halfa, Montgomery resumed his program of training, equipping, and revitalizing the army, and the troops' confidence rose under his energetic and careful leadership. Meanwhile, supplies continued to pour in; new Sherman tanks arrived from America, huge forward supply depots were established, and elaborate deception plans were implemented. Again, political pressure built up for an attack.

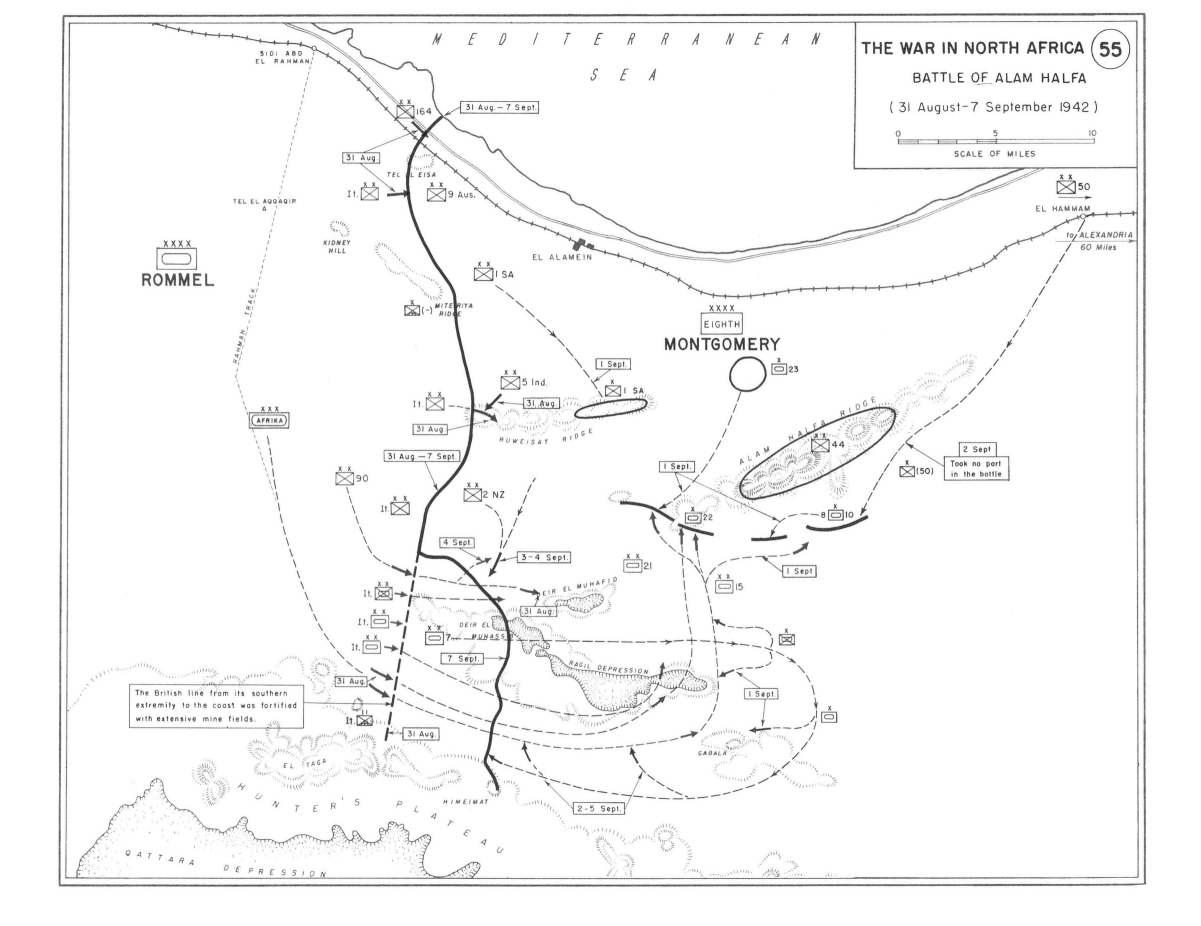

MEDITERRANEAN SEA

SIDI ABD EL RAHMAN

THE WAR IN NORTH AFRICA 55

BATTLE OF ALAM HALFA

(31 August–7 September 1942)

0   5   10
SCALE OF MILES

164   31 Aug.–7 Sept.

31 Aug.

TEL EL EISA

It. 9 Aus.

TEL EL AQQAQIR

KIDNEY HILL

EL ALAMEIN

50

EL HAMMAM

to ALEXANDRIA
60 Miles

ROMMEL

I SA

MITEIRIYA RIDGE (-)

EIGHTH

MONTGOMERY

23

AFRIKA

5 Ind.

1 Sept.

I SA

It.   31 Aug.

31 Aug.

RUWEISAT RIDGE

ALAM HALFA RIDGE

44

2 Sept
Took no part
in the battle

(50)

31 Aug.–7 Sept.

90

It.

2 NZ

1 Sept.

22

8   10

1 Sept

4 Sept.

3–4 Sept.

21

15

It.

DEIR EL MUHAFID

31 Aug.

It.

DEIR EL MUNASSIB

7

7 Sept.

RAGIL DEPRESSION

1 Sept

It.

31 Aug.

The British line from its southern
extremity to the coast was fortified
with extensive mine fields.

It.

GABALA

31 Aug.

EL TAQA

HIMEIMAT

HUNTER'S PLATEAU

2–5 Sept.

QATTARA DEPRESSION

BATTLE OF EL ALAMEIN

★

Montgomery would not be pushed into battle until he was ready. And he was ready by the 23 October. On that day he ordered XXX Corps in the north to drive two corridors through Rommel's minefields, while XIII Corps in the south simultaneously launched a secondary attack designed to hold 21st Panzer in place. The X Armoured Corps would pass through the corridors created by XXX Corps and block the enemy's armor, while XXX Corps eliminated the Axis infantry and Rommel's panzers.

Rommel used the period from 7 September to 23 October to build defenses for the inevitable Allied assault. Logistical support continued to be inadequate, while Montgomery built up a two-to-one preponderance in men, tanks, artillery, and aircraft. Rommel's deep, static defenses were held by the Italian infantry divisions, stiffened by German paratroopers, except in the vital coastal sector which was defended by German infantry. On 22 September a very sick Rommel was flown back to Germany for treatment, only to fly back to Africa once he heard of the battle's start (he was back by 25 October).

The offensive started at 2140, 23 October, with a tremendous artillery barrage, followed twenty minutes later by the infantry assault which opened up the planned corridors, and was followed four hours later by X Corps armor. Heavy fighting continued all night as the Axis troops, recovering from the initial shock, concentrated artillery fire on the corridor and struck back with 15th Panzer. Modest gains had been made by Montgomery's forces, but the armor had not reached the hope-for blocking positions.

Now began the "dogfight," as Montgomery described the bitter fighting of the ensuing week, but when the attack by 50th Division failed on 24th, and it became apparent that the gains in the south were too costly, Montgomery ordered XIII Corps to suspend its attacks. Also on the 25th, he switched his main effort from the corridors to the Australian 9th Division sector, but ordered 1st Armoured to fight its way beyond Kidney Hill. Throughout the period 26–29 October, the Australians made good progress, but the armor, although finally taking Kidney Hill, suffered at the hands of repeated German counterattacks. On the night of the 26th, Rommel moved 21st Panzer north for an attack next day, and Montgomery countered by moving 7th Armoured north and withdrew 1 Armoured and the New Zealand 2nd Division into reserve, preparatory to regrouping for the final "breakout." During this attritional phase of the dogfight, Rommel's tank losses mounted rapidly and, desperately short of fuel, he was forced to commit his armor piecemeal.

The final phase of the battle began at 0100 on 2 November. Montgomery planned for an infantry penetration of the Axis lines just north of Kidney Hill, to be followed by armor fanning out into the open countryside where it would complete the destruction of Rommel's army. The area of attack was selected to avoid the higher concentrations of German troops on the coast while hitting the weaker Italian formations further inland.

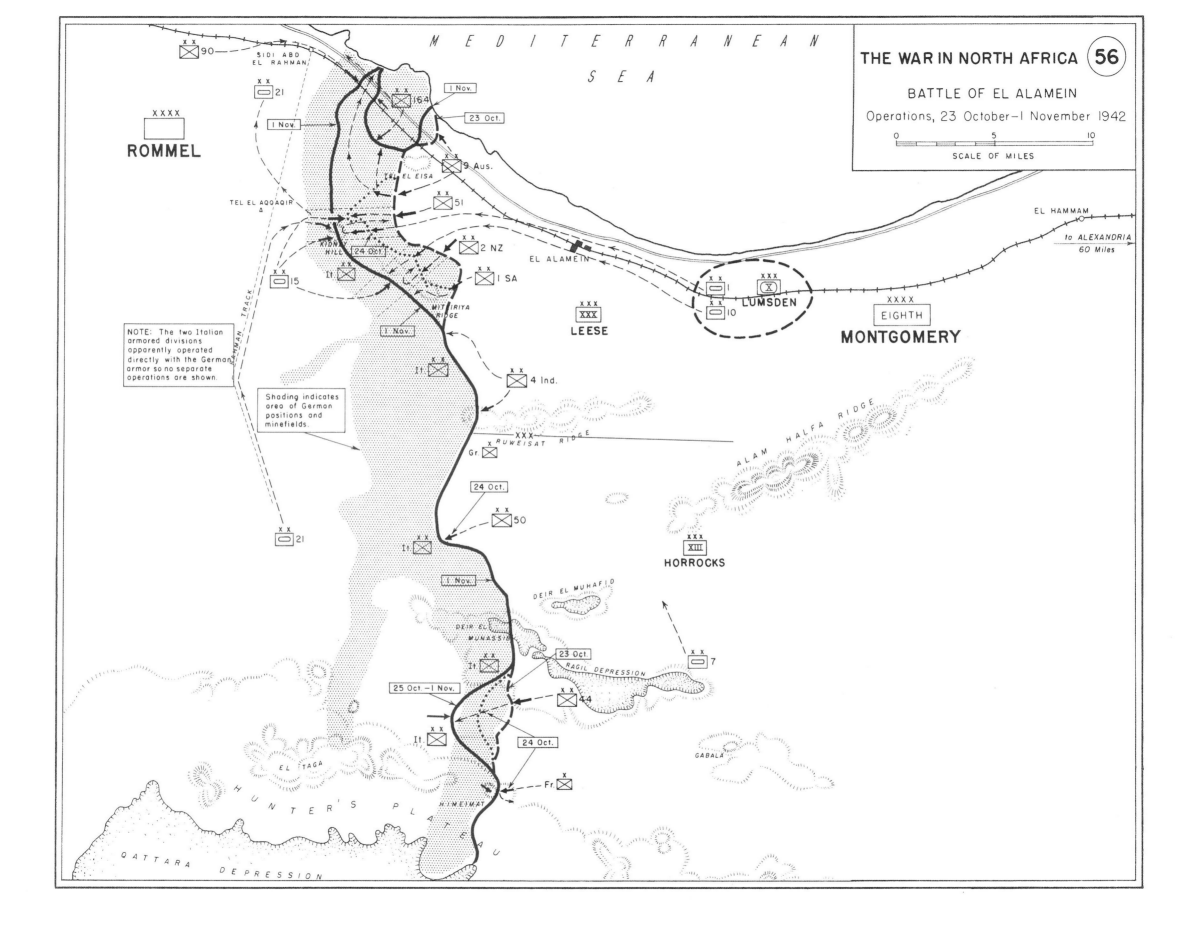

MEDITERRANEAN
SEA

XX 90 — SIDI ABD EL RAHMAN

XX 21

XXXX
ROMMEL

1 Nov.

XX 164 — 1 Nov.
23 Oct.

EL EISA

XX 9 Aus.

TEL EL AQQAQIR

XX 51

KIDN HILL — 24 Oct.

XX 2 NZ

EL ALAMEIN

XX It.

XX 15

XX 1 SA

MITEIRIYA RIDGE

1 Nov.

NOTE: The two Italian armored divisions apparently operated directly with the German armor so no separate operations are shown.

Shading indicates area of German positions and minefields.

XXX XXX
LEESE

XX 1
X
XXX
LUMSDEN
XX 10

XXXX
EIGHTH
MONTGOMERY

to ALEXANDRIA
60 Miles

EL HAMMAM

ALAM HALFA RIDGE

XX It.

XX 4 Ind.

XXX RUWEISAT RIDGE
Gr. XX

24 Oct.

XX 21

XX 50

XX It.

XXX
XIII
HORROCKS

1 Nov.

DEIR EL MUHAFID

DEIR EL MUNASSIB

23 Oct.

RAGIL DEPRESSION

XX 7

25 Oct.-1 Nov.

XX It.

XX 44

XX It.

24 Oct.

GABALA

EL TAGA

HIMEIMAT

Fr. XX

HUNTER'S PLATEAU

QATTARA DEPRESSION

THE WAR IN NORTH AFRICA 56

BATTLE OF EL ALAMEIN

Operations, 23 October–1 November 1942

0   5   10
SCALE OF MILES

BATTLE OF EL ALAMEIN

★

The stalwart New Zealand 2nd Division, rested since its mauling at Alam Halfa, led the attack on the 2nd behind a heavy rolling barrage, and by dawn a new corridor had been carved out, enabling 9th Armoured Brigade to establish a bridgehead across the Rahman Track. But in attempting to expand it, the brigade ran into another of Rommel's skillfully deployed antitank screens and suffered 75 percent casualties, yet still managed to hold the salient. Meanwhile 1st Armoured debouched from the bridgehead and collided head-on with 15th Panzer. A violent tank battle ensued for the rest of the day in which elements of 21st Panzer and Italian joined. Rommel finally sealed off the penetration, but the attrition rate was reaching catastrophic proportions. When the day ended the DAK had only thirty-five operational tanks. In addition, his antitank guns were being knocked out at a steady rate. On the night of the 2nd he acknowledged defeat and decided to withdraw. Hitler, however, absolutely forbade it. Dejected, Rommel ordered the withdrawal halted, but along the coastal road, now clogged with retreating troops, confusion reigned and British air attacks took a heavy toll.

On the night of 3 November, unwilling to continue his breakout efforts in the established bridgehead, Montgomery ordered an attack astride Kidney Hill. It was launched just before dawn on 4 November by 51st and Indian 4th Divisions and achieved a clean breakthrough. Montgomery poured the 7th and 10th Armoured Divisions through the gap and also diverted 1st Armoured and the New Zealand 2nd Divisions to the area. The full onslaught fell on the Ariete Division which, by the afternoon, had been completely surrounded and destroyed.

At 1530, in defiance of Hitler's edict, Rommel ordered a withdrawal (sanctioned by Hitler two days later), but the Italian divisions isolated in the south were abandoned, and during the next few days were rounded up by XIII Corps. The remainder of the beaten army struck out westward on a broad front near the coastal road, on foot or in whatever vehicles still ran.

After stopping on the 5 November for regroupment, Montgomery began a determined pursuit, and on that day the New Zealand 2nd Division almost blocked the retreating Germans at Fuka. An even greater opportunity fell to X Corps two days later at Charing Cross–Mersa Matruh, but its supply trucks became bogged down by torrential rain. Montgomery gave up on bringing Rommel to a final showdown and concentrated on a long harrying race westward that would give his foe no rest.

On 8 November, the British continued the pursuit with one division (7th Armoured: the "Desert Rats"), and on that date, Allied forces landed in Algeria and French Morocco; on the 11th Axis forces were ejected from Egypt, and Rommel refueled with his last stocks in Cyrenaica (for the next two weeks he would rely on air supply). Montgomery attacked the El Agheila position on 11 December but Rommel withdrew when threatened with encirclement and Montgomery entered Tripoli on 23 January. In three months, the Eighth Army had driven Rommel 1,400 miles. But Rommel was now waiting behind the Mareth line; and, as the Allies were to discover, he would not be waiting long.

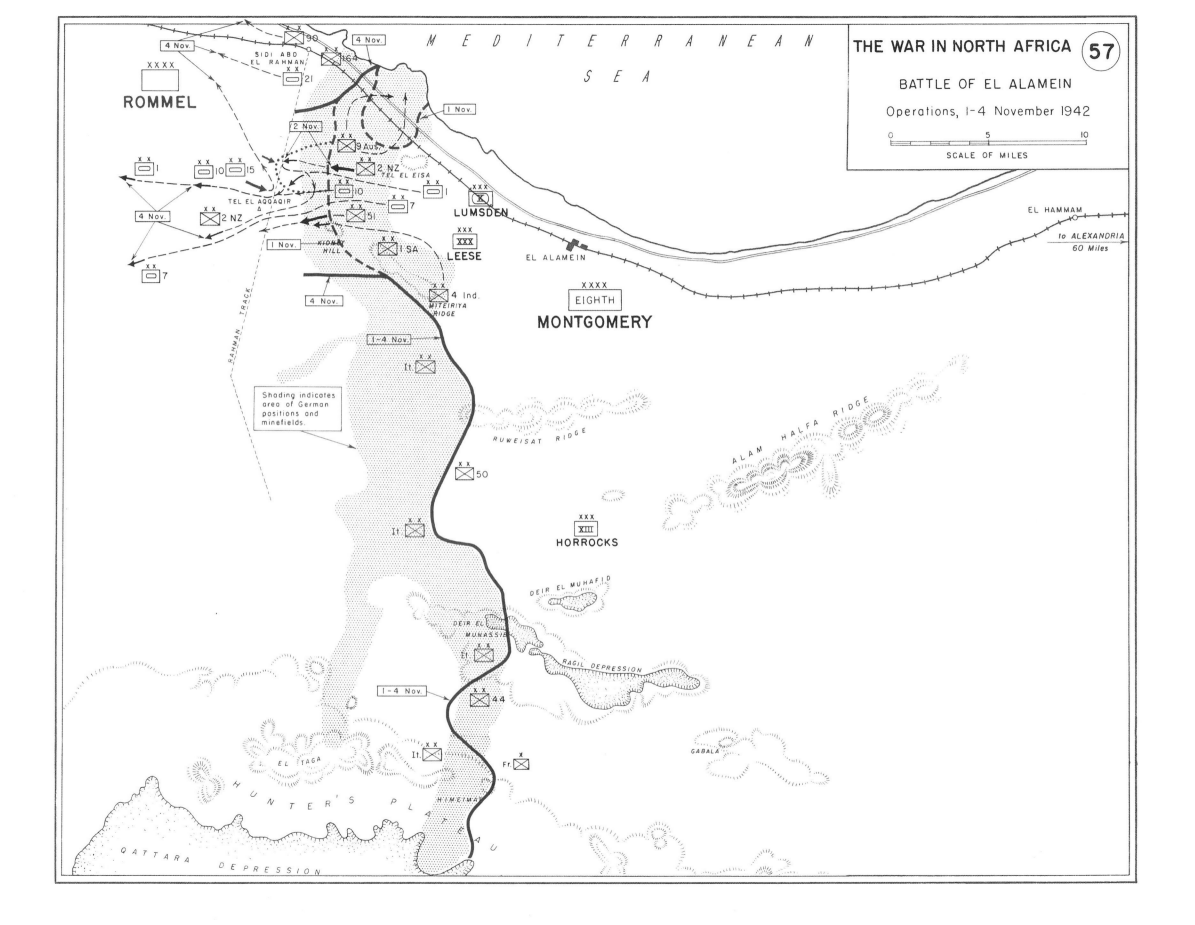

SCALE OF MILES

MEDITERRANEAN

SEA

ROMMEL

4 Nov.

SIDI ABD
EL RAHMAN

4 Nov.

90

164

21

1 Nov.

2 Nov.

9 Aus.

2 NZ
TEL EL EISA

1

10 15

10

1 Nov.

7

TEL EL AQQAQIR

LUMSDEN

2 NZ

4 Nov.

51

7

KIDNEY
HILL

1 SA

LEESE

EL ALAMEIN

EL HAMMAM

to ALEXANDRIA
60 Miles

7

4 Nov.

RAHMAN TRACK

1 Nov.

4 Nov.

4 Ind.
MITEIRIYA
RIDGE

EIGHTH

MONTGOMERY

1-4 Nov.

It.

Shading indicates
area of German
positions and
minefields.

RUWEISAT RIDGE

ALAM HALFA RIDGE

50

It.

XIII

HORROCKS

DEIR EL MUHAFID

DEIR EL
MUNASSIB

It.

RAGIL DEPRESSION

1-4 Nov.

44

GABALA

It.

Fr.

EL TAGA

HIMEIMAT

HUNTER'S PLATEAU

QATTARA DEPRESSION

ALLIED INVASION

★

The Allied landings in North Africa (Operation TORCH) on 8 November were the culmination of almost a year of Anglo-American debate. The British saw it as a chance to take the initiative from Hitler at relatively low cost. In addition, it offered the possibility of striking at Germany up through the soft underbelly of Italy. The U.S. Joint Chiefs of Staff, however, were not convinced. They saw it as a dissipation of effort, when the main thrust should be at France from Britain. In July 1942, Roosevelt finally resolved the matter by ordering the Joint Chiefs to prepare for TORCH. Eisenhower (then in command of American forces in Britain) was appointed Commander, Allied Expeditionary Force and established his Allied Force Headquarters (AFHQ). In the final plan, the Center and Western Task Forces were wholly American, while the Eastern Task Force was a composite British-American effort.

Before dawn on 8 November, the three Allied Task Forces landed with strikingly similar battle plans. Each one would aim to land on either side of its target city and pinch it out. Elements of Gen. George Patton's Western Task Force landed between 0400 and 0600 hours. It had been hoped that pro-Allied officers in Morocco would seize control and allow unopposed landings, but Patton's forces met with the strongest resistance of the day from tough French colonial troops. However, Maj. Gen. Ernest Harmon's force secured Safi by 1015, and early on 10 November started Combat Command B (2nd Armored Divi-

sion) toward Casablanca, capturing Mazagan the next morning. Meanwhile, north of Casablanca, the other two of Patton's landing forces were encountering stiffer resistance. Fire from shore batteries (soon neutralized) plus failures to land at designated beaches caused considerable confusion, but by 1500 3rd Division had captured Fédala. At Casablanca, French naval vessels took heavy losses in an engagement with the American fleet. On 9–10 November, Port Lyautey airfield was taken in hard fighting along the city's waterways. After difficulty in building up adequate supplies, 3rd Division closed in on Casablanca, and at 0700 on 11 November, the city surrendered.

Meanwhile, the Center and Eastern Task Forces, entering the Mediterranean on 5–6 November, had veered sharply southward at the last minute to their landing areas. At Oran, Maj. Gen. Lloyd Fredendall's force began landing at 0135 on 8 November, against sporadic resistance, but even so, they made heavy weather of it (two cutters, attempting to surprise the harbor defenses were forced to surrender, and airborne landings were ineffective). But eventually, Fredendall's troops tightened the ring around Oran, and at 1230 on 10 November, the French capitulated.

At Algiers, the Allies met the least resistance, primarily because the area had already been seized temporarily by friendly forces. Pro-Vichy troops made a short comeback, but by 1900 hours, they had been defeated.

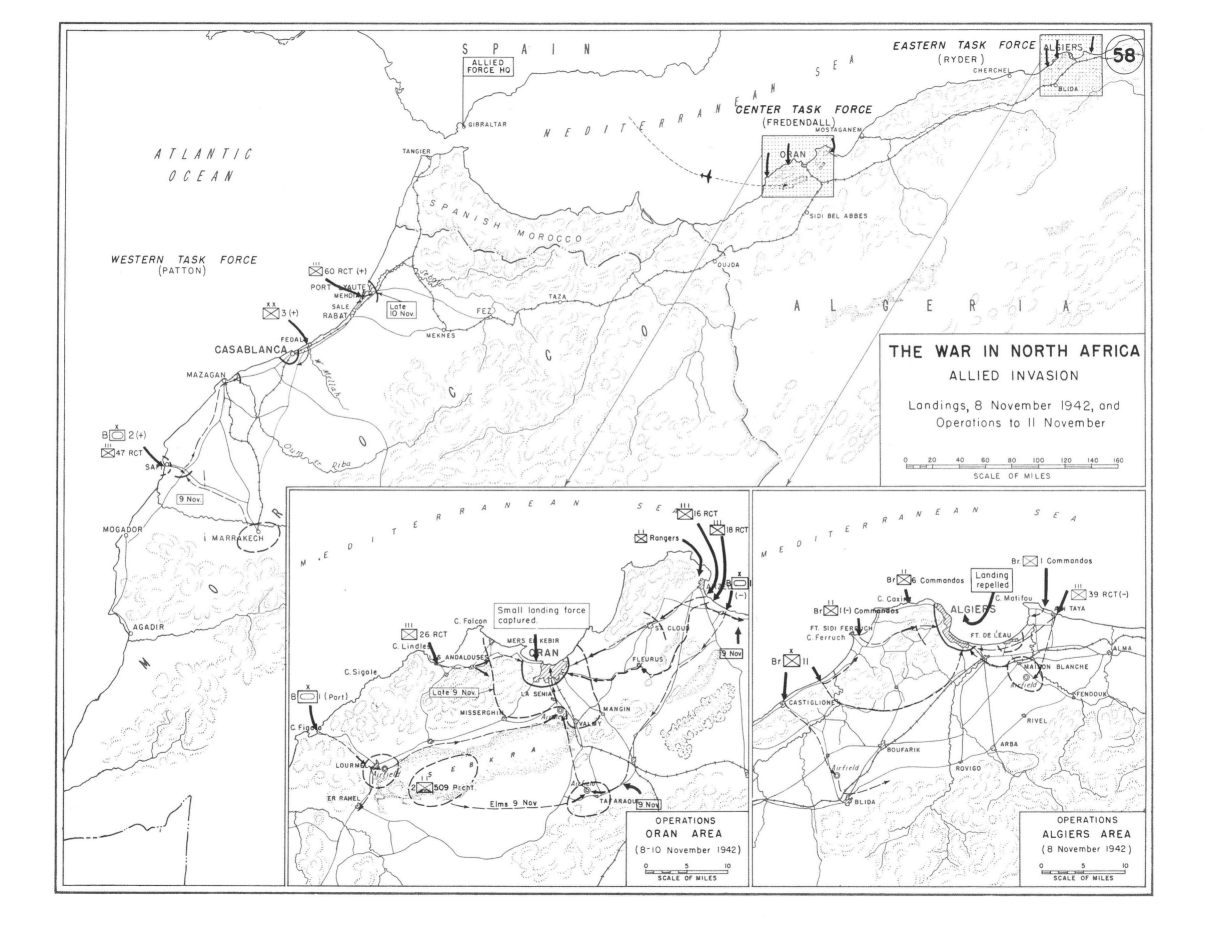

SPAIN

ALLIED FORCE HQ

GIBRALTAR

M E D I T E R R A N E A N   S E A

EASTERN TASK FORCE
(RYDER)

ALGIERS

CHERCHEL

BLIDA

58

CENTER TASK FORCE
(FREDENDALL)

MOSTAGANEM

ORAN

SIDI BEL ABBES

*ATLANTIC
OCEAN*

S P A N I S H   M O R O C C O

TANGIER

A L G E R I A

WESTERN TASK FORCE
(PATTON)

60 RCT (+)

PORT LYAUTEY
MEHDIA

SALE
RABAT

Late
10 Nov.

TAZA

FEZ

MEKNES

OUJDA

3 (+)

FEDALA

CASABLANCA

MAZAGAN

Oum er Riba

THE WAR IN NORTH AFRICA

ALLIED INVASION

Landings, 8 November 1942, and
Operations to 11 November

B 2 (+)

47 RCT

SAFI

9 Nov.

0 20 40 60 80 100 120 140 160
SCALE OF MILES

MOGADOR

MARRAKECH

AGADIR

M

O
R
O
C
C
O

OPERATIONS ORAN AREA

M E D I T E R R A N E A N   S E A

16 RCT

18 RCT

Rangers

Small landing force
captured.

C. Falcon

26 RCT

C. Lindles

C. Sigale

MERS EL KEBIR

ORAN

ST. CLOUD

FLEURUS

9 Nov

B 1 (Part)

C. Figalo

LAS ANDALOUSES

Late 9 Nov.

LA SENIA

MISSERGHIN

MANGIN

VALMY

LOURMEL

Airfield

2 509 Prcht.

S   E   B   K   R   A

Airfield

Elms 9 Nov.

TAFARAOUI

9 Nov

ER RAHEL

**OPERATIONS
ORAN AREA**
(8-10 November 1942)

0   5   10
SCALE OF MILES

OPERATIONS ALGIERS AREA

M E D I T E R R A N E A N   S E A

Br. 1 Commandos

Br. 6 Commandos

C. Caxine

Landing
repelled

39 RCT (-)

C. Matifou

Br. 1 (-) Commandos

ALGIERS

CAPE TAYA

FT. SIDI FERRUCH
C. Ferruch

FT. DE L'EAU

ALMA

MAISON BLANCHE
Airfield

Br. 11

CASTIGLIONE

FENDOUK

BOUFARIK

RIVET

ARBA

ROVIGO

Airfield

BLIDA

**OPERATIONS
ALGIERS AREA**
(8 November 1942)

0   5   10
SCALE OF MILES

THE RACE FOR TUNISIA & AXIS INITIATIVE

★

The race for Tunis began on 9 November, the day after the Allied landings. Hitler started to airlift troops into Bizerte, while British troops were leapfrogged to Bougie and Bone. Admiral Darlan, the commander of Vichy forces in North Africa, was pulled hither and thither by conflicting demands. Maj. Gen. Mark W. Clark (Eisenhower's second-in-command) met with Darlan and got him to sign a cease-fire order; but under pressure from Vichy Premier Pierre Laval, he rescinded it, only later to reinstate it under pressure from Clark. In the meanwhile, Axis troops were entering Tunis in increasing, and unopposed, numbers. This, understandably, caused much confusion among French troops, but General Georges Barré, the commander in Tunis, kept his head and withdrew his troops into the mountains, where he made contact with Allied columns.

British commando and paratroop landing at Bône were unopposed, and advanced spearheads were sent across the Tunisian border. By 17 November, Allied forces were in close proximity to Axis forces in northern Tunisia, and the race for Tunisia was about to be decided by a clash of arms.

On 16 November, General Walther Nehring arrived in Tunis to assume command of the Axis forces there. During 17–23 November aggressive German patrols pushed westward and fought with advanced elements of British and French forces. The commander of British First Army, Gen. Kenneth A.N. Anderson, reinforced by Combat Command B of the U.S. 1st Armored Division, launched an attack along three axes toward Mateur and Djedeida, but the results were disappointing, and one of the most significant factors had been the failure of the Allies to gain air superiority over the Luftwaffe.

Although Eisenhower ordered the attacks continued, it was Nehring who took the initiative, and pushed the Allies back. On 9 December, Gen. Juergan von Arnim assumed command of the Axis forces, now renamed Fifth Panzer Army. After Anderson made another, failed, thrust for Tunis, Eisenhower conceded defeat and switched his attention to the Germans at Sousse, Sfax, and Gabes. Fredendall's II Corps arrived in the Sbeitla area in early January. Originally, he was to attack toward Sfax to cut the Axis coastal corridor, but when Eisenhower learned that Montgomery could not reach Tunisia until mid-February, he directed Fredendall to defend the extended ridge chain called the Eastern Dorsal.

Meanwhile, Arnim continued to launch attacks, and on 2 January captured Fondouk from the French XIX Corps. On the 18 January he switched his attacks back north, and by the 25th had penetrated the undermanned French sector, which had to be propped up by American units. On 30 January, Arnim attacked to secure the pass at Faid, and again the blow fell on the French, and by the 14 February had secured commanding positions along the Eastern Dorsal. Worse, II Corps units were badly intermingled, 1st Armored was widely dispersed, and Rommel was about to join Arnim in an attack on II Corps.

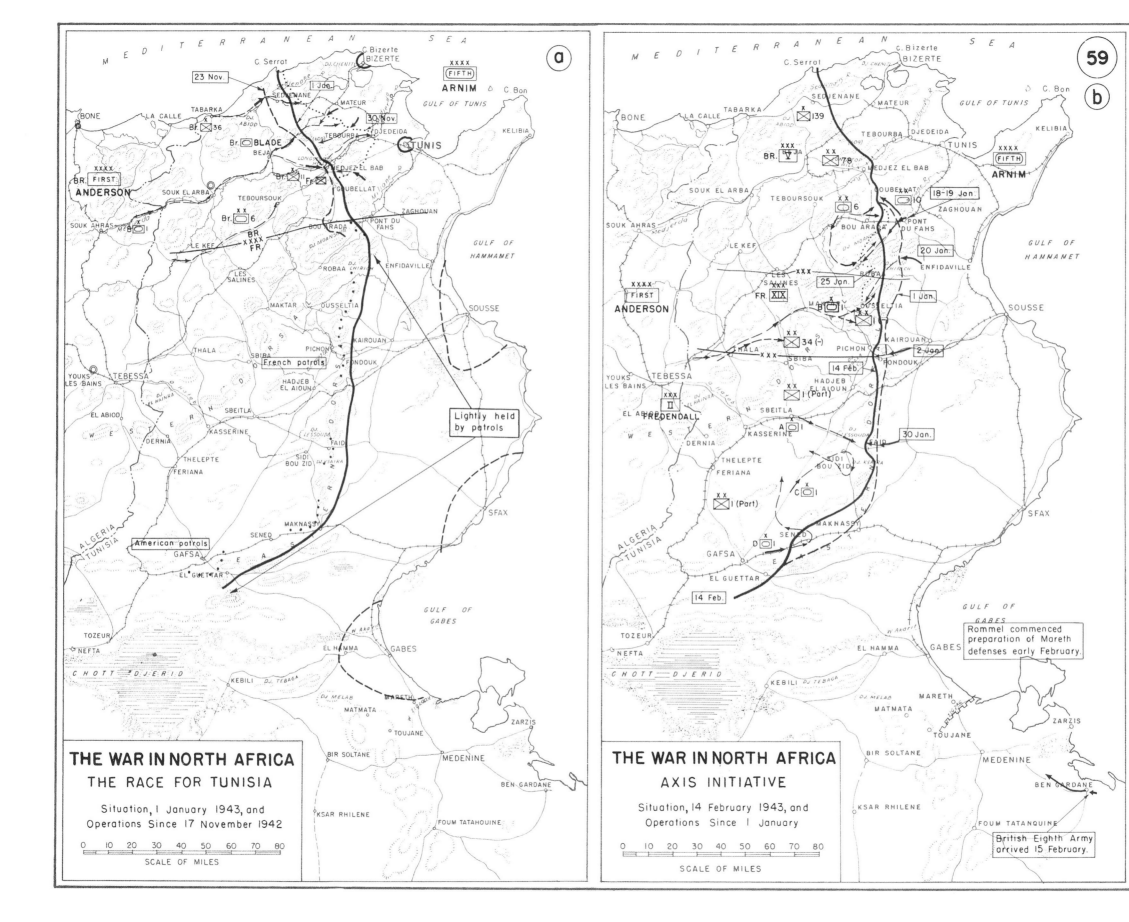

THE WAR IN NORTH AFRICA
THE RACE FOR TUNISIA

Situation, 1 January 1943, and
Operations Since 17 November 1942

0 10 20 30 40 50 60 70 80
SCALE OF MILES

THE WAR IN NORTH AFRICA
AXIS INITIATIVE

Situation, 14 February 1943, and
Operations Since 1 January

0 10 20 30 40 50 60 70 80
SCALE OF MILES

BATTLE OF KASSERINE PASS

★

Early in February 1943, the Germans, at Rommel's suggestion, planned a limited dual offensive. Arnim was to lead off with an attack against Sidi Bou Zid, while Rommel would move up and take Gafsa.

Early on 14 February 10th and 21st Panzer Divisions moved through the passes and attacked the Americans at Sidi Bou Zid. Although the Allies had expected such a move, they had not thought it would be in such strength; and, to make matters worse, II Corps was badly dispersed. The main strike force, 1st Armored Division, with its best unit, Combat Command B (CCB), was still attached to XIX Corps at Maktar, a good way north. Only Combat Command A (CCA) was with 168th Regimental Combat Team (RCT) to face the panzers that morning. Supported by Stukas, the panzers quickly outflanked Sidi Bou Zid and cut off the 168th RCT on the two heights. That afternoon, CCA withdrew to the February 15–16 line, having suffered heavy tank losses, and barely escaped being surrounded.

Underestimating the German strength, Maj. Gen. Orlando Ward (1st Armored) planned to hit back the next day with Combat Command C (CCC), reinforced by one battalion from CCB. The counterattack by CCC on the 15th was a disaster. The veteran panzers, again ably assisted by the Luftwaffe, enveloped the advancing column, practically wiped out one tank battalion, and sent the rest of the force scurrying back to the 15–16 February line. The 168th RCT, cut off and short of food and water was trapped, and although it attempted to break out on 17 February, few escaped.

On 15 February, Anderson, finally releasing the remainder of CCB to Ward, ordered II Corps to withdraw to the Western Dorsal but to maintain control of Sbeitla, Kasserine, and Feriana. By early evening, 16 February, 1st Armored Division was concentrated at Sbeitla, while the weak Allied force at Gafsa had withdrawn, and Rommel entered the town the next day. Arnim now turned his attention to Sbeitla, and attacked on the night of 16 February. Some of the American troops panicked in their first night combat, and a rout was barely averted. But CCB, in particular, fought well until the town was evacuated on the 17th. Ward's division now moved back to Tebessa as other units moved in to block the passes at Sbiba and Kasserine.

Having occupied Feriana on the 17th, Rommel concluded that a quick thrust through Tebessa northward might force a major Allied withdrawal. Appealing directly to Kesselring over Arnim's objections, Rommel was given command of all available panzers, and on the 19th ordered attacks on Sbiba and Kasserine, intending to exploit the more successful one. Additionally, he directed 10th Panzer to move from Fondouk to Kasserine. Neither drive achieved much success on the 19th: DAK tried to force Kasserine without having seized the heights and failed; while at Sbiba the Allied resistance was too strong. The next day, 10th Panzer joined the attack at Kasserine and, although the defenders were outflanked and forced back, the decisive thrust toward Thala was stopped by a tenacious British defense aided by U.S. 9th Division artillery. Overworked CCB and 1st Division stopped the DAK drive toward Tebessa, and on 22 February Rommel concede failure and began to withdraw.

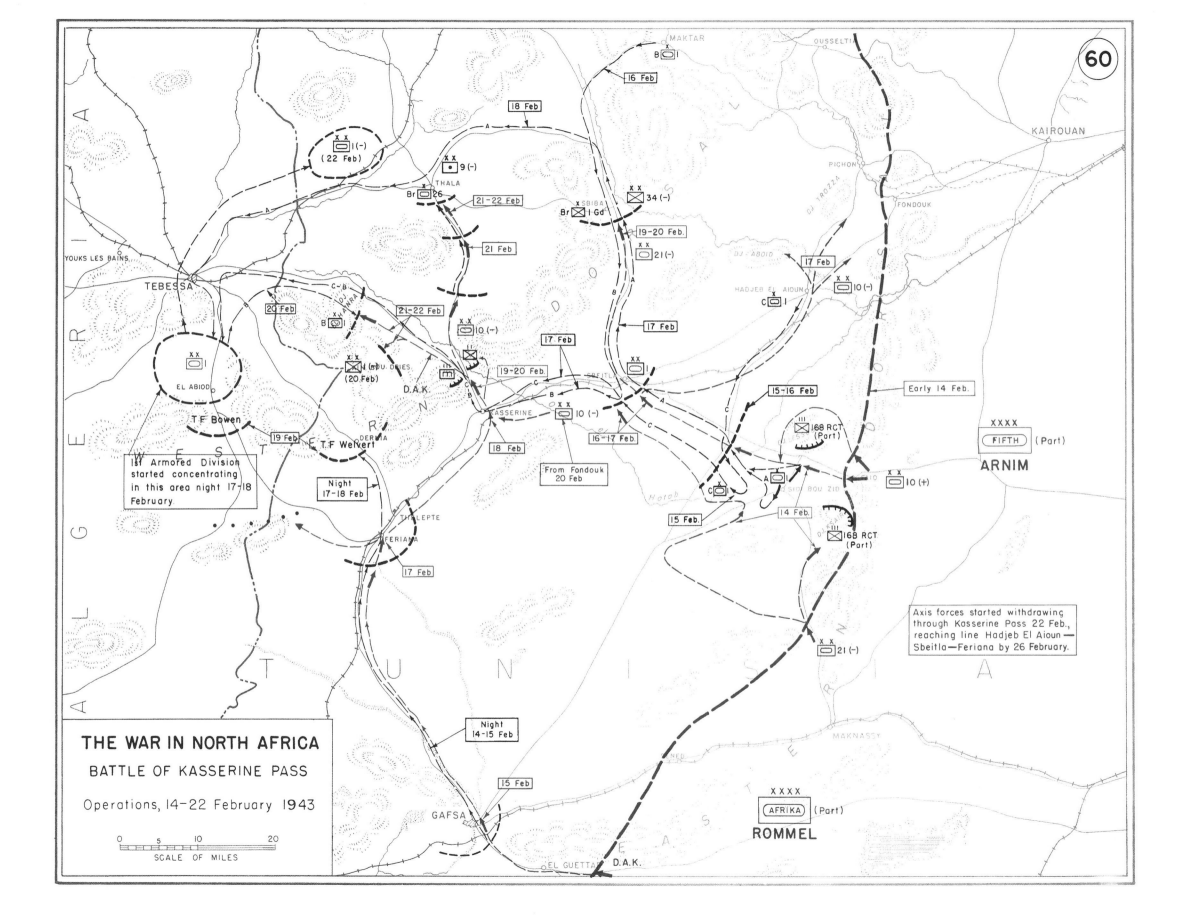

60

KAIROUAN

MAKTAR
B □ I
16 Feb

18 Feb

XX
1 (-)
(22 Feb)

XX
9 (-)

THALA
Br □ 26

21-22 Feb

XX
34 (-)
X SBIBA
Br ⊠ I Gd

21 Feb

19-20 Feb.

XX
21 (-)

DJ ABOID

17 Feb

XX
10 (-)

HADJEB EL AIOUN
C □ I

17 Feb

OUSSELTIA

PICHON

FONDOUK

YOUKS LES BAINS

TEBESSA

C-B

20 Feb

B ⊡ I

XX
I

EL ABIOD

T. F. Bowen

T. F. Welvert

19 Feb

DERNIA

XX
I (BOU DRIES)
(20 Feb)

21-22 Feb

D.A.K.

XX
10 (-)

19-20 Feb.

17 Feb

XX
I

SBEITLA

C

B

KASSERINE

XX
10 (-)

16-17 Feb.

15-16 Feb

Early 14 Feb.

XXXX
FIFTH (Part)

ARNIM

III
168 RCT
(Part)

From Fondouk
20 Feb

C

A

XX
10 (+)

1st Armored Division
started concentrating
in this area night 17-18
February.

Night
17-18 Feb

THELEPTE

FERIANA

17 Feb

Night
14-15 Feb

15 Feb.

18 Feb

Hatab

14 Feb.

III
168 RCT
(Part)

Axis forces started withdrawing
through Kasserine Pass 22 Feb.,
reaching line Hadjeb El Aioun —
Sbeitla—Feriana by 26 February.

XX
21 (-)

MAKNASSY

THE WAR IN NORTH AFRICA

BATTLE OF KASSERINE PASS

Operations, 14-22 February 1943

0   5   10   20
SCALE OF MILES

GAFSA

15 Feb

EL GUETTAR

D.A.K.

XXXX
AFRIKA (Part)

ROMMEL

ALGERIA

TUNISIA

THE BATTLE OF MARETH & PURSUIT OF ENFIDAVILLE

★

With Rommel's withdrawal, the Allies made plans for regaining the initiative. And Alexander's primary goal was to coordinate the Montgomery's role with that of the armies in Tunisia. Arnim tried a spoiling attack in late February, but by the end of March had been pushed back to the 31 March line.

In the meantime, Rommel attacked Montgomery at Médenine on 6 March. Only XXX Corps was present, but was well positioned, with 300 tanks, 350 artillery pieces, and 450 antitank guns. Rommel, with inferior equipment, attacked with 10th, 15th, and 21st Panzer, without adequate reconnaissance or strong infantry support, and was repulsed with the loss of more than a third of his tanks. Three days later, a sick man, he left Africa for good.

On 6 March, Patton assumed command of U.S. II Corps and immediately began to revitalize it. The corps now consisted of the 1st, 9th, and 34th Infantry Divisions and 1st Armored Division. Its poor performance at Sidi Bou Kid and Kasserine, convinced Alexander that it needed more time to recover, and so Patton's mission was limited to seizing Gafsa and to reconnoiter toward Maknassy without becoming heavily engaged.

Although Rommel had recommended a general withdrawal to Enfidaville, Kesselring and Hitler insisted on standing at the Mareth Line. By 20 March Montgomery had built up a four-to-one superiority and was ready to attack. The XXX Corps was to make the main assault on a narrow front, while the New Zealand Corps would outflank the line to the west and move into the enemy rear. XXX Corps' moonlit attack made some progress but was pushed back by counterattacks and could not beach the line. Montgomery now shifted the emphasis, and sent X Corps with 1st Armoured Division to join the New Zealanders who were already heavily engaged in the Axis rear. The combined attack paid off, and the defenses were breached southwest of El Hamma, with the Italian forces narrowly evading encirclement.

Meanwhile, Patton's attacks at El Guettar–Maknassy so worried Arnim that he ordered 10th Panzer to counterattack, but the 1st Division handily repulsed it on the 23rd. Now the 9th and 34th Divisions were released to Patton and he was ordered to break out on the coastal plain west of El Guettar and Fondouk, but his attacks made little progress against stiff resistance. When Montgomery lunged forward on 6 April, Gen. Giovanni Messe withdrew toward Enfidaville, so that when II Corps and Eighth Army joined up north of El Hamma, they ensnared no Axis forces.

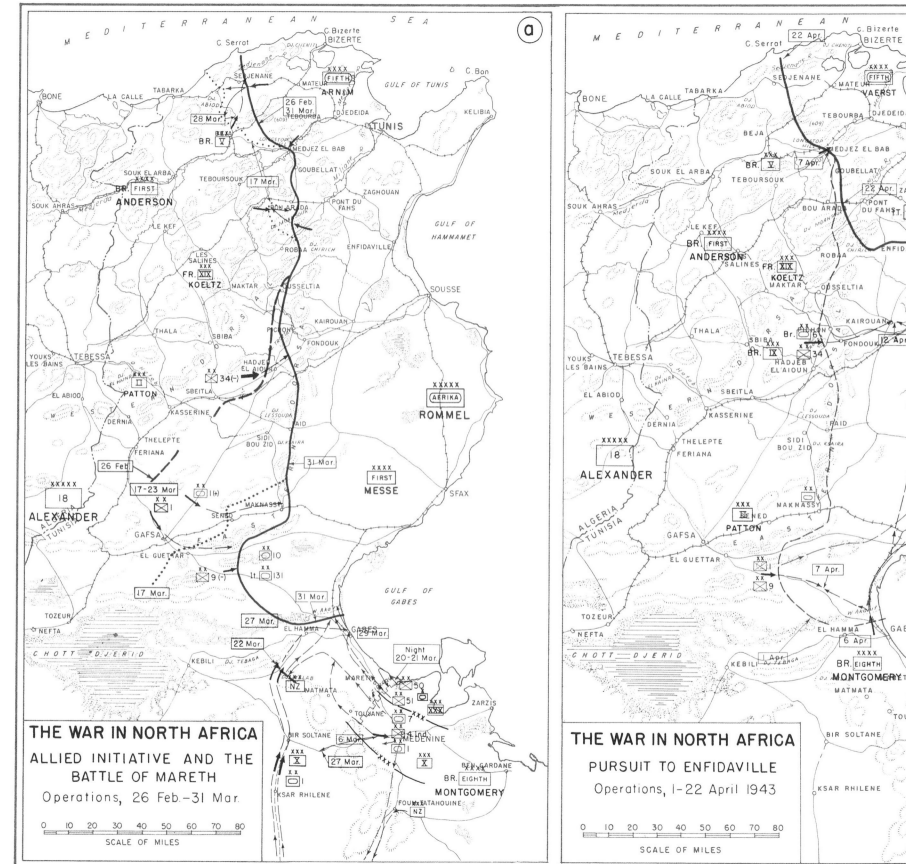

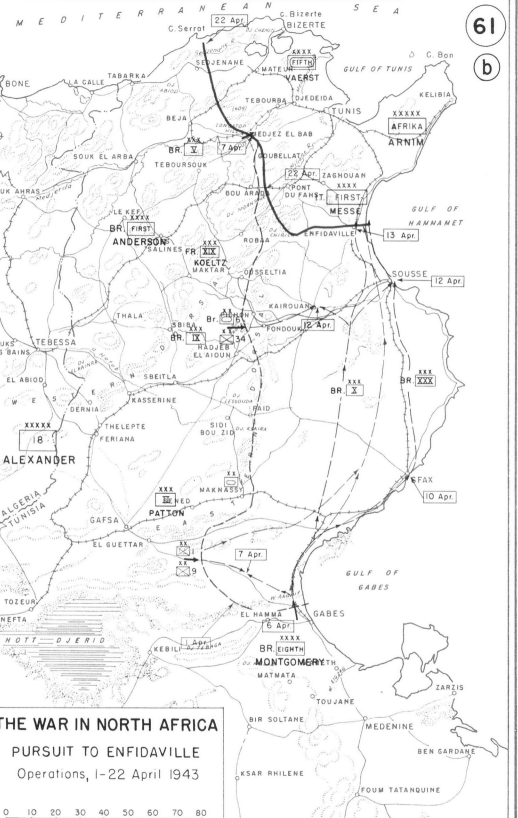

THE WAR IN NORTH AFRICA

ALLIED INITIATIVE AND THE BATTLE OF MARETH

Operations, 26 Feb.–31 Mar.

0 10 20 30 40 50 60 70 80
SCALE OF MILES

THE WAR IN NORTH AFRICA

PURSUIT TO ENFIDAVILLE

Operations, 1–22 April 1943

0 10 20 30 40 50 60 70 80
SCALE OF MILES

BATTLE OF TUNIS

★

Since the Allies had decided at the Casablanca Conference in January 1943 that Sicily would be invaded in July that year, it was imperative to clear North Africa of Axis forces quickly. Alexander's planned that the British First Army would make the main effort while U.S. II Corps (now under Maj. Gen. Omar N. Bradley) to the north, and Montgomery's Eighth Army to the south, would play supporting roles.

Montgomery kicked off the attack on the night of the 19 April, and when his initial gains proved disappointing, he regrouped and concentrated along the coast. On the 22nd, IX Corps moved forward, and the following day V Corps joined the attack, and during four days of bloody fighting, Anderson's troops inched ahead but could not break out his armor toward Tunis. While the British and French were being held by a tenacious defense, Bradley's lightly regarded II Corps was achieving the greatest gains of the period. On 23 April, the 1st and 9th Divisions attacked in practically independent actions, and by 3 May, 1st Armored had entered Mateur.

British IX Corps had been slated to make the main attack on a 3,000 yard front, with overwhelming air and artillery support, toward Massicault and Tunis. Indian 4th and 4th Infantry Divisions would open a hole through which 6th and 7th Armoured would pour. After seizing Tunis, First Army would rapidly move east and south to link up with Eighth Army and prevent Axis forces moving out to the Cap Bon peninsula. The offensive got underway as planned on 4 May with the attacks by XIX and V Corps. In the meantime, behind a 600-gun artillery barrage and the most devastating air attack yet launched in Africa, British IX Corps rolled forward at 0303 on 6 May. At 1100, the armor passed through the infantry and had advance elements in Massicault that night. The battered Germans fell back toward Tunis and attempted to establish another line, but their lack of mobility soon reduced them to a desperate state.

Also on 6 May, Bradley's three southernmost divisions launched their attacks, and on 7 May, Tunis and Bizerte fell to the British 7th Armoured and U.S. 9th Division respectively. The following day, German resistance slackened everywhere, and Allied units began to fan out in exploitation. On 9 May, U.S. 1st Armored cut the Tunis–Bizerte road and linked up with the British at Protville. By now, encircled Axis forces, desperately short of ammunition and fuel and despairing of evacuation, were surrendering all along the front. On 13 May, Messe surrendered his Italian First Army to Montgomery, and in all, the Allies took 275,000 prisoners, including the top commanders, in the last week of fighting.

The conquest of North Africa substantially cleared the Mediterranean for Allied shipping, and provided air bases for heavy bomber attacks against southern Europe. Equally important, Tunisia had taught the Americans valuable combat lessons and welded Allied unity in the first experiment in combined operations. Hitler had lost a complete army, but he managed to convince himself that the campaign had delayed an Allied invasion of Europe.

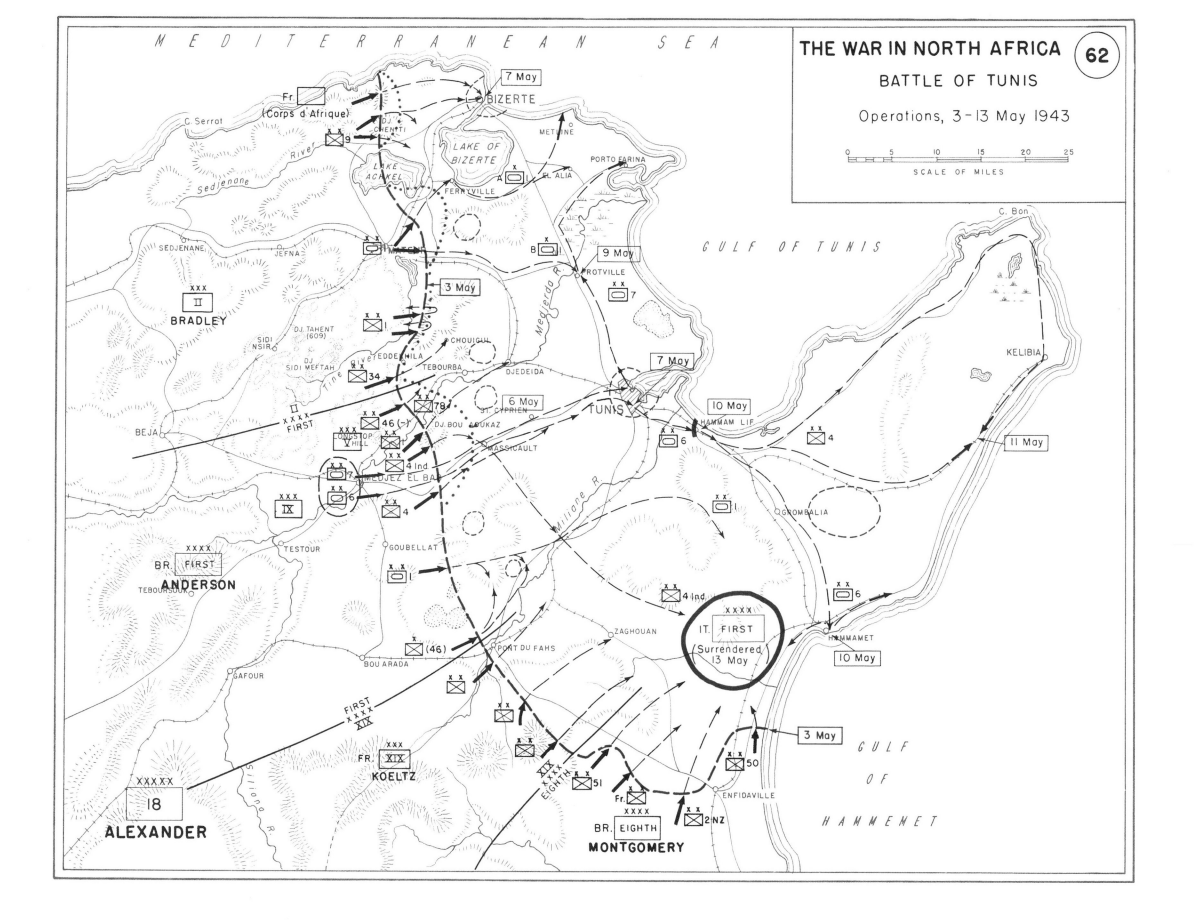

MEDITERRANEAN SEA

C. Serrat

7 May

Fr.
(Corps d'Afrique)

DJ. CHENTI

9

BIZERTE

LAKE OF BIZERTE

LAKE ACHKEL

METLINE

PORTO FARINA

FERRYVILLE

A

EL ALIA

C. Bon

River

Sedjenane

SEDJENANE

JEFNA

9 May

B

PROTVILLE

GULF OF TUNIS

XXX
II
BRADLEY

3 May

1

DJ. TAHENT (609)

CHOUIGUI

Medjerda R.

7

KELIBIA

SIDI NSIR

DJ. SIDI MEFTAH

34

River
TEDDE HILA

TEBOURBA

DJEDEIDA

7 May

6 May

10 May

Tine

78

ST. CYPRIEN

TUNIS

HAMMAM LIF

11 May

BEJA

II
FIRST

46 (-)

DJ. BOU AOUKAZ

MASSICAULT

6

4

Miliane R.

LONGSTOP HILL

1

4 Ind

MEDJEZ EL BAB

XXXX
BR. FIRST
ANDERSON

7

XXX
IX

6

4

GOUBELLAT

1

4 Ind

GROMBALIA

TESTOUR

TEBOURSOUK

XXXX
IT. FIRST
(Surrendered)
13 May

6

HAMMAMET

ZAGHOUAN

10 May

FIRST
XIX

(46)

PONT DU FAHS

GAFOUR

BOU ARADA

3 May

FR.
XIX
KOELTZ

50

Silana R.

ENFIDAVILLE

XXXXX
18
ALEXANDER

EIGHTH

51

Fr.

2 NZ

BR. EIGHTH
MONTGOMERY

GULF OF HAMMEMET

SCALE OF MILES
0 5 10 15 20 25

PLAN FOR LANDINGS, JULY 10, 1943

★

Operation HUSKY, the invasion of Sicily, was not an entirely unanimous decision. American planners saw it as a distraction from the cross-Channel invasion of France they were advocating. The British, on the other hand, were not as sanguine about the cross-Channel strategy in 1943, and favored a "softening-up" operation that would bleed Axis resources. In any event, both groups came to the conclusion that troop strengths in Britain could not be built to the required level to take on the Germans in France in 1943.

Two major tactical factors exerted their influence on the landings: the early seizure of ports and the rapid capture of airfields to be used for close-support missions.

Sicily is about the size of Vermont and is largely mountainous, although there is a sizable plain near Catania, which merges into the 10,686 foot-high Mt. Etna to the north. Movement along the coastal stretch between Messina and Catania is restricted to the main roads. The main mountain range runs along the northern coast, with spurs from it running south. The rivers and streams, many of which dry up in the summer, are not major obstacles.

As soon as the Tunisia campaign had been concluded, the Allied Mediterranean air forces turned their full attention to preparing the way for HUSKY. Enemy air bases in Sicily, Sardinia, and Italy were subjected to constant attacks by medium and heavy bombers. In daily raids during the month preceding the landings, Allied air power hammered at Axis air fields so that, by 1 July, enemy aircraft numbered only 1,400 (including 600 inferior Italian planes); the Allies had 3,680.

The final landing plan concentrated the might of two armies on southeastern Sicily. Under Alexander's overall control, Patton would lead Seventh Army; Montgomery, Eighth Army. Most of the units had seen action in North Africa, but some had just arrived from the USA and Britain. In general, Alexander's plan called initially for the seizure of Licata (by Patton), and Syracuse (by Montgomery) and the early capture of key airdromes, followed by the juncture of the two armies along their common boundary.

Montgomery was to move toward Messina, while Seventh Army was to take up Line Yellow to defend Eighth Army's left flank, and protected the beachheads from long-range enemy artillery. Line Blue, along commanding terrain, would forestall Axis counterattacks, and was Patton's second objective. The Axis defenders' greatest potential combat strength was in the six mobile Italian and German divisions (those not labeled "Coast"). General Alfred Guzzoni wanted to concentrate the two German divisions in the eastern half of the island, ready for a strong counterattack, but the optimistic Kesselring advocated a cordon defense to defeat the invader on the beaches (a strategy that would be later employed, equally unsuccessfully at Normandy almost one year later).

As the convoys made their way toward Sicily on 9 July 1943 bad weather threw some of them off course, and even threatened the whole operation; but eventually the winds died down, and the landings began on schedule. The bad weather had an unexpected benefit in that it also put the defenders off their guard (as it would do again at Normandy), and the landing troops did not have to face significant opposition.

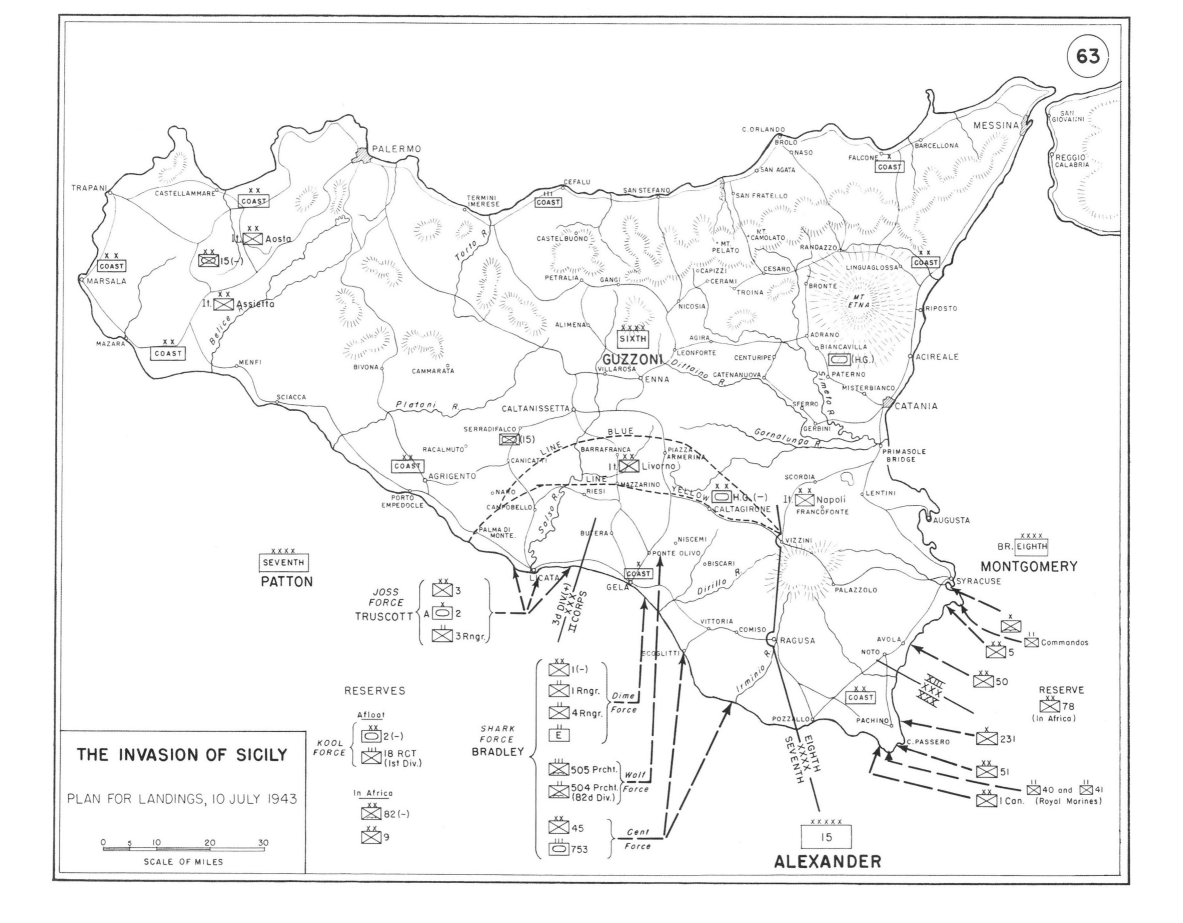

63

THE INVASION OF SICILY

PLAN FOR LANDINGS, 10 JULY 1943

0 5 10   20   30
SCALE OF MILES

SITUATION JULY 23, 1943

★

By nightfall of 10 July, the assault divisions had secured their beachheads, and at Licata, an innovation proved to be a resounding success: the 3rd Division was landed by a series of new ship-to-shore craft—Landing Craft Tank (LCT), and Landing Craft Infantry (LCI)—that allowed direct access to the beaches without an intermediary transfer. The airborne assaults, however, were not as successful, were blown off course, and scattered all over the southeastern end of the island. Friendly fire was also a significant problem for both American and British paratroopers. Pre-invasion planning was also faulty in not providing an air umbrella over the landing points, so allowing the Luftwaffe exceptional freedom to attack.

The 11 July was a critical day for the Allies. The German armor launched a counterattack toward the Americans at Gela, but it was repelled by superb naval gunnery and dogged infantry action. On the 13th, Guzzoni, with Kesselring's approval, ordered most of his mobile units out of western Sicily and began to concentrate his strength to cover the Catania plain. Hitler concurred, and ordered more troops to Sicily.

Alexander, now more conversant with Axis dispositions, ordered Eighth Army to advance on either side of Etna, with Messina as its ultimate objective; Seventh Army would push north to the coast and bisect the island. Patton captured Agrigento on 17 July and drove toward Palermo, while the western part of the island was taken with relative ease against Italian units that had pretty much thrown in the towel. Maj. Gen. Lucian K. Truscott's 3rd Division, in a march reminiscent of Stonewall Jackson's Civil War "foot cavalry," made the 100-mile march to Palermo in four days, despite rugged country and skillful rearguard action. The city, shattered by Allied bombing, surrendered on 22 July, and the next day, Patton entered in triumph.

Meanwhile, Eighth Army was encountering stiff opposition in its drive toward Catania, as Guzzoni shifted his better divisions to that front.

On 20 July, Alexander, aware of Montgomery's reluctance to continue a costly coastal attack, modified his strategy and ordered Patton to drive eastward along the northern coast toward Messina. Montgomery would make a sharp hook around Mt. Etna with the Canadians to afford Seventh Army the necessary room, and would hold off offensive operations south of Catania, in order to minimize his casualties. However, the resulting intermission gave the Germans breathing space and time to organize a strong position in the mountains.

On Alexander's directive, Patton turned the 1st, 3rd, and 45th Divisions eastward, and by 23 July Kesselring had already moved the 29th Panzer Grenadier Division and two regiments of the 1st Parachute Division to Sicily; Gen. Hube had now arrived to take command of German troops on the island.

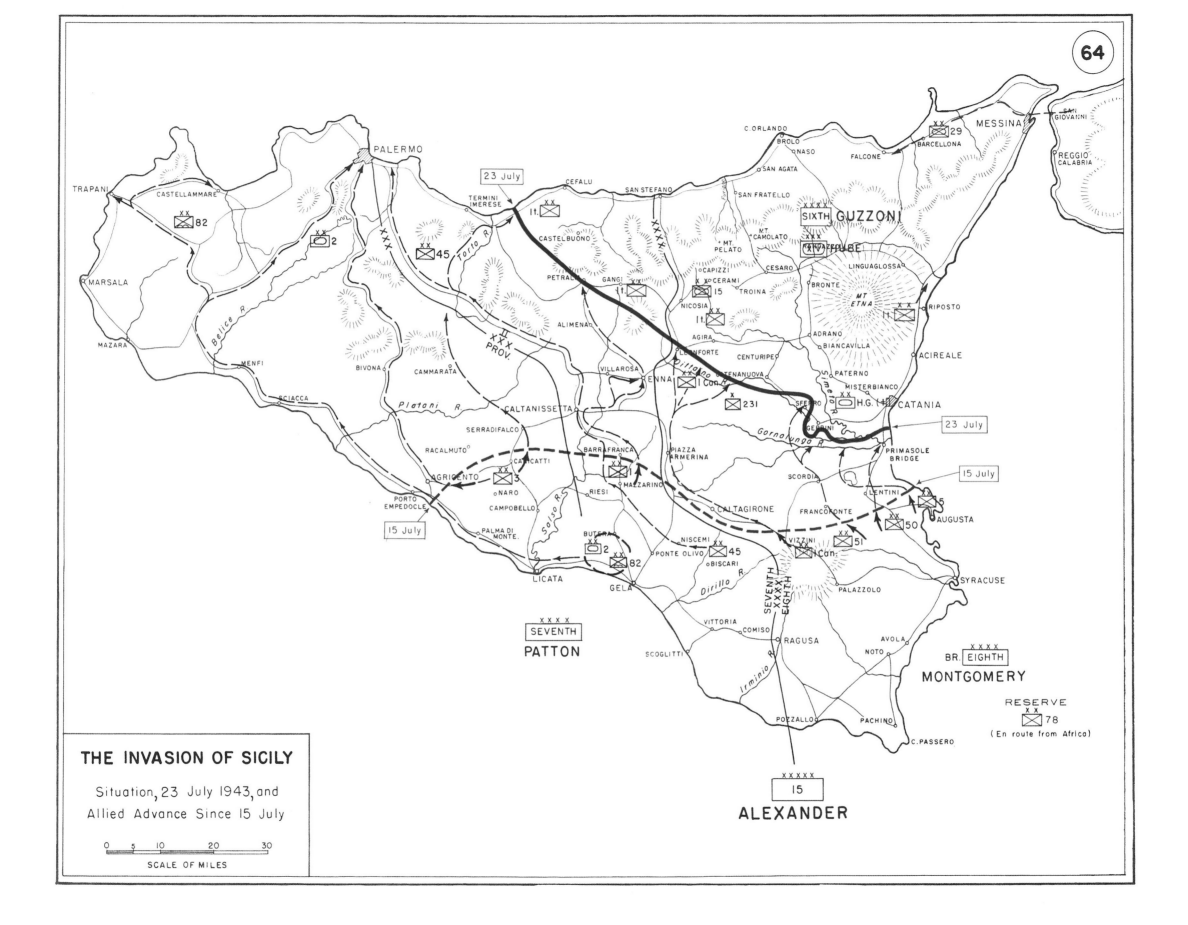

64

THE INVASION OF SICILY

Situation, 23 July 1943, and
Allied Advance Since 15 July

0   5   10   20   30
SCALE OF MILES

MESSINA
SAN GIOVANNI
REGGIO CALABRIA
TRAPANI
CASTELLAMMARE
MARSALA
MAZARA
PALERMO
TERMINI IMERESE
CEFALU
SAN STEFANO
C. ORLANDO
BROLO
NASO
FALCONE
BARCELLONA
29
82
2
45
SIXTH GUZZONI
HUBE
SAN AGATA
SAN FRATELLO
MT. CAMOLATO
LINGUAGLOSSA
MENFI
SCIACCA
BIVONA
CAMMARATA
PETRALIA
GANGI
CASTELBUONO
MT. PELATO
CAPIZZI
CERAMI
CESARO
BRONTE
MT ETNA
RIPOSTO
ACIREALE
15
NICOSIA
TROINA
ALIMENA
AGIRA
LEONFORTE
CENTURIPE
ADRANO
BIANCAVILLA
PATERNO
MISTERBIANCO
CATANIA
H.G.
VILLAROSA
ENNA
CALTANISSETTA
SERRADIFALCO
231
SFERRO
GERBINI
PRIMASOLE BRIDGE
RACALMUTO
AGRIGENTO
CANICATTI
3
NARO
BARRAFRANCA
1
PIAZZA ARMERINA
1 Can.
SCORDIA
LENTINI
50
AUGUSTA
15
PORTO EMPEDOCLE
CAMPOBELLO
RIESI
MAZZARINO
CALTAGIRONE
FRANCOFONTE
VIZZINI
51
1 Can.
PALMA DI MONTE.
BUTERA
2
82
NISCEMI
PONTE OLIVO
45
BISCARI
PALAZZOLO
SYRACUSE
LICATA
GELA
VITTORIA
COMISO
RAGUSA
AVOLA
NOTO
SCOGLITTI
POZZALLO
PACHINO
C. PASSERO

SEVENTH
PATTON

BR. EIGHTH
MONTGOMERY

RESERVE
78
(En route from Africa)

SEVENTH
EIGHTH

15
ALEXANDER

23 July
15 July

ALLIED ADVANCE TO MESSINA

★

Patton's drive to Messina utilized two routes: the coastal road, and the more difficult mountain route through Gangi–Nicosia–Randazzo. The 45th Division started down the coastal road, while 1st Division headed over the mountains. The 45th was relieved by 3rd Division in time for the assault on the strong German-held defenses at San Fratello. The 1st (augmented by a combat team from 9th Division), made plans for the capture of Troina.

Meanwhile, in the Eighth Army sector, Montgomery had moved 5th and 51st Divisions inland, and had them attack on 31 July in conjunction with 78th Division and the Canadians; together they pushed the Germans back to the Simeto River. With their key position, Adriano, at the southern base of Mt. Etna, now threatened, the Germans began to pull back from their Catania positions.

On 3 August, 1st and 3rd Divisions launched their attacks in the north, and broke through to the Furiano River, where they were held up for three days. At Troina, 1st Division, although supported by overwhelming artillery and air support, could not crack defenses augmented with extensive minefields, road blocks, and demolitions. On the 5 August, 9th Division attacked through the mountains toward Cesaro, forcing the Germans to evacuate Troina, which 1st Division promptly occupied until relieved by 9th Division. On

6 August, Hube also abandoned the San Fratello position in time to evade the amphibious leapfrog down the northern coast that Patton used on the 11th and 15th.

By 8 August, the Allies were advancing slowly all along the front. Montgomery had finally occupied an abandoned Catania on the 5th and Adrano on the 7th, and the British threat to Bronte forced the Germans to pull back from the 9th Division front. On the 17 August the Allies entered Messina, but it was too late. Hube and the Germans had gone across the Straits of Messina to mainland Italy to fight another day.

The Germans had delayed skillfully and methodically as the evacuation from Messina proceeded in an orderly manner. In spite of Allied naval and air superiority, the Axis evacuated some 100,000 troops, 9,800 vehicles, and 47 tanks during the 3–17 August period. The haphazard Allied attempts to stop the evacuation only succeeded in sinking seven boats.

Two events associated with the conquest of Sicily exerted considerable influence on Allied global strategy. Three days after the fall of Palermo, Mussolini was ousted as Italy's ruler. News of Mussolini's overthrow triggered the second event. On 26 July, the Combined Chiefs of Staff ordered Eisenhower to prepare for the invasion of the Italian mainland.

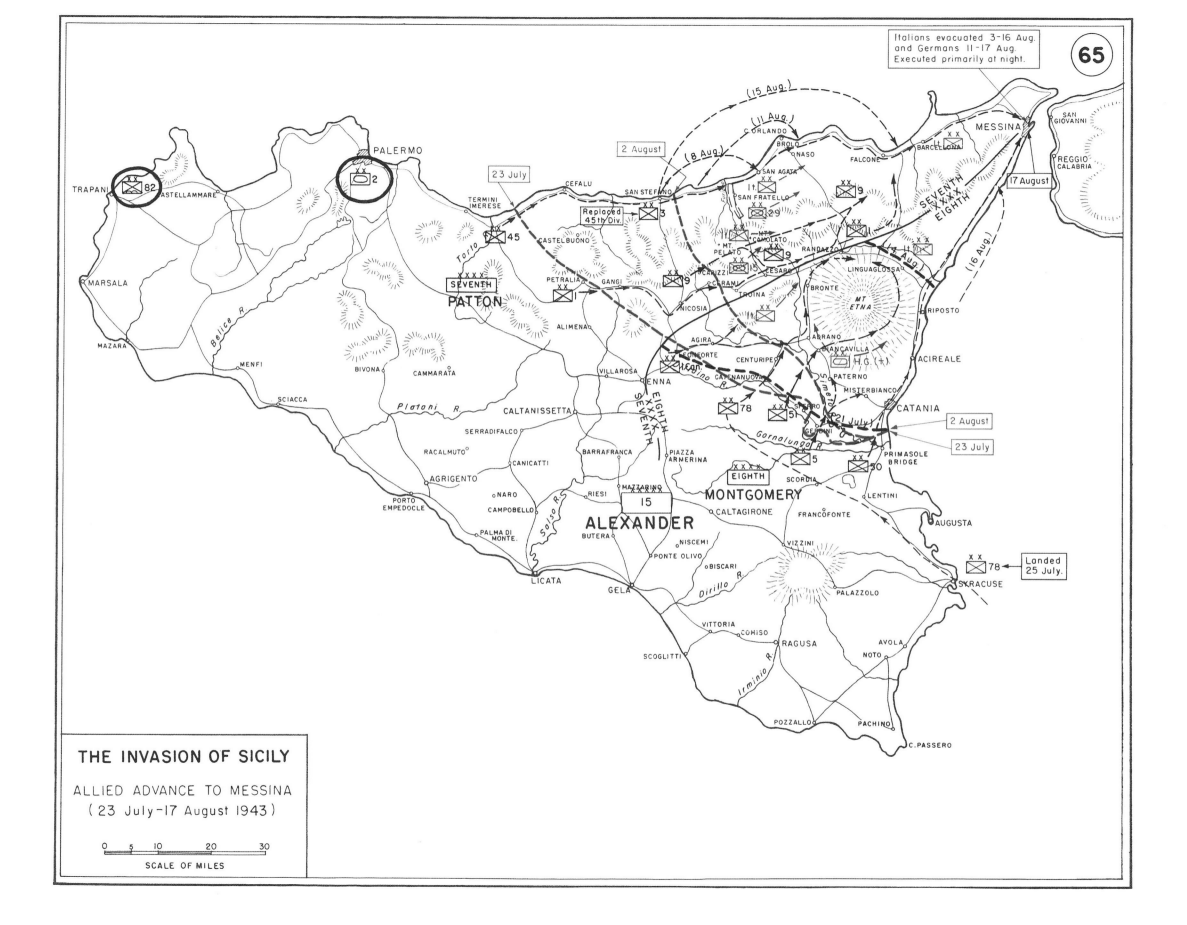

65

Italians evacuated 3-16 Aug.
and Germans 11-17 Aug.
Executed primarily at night.

THE INVASION OF SICILY

ALLIED ADVANCE TO MESSINA
(23 July-17 August 1943)

0 5 10   20   30

SCALE OF MILES

SALERNO CAMPAIGN

★

On 24–25 July a revolt in Italy overthrew Mussolini, and his successor, Marshal Pietro Badoglio soon began secret negotiations with the Allies (a secret armistice would be signed on 3 September). On 27 July, Maj. Gen. Mark Clark, commanding the American V Army, was directed to prepare plans for the capture of Naples. On 3 September elements of Eighth Army crossed the Straits of Messina and moved inland against negligible resistance. On 9 September Fifth Army launched its amphibious attack on Salerno in preparation for its move on Naples.

The Salerno area offered excellent beaches, but its narrow coastal plain was dominated from three sides by steep, high hill masses. German intelligence, reckoning on the usual Allied dependence on tactical air support, had concluded that Salerno (at the furthest range for fighter air support from Sicily) would be the likeliest landing site, and as such had to be held until German divisions could extricate themselves. Lacking the manpower, time, and materials to develop a strong coastal defensive position, 16th Panzer organized a mobile defense: mine fields along the shore; strong points sited to block exits from the beaches; supporting mortars and artillery emplaced to cover the whole area; and tank units in reserve for counterattacks.

Clark launched his assault at 0330 9 September. On his left, the Rangers landed unopposed and advanced inland toward the pass at Nocera. The Commandos moved into Salerno against light resistance. The British 46th and 56th Divisions, covered by a heavy naval bombardment, fought their way ashore against determined opposition. To the south,

vainly hoping for surprise, the American VI Corps sent its inexperienced 36th Division without either naval or air support. The Germans were waiting, and caused heavy casualties. Nevertheless, the American attack went forward energetically, and by the night of the 9th held four separate beachheads. As they congratulated themselves on their success, the outnumbered Germans could not believe their luck that the Allies' had not pressed home their advantage.

On the 10th, the Germans shifted most of their strength northward to protect their communications with Naples, which allowed to 36th Division to move forward to Ogliastro and Trentinara. Maj. Gen. Ernest J. Dawley planned to go northward to cut Highway 19 in the Ponte Sele–Serre area. He sent a regimental combat team of 45th Division eastward between the Sele and Calore Rivers, where it was hit in the flank by a German counterattack from Eboli and driven back; the other combat team, sent to the restore the situation was stopped quickly by 16th Panzer, as was the British 56th Division at Battipaglia. When night fell on the 10th, the Allied position remained uncomfortably fluid.

Despite Allied gains, the German position at Salerno had improved considerably by the night of the 11th. German troops in southern Italy had eluded Eighth Army, while those in central Italy had mainly disarmed Italian army and air force troops. Consequently, elements of five German panzer or panzer grenadier divisions had arrived to reinforce 16th Panzer. Kesselring now had hopes of destroying the beachhead before Eighth Army could arrive from the south.

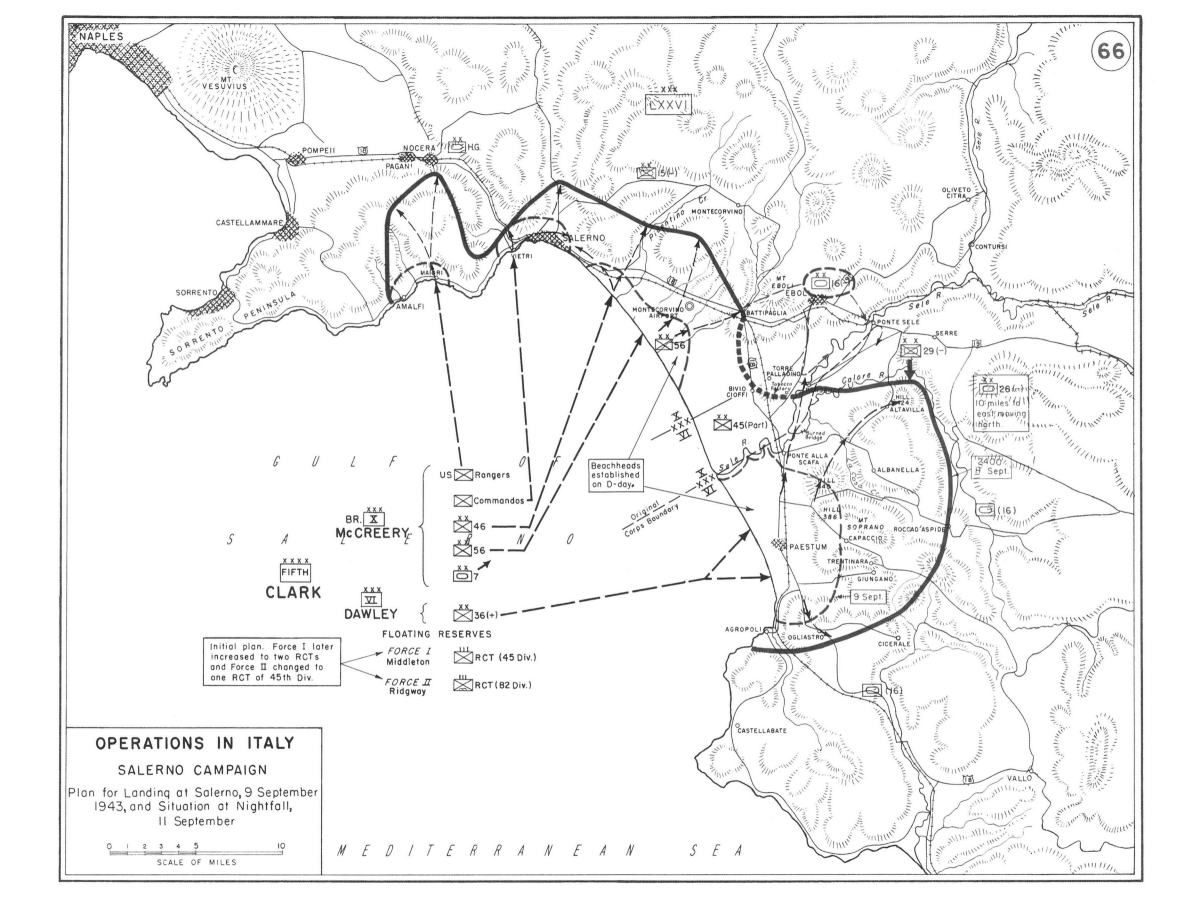

66

NAPLES

MT VESUVIUS

POMPEII · NOCERA · HG.

PAGANI

CASTELLAMMARE

SORRENTO

SORRENTO PENINSULA

AMALFI

MAIORI

SALERNO

VIETRI

MONTECORVINO AIRPORT

56

LXXVI

15(L)

MONTECORVINO

MT EBOLI

EBOLI

BATTIPAGLIA

PONTE SELE

SERRE

TORRE PALLADINO

BIVIO CIOFFI

Tobacco Factory

Calore R.

29(-)

26(-)

10 miles to east moving north.

OLIVETO CITRA

CONTURSI

Sele R.

Beachheads established on D-day.

Original Corps Boundary

45 (Part)

Burned Bridge

PONTE ALLA SCAFA

ALBANELLA

2400 11 Sept.

HILL 424 ALTAVILLA

HILL 424

HILL 386

MT SORPANO

CAPACCIO

ROCCAD ASPIDE

(16)

GULF

OF

SALERNO

SEA

US ⊠ Rangers

⊠ Commandos

BR. X
McCREERY

46

56

7

XXXX
FIFTH
CLARK

VI
DAWLEY

36(+)

PAESTUM

TRENTINARA

CAPACCIO

GIUNGANO

9 Sept.

AGROPOLI

OGLIASTRO

CICERALE

(16)

FLOATING RESERVES

Initial plan. Force I later increased to two RCTs and Force II changed to one RCT of 45th Div.

FORCE I Middleton → RCT (45 Div.)

FORCE II Ridgway → RCT (82 Div.)

CASTELLABATE

VALLO

OPERATIONS IN ITALY

SALERNO CAMPAIGN

Plan for Landing at Salerno, 9 September 1943, and Situation at Nightfall, 11 September

0 1 2 3 4 5   10
SCALE OF MILES

M E D I T E R R A N E A N   S E A

SALERNO CAMPAIGN

★

At daybreak on 12 September, the Germans assaulted Hill 424, finally recapturing it during the afternoon. Meanwhile, in the center, the battle had surged back and forth through the Tobacco Factory area. The 45th Division held it at nightfall, but contact between British X and American VI Corps remained tenuous in this area, a sector of some five miles wide held largely by a screen of reconnaissance units. After dark on the 12th, a driving German attack threw the British out of Battipaglia, further weakening this sector, and counterattacks failed to restore the position.

During the day, Dawley had decided to strengthen his left flank in order to close the gap between his forces and X Corps. Accordingly, he began shifting his troops northward: the 36th Division was ordered to take over the Calore–Sele sector from the 45th, and also to detach troops from the Ogliastro area to take over the extreme flank of the corps around Bivio Cioffi. At 1530 on 13 September, while this maneuver was underway, a powerful German attack suddenly developed along the north bank of the Sele River. Beating the right flank of the 45th Division away from Persano, the Germans forced the Sele there, overran a battalion from the 36th Division, and drove southeast for a ford on the Calore River. Once across the ford, they would be in the American rear areas along the beaches. The situation was desperate. The American infantry lines were broken and something very close to panic prevailed. But American artillerymen, standing to their guns in the best traditions of Antietam and Gettysburg, barred the way.

At nightfall, the German attacks ceased, but the exhausted Allies had to struggle to reestablish their lines along the best defensive positions available. Losses had been heavy, and many units had been completely scattered. During the night, two battalions of the 82nd Airborne were dropped into the beachhead. During 14 September, the Germans pushed constant probing attacks all along all along the Allied front, seeking a weak spot. But thanks to splendid naval and air force support, all the assaults were broken up, while more Allied reinforcements, including elements of the British 7th Armoured Division, poured in. By the 15th, the beachhead was safe.

On 16 September, leading elements of the British 5th Division made contact with a Fifth Army patrol forty miles southwest of Salerno. Kesselring, therefore, began a deliberate disengagement and withdrawal from the Salerno area on 18 September, falling back from one delaying position to the next through terrain ideally suited to suck tactics. Initially the Germans held the hill mass north of Salerno to gain time enough to destroy Naples harbor. Allied forces at the beachhead had now received significant reinforcements and pushed vigorously after the German rearguard. Naples was finally occupied on 1 October. By 6 October, Fifth Army had reached the Volturno River, to find all bridges down and streams swollen with autumn rains.

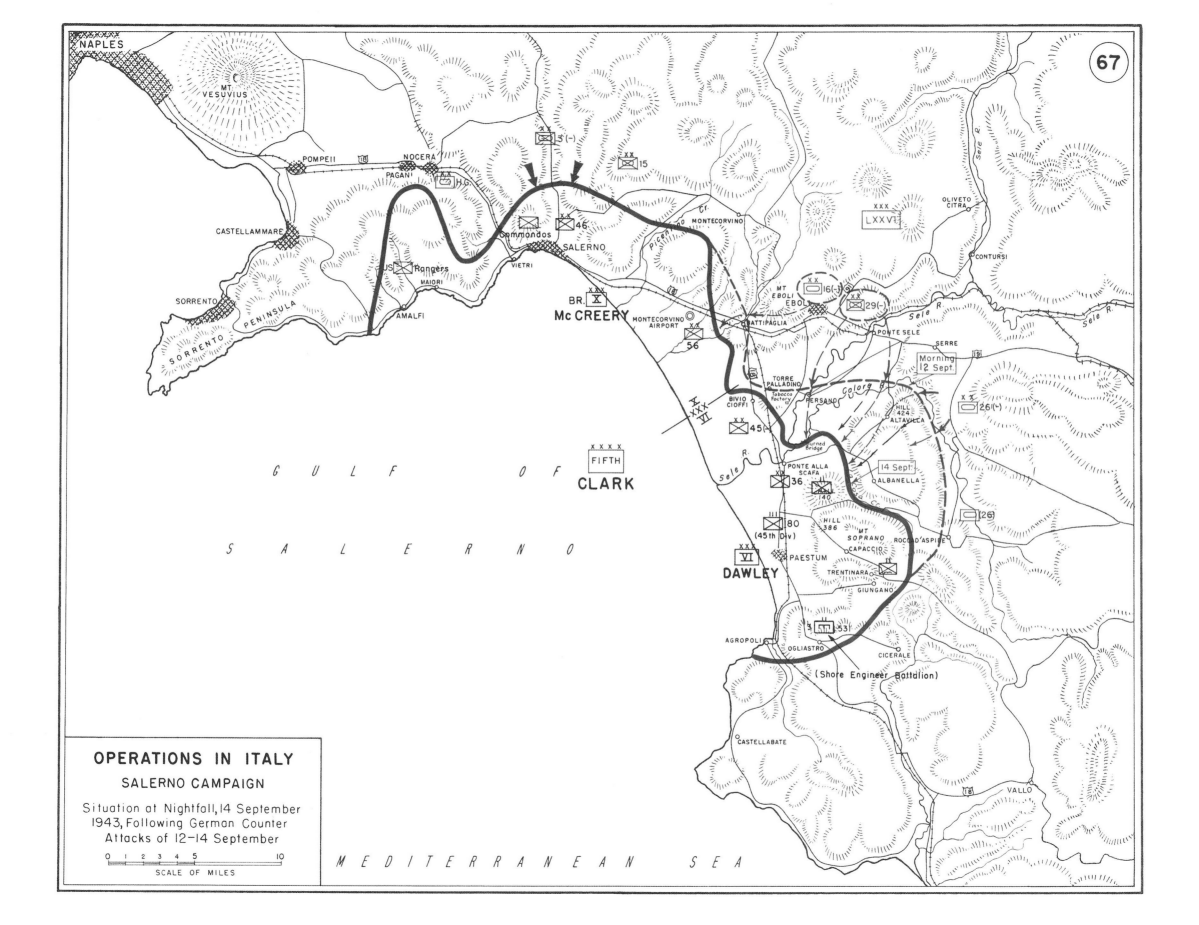

NAPLES

MT VESUVIUS

POMPEII 18 NOCERA PAGANI

CASTELLAMMARE

SORRENTO PENINSULA

SORRENTO

AMALFI

MAIORI

US Rangers

Commandos

SALERNO

VIETRI

BR. X McCREERY

Montecorvino Airport

56

3 (-)

15

H.G.

46

Montecorvino

Picentino Cr.

LXXVI

OLIVETO CITRA

CONTURSI

MT EBOLI EBOLI

16 (-)

29 (-)

Sele R.

BATTIPAGLIA

PONTE SELE

SERRE 19

Morning 12 Sept.

TORRE PALLADINO

Tobacco Factory

PERSANO

Calore R.

HILL 424

ALTAVILLA

26 (-)

BIVIO CIOFFI

45

Burned Bridge

Sele R.

14 Sept.

PONTE ALLA SCAFA

36

140

26

ALBANELLA

GULF OF SALERNO

FIFTH CLARK

80 (45th Div)

HILL 386

MT SOPRANO CAPACCIO

HILL 424

ROCCAD'ASPIDE

VI DAWLEY

PAESTUM

TRENTINARA

GIUNGANO

CICERALE

AGROPOLI OGLIASTRO

3 531

(Shore Engineer Battalion)

CASTELLABATE

VALLO 18

MEDITERRANEAN SEA

OPERATIONS IN ITALY

SALERNO CAMPAIGN

Situation at Nightfall, 14 September 1943, Following German Counter Attacks of 12–14 September

0 1 2 3 4 5 10
SCALE OF MILES

67

VOLTURNO RIVER CAMPAIGN

★

By early October 1943, the Allies had achieved their initial objectives; Italy had surrendered; the Germans had evacuated Sardinia and Corsica; the port of Naples was being rapidly restored; and the capture of the Foggia airfields gave the Allied air forces excellent bases for raids against the underbelly of Hitler's empire. With the wisdom of hindsight, some have suggested that the Allies should have taken a defensive posture in Italy. There were, however, important reasons to continue the advance: Rome was important politically and from a psychological point of view, and its liberation would be highly prestigious; capture of the numerous airfields around Rome would increase the range of Allied bombers; and finally, if the Allies sat back complacently they ran the risk of German counteroffensives that may wipe out much of their hard-won gains.

But the prospects for the advancing Allies were daunting. From the Volturno to Rome was over 100 miles of jumbled mountains, deeply cut by swift streams which usually ran east or west across the Allied line of advance. Such terrain was naturally designed for delaying actions, particularly in view of the Allies' lack of troops trained for mountain warfare. Autumn was the wettest season in Italy; coastal swamps would be flooded, and mountain streams would run in torrents. Allied navies might control the Mediterranean, but the chronic shortage of assault shipping would severely limit the potential for amphibious landings.

To gain time for the construction of his Winter Position (essentially a defensive line across the waist of Italy), Kesselring had ordered the Volturno River held until 15 October. After much careful reconnaissance to locate good crossing sites, Fifth Army opened its offensive across the river on the night of 12 October, each of its two corps attacking simultaneously, three divisions abreast. In generally bitter fighting, five of the six divisions finally gained bridgeheads during the night of the 13th, but German artillery fire held up the construction of bridges until the 14th and 15th. Showing a high order of leadership and skill (especially as they had no air cover), the Germans fell back in a series of delaying actions.

Eighth Army had become overextended during its drive to Termoli, and so Montgomery busied himself with his usual methodical preparations until 22 October, when he launched another of his characteristically deliberate offensives, forcing the Trigno River against vigorous opposition and closing to the south bank of the Sangro River. Meanwhile, Fifth Army had found German resistance stiffening again along the outposts of the Winter Position, and on 13 November, exhausted and drained by casualties, it stopped to rest and regroup. Constant rains turned roads into bogs and washed out the temporary bridges which had replaced those demolished by the retreating Germans (who had developed a murderous proficiency with demolitions, mines, and booby traps).

On 8 November, Alexander laid out his plan. Eighth Army would attack first, driving north to Pescara, then wheel westward toward Avezzano. Then Fifth Army would attack up the Liri and Sacco Valleys to Frosinone. Third, an amphibious landing south of Rome (by approximately two divisions from Fifth Army) would advance inland and seize the Alban Hills.

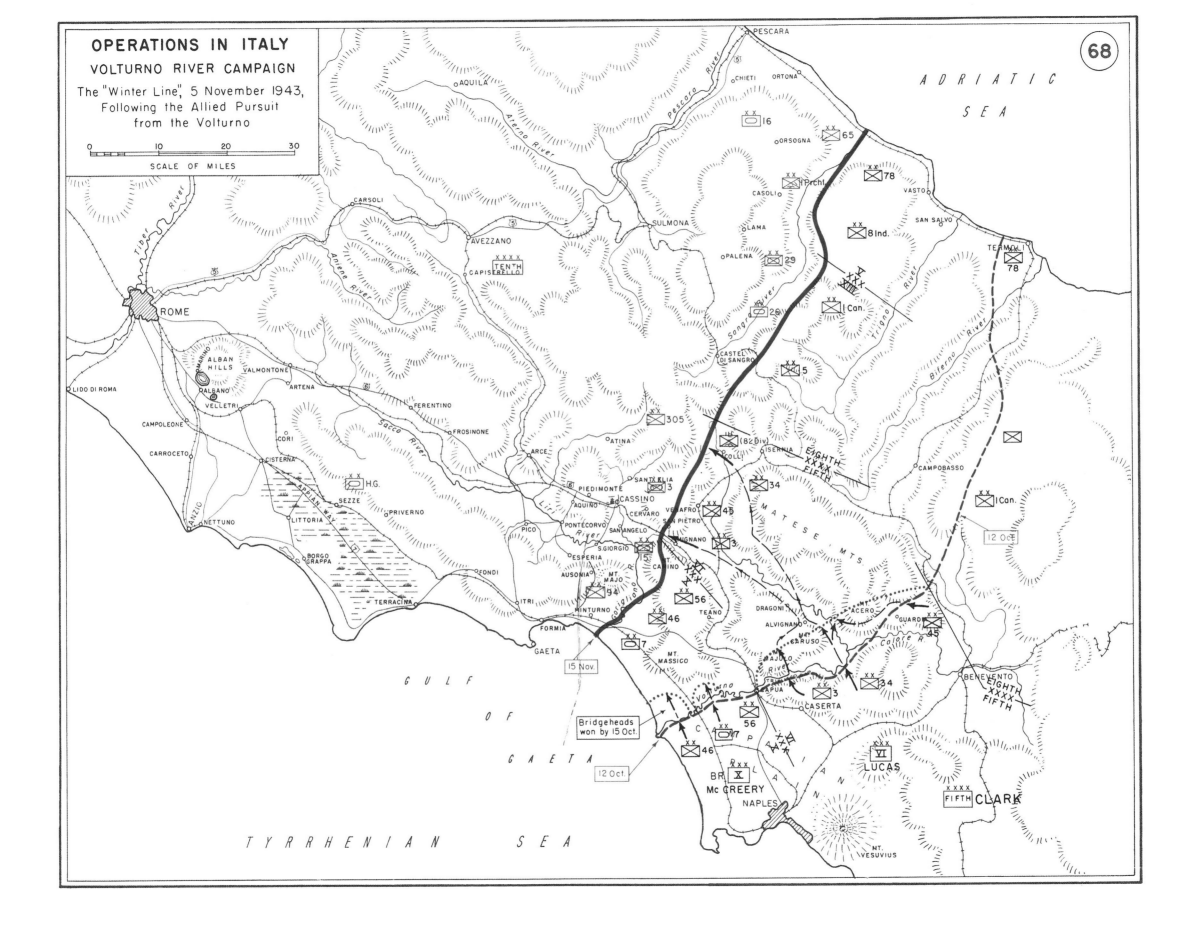

OPERATIONS IN ITALY

VOLTURNO RIVER CAMPAIGN

The "Winter Line", 5 November 1943,
Following the Allied Pursuit
from the Volturno

SCALE OF MILES
0   10   20   30

68

WINTER LINE CAMPAIGN

★

Meanwhile, Kesselring (now the commander in chief of German forces in Italy) strengthened his Winter Position. The most formidable portion lay behind the Garigliagno, Rapido, and Sangro Rivers; its southwest sector termed the "Gustav Line." A strong forward position (frequently termed the Winter Line) covered the approaches to the main position. Actually, the whole mountainous countryside had been organized into a series of defensive positions. Demolitions and mine fields blocked every avenue of approach; machine gun and mortar positions were well dug in (many blasted out of solid rock) and camouflaged to disappear into the rugged scenery; German artillery had registered on all roads, trails, and possible sites for bivouac and assembly areas.

Eighth Army opened its offensive on 20 November, rapidly establishing small footholds on the north bank of the Sangro, but torrential rain immediately stalled the attack until the 27th. By 2 December, the whole Eighth Army was across the Sangro, but both the weather and German resistance grew steadily worse. Ammunition supply became problematic, and because of the lack of reserves, local success could not be exploited. Air superiority was neutralized by the bad weather. Ortona was cleared on 27 December, but only after a week of vicious house-to-house fighting. There being no break in the weather, the offensive had to be called off, and on 30 December, Montgomery was recalled to Britain to prepare for D-Day.

The Liri Valley has been termed "the gateway to Rome," but it is not a very inviting portal. Fifth Army's X Corps faced the Garigliano, a narrow stream, but deep and swift, with its west bank walled by mountains from its junction with the Liri to the sea. VI Corps was confronted by a major hill mass, extending from the main ridge of the Apennine Mountains southward to Mount Sammucro. This was a particularly rough and barren region, studded with tall peaks and traversed by only two narrow and crooked roads. In the center, a mile-wide natural corridor, the Mignano Gap, faced II Corps. The gap, however, is dominated by the Mount Camino hill group. Within the gap is Mount Lungo, rising abruptly from the valley floor. Farther west are Mounts Porchia and Trocchio—all had been integrated into the German defenses, making the Mignano an ideal killing ground. The Germans had blocked it with mine fields, wire entanglements, and log-and-earth bunkers, and had converted the hillside villages (such as San Pietro) into strong points which could enfilade any Allied advance through the gap. The frustrating feature of these defenses was that nowhere was there any key point which, if captured, would shatter the intricately planned Winter Line. Each valley, hill, and village would have to be fought and paid for.

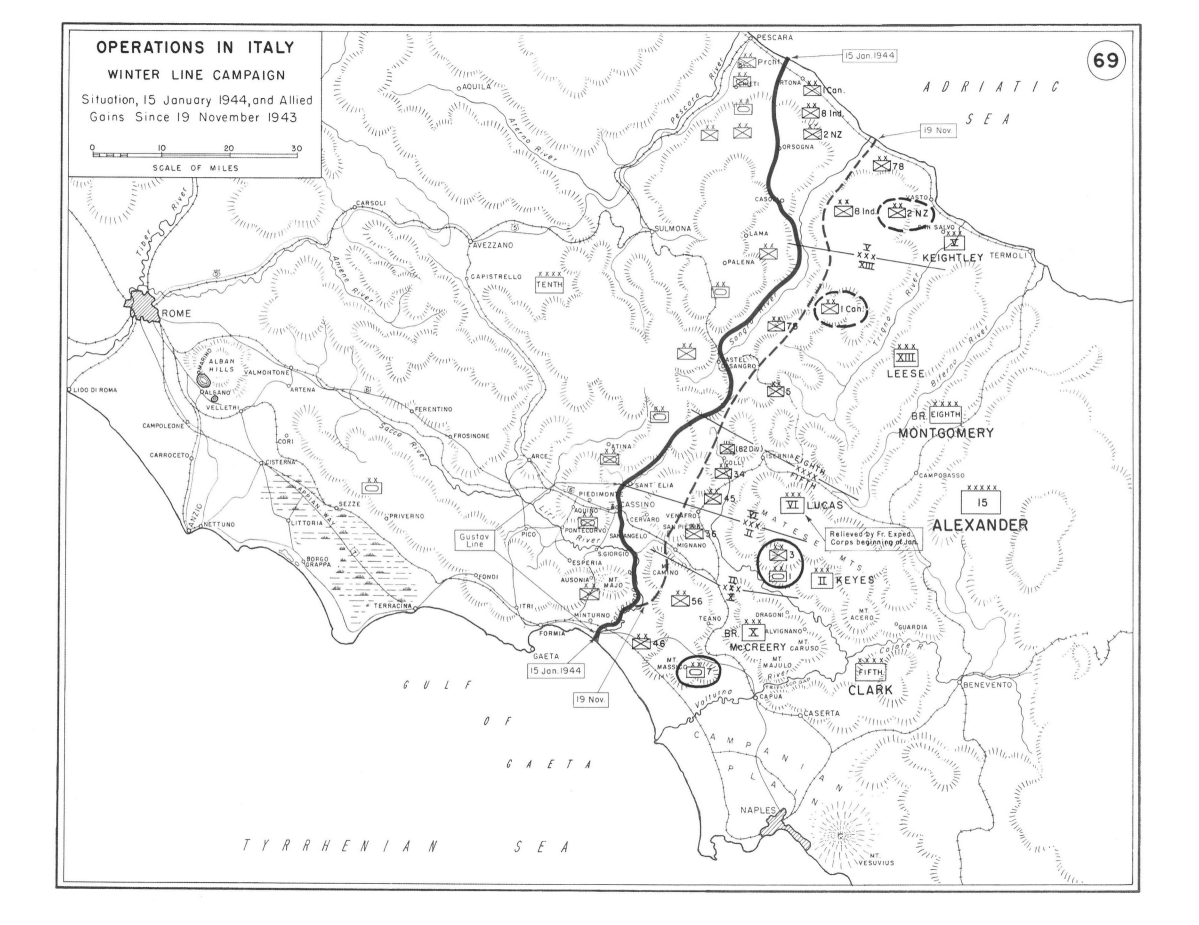

OPERATIONS IN ITALY

WINTER LINE CAMPAIGN

Situation, 15 January 1944, and Allied
Gains Since 19 November 1943

0   10   20   30
SCALE OF MILES

69

WINTER LINE CAMPAIGN

★

In accordance with phase two of Alexander's plan, II Corps would attack north of the Mignano Gap against the Mount Lungo–Mount Sammucro area, and VI Corps would support it by attacking toward the hills northwest of Cassino. Fifth Army would crush remaining resistance and advance into the Liri Valley. Elements of 45th and 34th Divisions jumped off on 29 November, and to the south the main attack began on the night of 1 December as the British 46th Division attacked the southern tip of the Mount Camino hill mass. With the Germans thus engaged, the 1st Special Service Force attacked Camino that night, while the 142nd Infantry Regiment of 36th Division advanced on Mount Maggiore at 0300 on 3 December, and captured it by 1700, although the outnumbered Germans fought savagely. By 10 December, the Camino area was completely cleared.

Now the Fifth Army offensive, designed to catch the Germans still disorganized after the loss of Mount Camino, opened on 8 December. In the Mignano Gap, the Italian 1st Motorized Group (now fighting with the Allies) would attack Mount Lungo. On their right, two battalions of the 143rd Infantry Regiment of 36th Division would move across the southern slopes of Mount Sammucro, while the rest of the regiment and 3rd Rangers would attack the crest. The battalion of panzer grenadiers on Lungo had little difficulty repelling the attack, and found opportunity to use much of its fire power against the American drive on San Pietro. (Two battalions of 143rd Infantry Regiment got within 400 yards of the town, but were then pinned down. They tried again on the 9th, but with equal lack of success).

The other battalion of the 143rd had successfully rushed the peak of Mount Sammucro at dawn, 8 December, thanks to a skillfully led approach march that enabled it to get within hand-grenade distance before being discovered. Though the Germans counterattacked vigorously, they could not regain the peak.

The 36th Division regrouped and prepared for a heavier attack for 15 December, to be launched simultaneously with VI Corps' secondary attack further north. One column would move down from the crest of Sammucro and seize the western end of the mountain; a second, reinforced by a company of tanks, would renew the advance on San Pietro. The attacks, although pressed courageously through the 16th, failed with heavy losses, including most of the tanks. The 142nd Infantry Regiment, however, did succeed in overrunning Mount Lungo on the 16th by an assault from the south.

With Americans on both Lungo and Sammucro, San Pietro became more of a trap than a strong point for the Germans, and under the cover of a fierce counterattack, they evacuated the town and fell back to their next position: the line Cedro Hill–Mount Porchia–San Vittore–western edge of Sammucro. Allied attempts to storm San Vittore on 19–21 December were expensive failures.

VI Corps' attacks in the north met tough resistance, but through many small, and bloody, actions, the corps got forward, by 21 December, to Casale–Cardito.

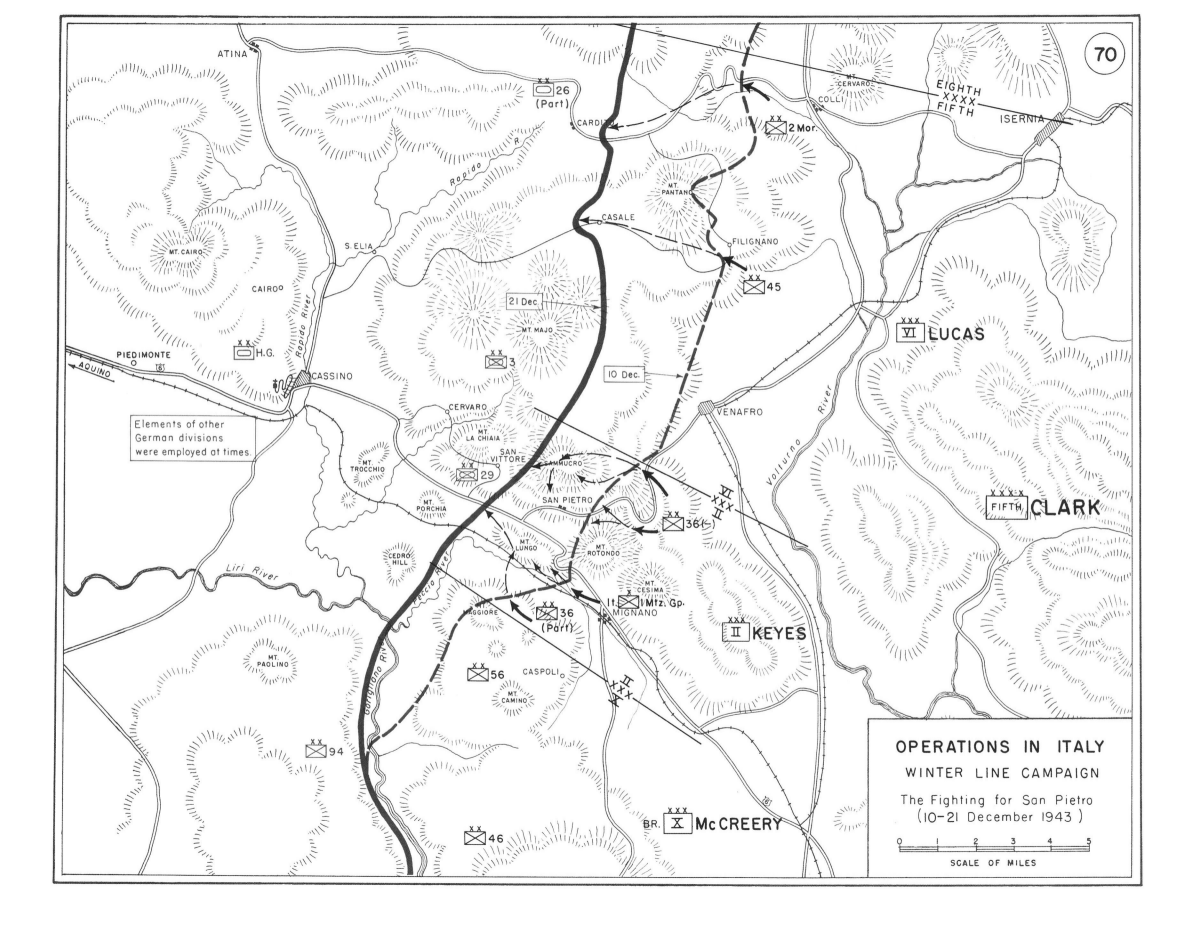

70

ATINA

MT. CERVARO

EIGHTH
XXXX
FIFTH

ISERNIA

COLLI

26
(Part)

CARDI

2 Mor.

Rapido R.

MT. PANTANO

CASALE

FILIGNANO

S. ELIA

45

MT. CAIRO

CAIRO

21 Dec.

Rapido River

MT. MAJO

H.G.

3

10 Dec.

XXX
VI LUCAS

AQUINO

PIEDIMONTE

CASSINO

Volturno River

VENAFRO

CERVARO

Elements of other
German divisions
were employed at times.

MT. LA CHIAIA

SAN
VITTORE

SAMMUCRO

XXXX
FIFTH CLARK

MT.
TROCCHIO

29

SAN PIETRO

XX VI
XXX

36(−)

Liri River

MT.
PORCHIA

CEDRO
HILL

MT.
LUNGO

MT.
ROTONDO

Gorgliano River

Peccia River

MAGGIORE

36
(Part)

MT.
CESIMA

It. I Mtz. Gp.
MIGNANO

XXX
II KEYES

MT.
PAOLINO

56

CASPOLI

II
XXX

MT. CAMINO

94

BR. XXX
X McCREERY

46

OPERATIONS IN ITALY

WINTER LINE CAMPAIGN

The Fighting for San Pietro
(10−21 December 1943)

0   1   2   3   4   5

SCALE OF MILES

WINTER LINE CAMPAIGN

★

Early in January, Fifth Army regrouped. The 34th Division relieved the hard-working 36th, and the Algerian 3rd Division replaced the 45th. The French Expeditionary Corps replaced VI Corps, and the arrival of the veteran 1st Armored gave Gen. Clark a strong mobile reserve.

The third phase of Fifth Army's offensive had been intended to break through the remaining German defenses and into the Liri Valley. II Corps would make the main attack along the general axis of Highway 6; X Corps and the French would deliver supporting attacks on either flank. In its attack, II Corps planned to make its main effort with 34th Division against Mount Chiaia, and outflanking the stronghold from the north. Still further north, 1st Special Service Force would strike across the mountains to clear out the Mount Majo area; Task Force A (6th Armored Infantry Regiment of the newly arrived 1st Armored Division) would seize Mount Porchia.

The 1st Special Service Force began its advance at 2120 on 3 January 1944, and moved swiftly along the twisting ridges. Two infantry battalions (one being the 100th Battalion composed of Japanese-Americans) were attached to the 6th, to consolidate and defend the ground gained. At 0520, 7 January, the right-flank column of Special Services Force over-ran Mount Majo. Its left-flank column had pushed toward the ridges north of Cervaro. Reaching them early on the 7th, it was forced back by counterattacks, but outmaneuvered the Germans during the night and seized its objectives early on the 8th. Repeated German counterattacks were broken up, usually by massed American artillery.

In the meantime, 34th Division had jumped off at 0550 on 5 January. The Mount Chiaia terrain was extremely rugged, the defense expert and determined, but San Vittore fell on the 6th and Chiaia itself on the 7th. Farther south, Task Force A finally occupied Mount Porchia that same day, after very costly fighting.

Quickly regrouping, II Corps drove forward again on the 10th, with Mount Trocchio as its objective. First, it was necessary to clear out the remaining German positions in the Cervaro area, which still flanked any Allied egress from the Mignano Gap. Even with heavy air and artillery support, this took three more days. On 14 January, II Corps was closing against Mount Trocchio, and a massive attack against it the next day found it abandoned, the Germans having withdrawn behind the Rapido River that night.

It was a testament to the tenacity of German skill in delaying rearguard actions that the fighting had been as prolonged and bloody as it had been. Both the Eighth and Fifth Armies had failed to achieve their objectives, and both were completely, although temporarily, fought out. Fifth Army now faced the Gustav Line. Its outpost skirmishing was over, and the real battle for Rome was about to begin.

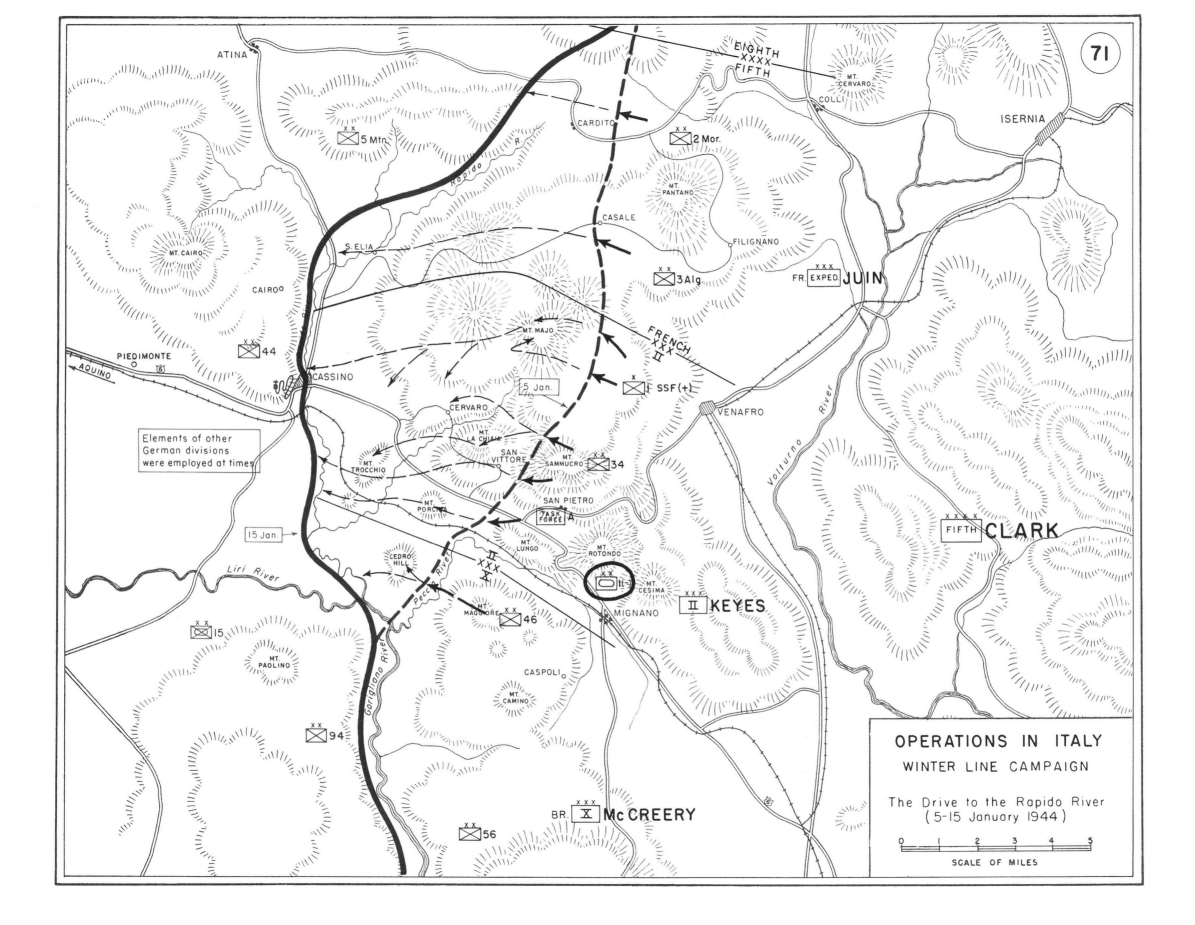

ATINA

MT. CERVARO

EIGHTH
XXXX
FIFTH

COLLI

ISERNIA

CARDITO

☒☒ 5 Mtn.

☒☒ 2 Mor.

Rapido R.

MT. PANTANO

FILIGNANO

CASALE

S. ELIA

☒☒ 3 Alg.

FR. EXPED. XXX JUIN

MT. CAIRO

CAIROO

MT. MAJO

FRENCH XXX II

5 Jan.

☒ I SSF (+)

VENAFRO

PIEDIMONTE

AQUINO

☒☒ 44

CASSINO

CERVARO

Volturno River

MT. LA CHIAIA

SAN VITTORE

MT. SAMMUCRO

☒☒ 34

Elements of other German divisions were employed at times

MT. TROCCHIO

MT. PORCHIA

SAN PIETRO

TASK FORCE A

FIFTH XXXX CLARK

15 Jan.

MT. LUNGO

MT. ROTONDO

CEDRO HILL

Peccia River

II XXX X

MT. CESIMA

☒☒ II

II KEYES

Liri River

☒☒ 15

MT. MAGGIORE

☒☒ 46

MIGNANO

Garigliano River

MT. PAOLINO

CASPOLI

MT. CAMINO

☒☒ 94

OPERATIONS IN ITALY

WINTER LINE CAMPAIGN

The Drive to the Rapido River
(5-15 January 1944)

BR. X McCREERY

☒☒ 56

0 1 2 3 4 5

SCALE OF MILES

71

CASSINO-ANZIO CAMPAIGN

★

Unlike the Winter Line, the Gustav Line had a definite key point—the massively built monastery and town of Monte Cassino lying at the foot of the Mount Cairo hill mass, at the junction of the Rapido and Liri valleys. Alexander's new plan provided for an initial secondary attack across the lower Garigliano River by X Corps, to pull the German reserves out of position. II Corps would then attack up the Liri Valley toward Frosinone. When these operations were well begun, VI Corps would make an amphibious landing in the Anzio area. Once ashore, it would drive northward and seize the Alban Hills, thus cutting the German Tenth Army's main line of communications, and would force Kesselring to evacuate the Gustav Line and retreat north of Rome.

Late on 17 January, X Corps stormed the Garigliano and established a considerable bridgehead. By the 20th, it had attracted all of Generaloberst Heinrich von Vietinghoff's available reserves. Also on the 20th, the 36th Division attempted to force the Rapido, two miles below Cassino, in one of the strongest sectors of the Gustav Line. Its assault was poorly organized and ended in bloody and complete failure.

The amphibious expedition sailed from Naples on 21 January, making a surprise and unopposed landing at Anzio at 0200 the next morning. An immediately bold advance might have swept into Rome, but Maj. Gen. John P. Lucas paused to organize his beachhead. When he attempted to move inland on the 30th, he found himself penned against the sea. Kesselring had foreseen and planned for such an emergency. German reserves were rushed in from the north, and quiet sectors of the Gustav Line were stripped of troops. Waiting until bad weather hampered Allied air and naval support, the German Fourteenth Army attacked on 15 February. Its initial assault penetrated deeply into the Allied position along the Anzio–Albano road; on the 18th however, Mackenson failed to commit his whole reserve for a knock-out blow. Reinforced only by driblets, his offensive rapidly lost momentum, and a VI Corps counterattack on 19 February checked it. Subsequent German assaults in the Cisterna area had little success, and early in March, the Germans halted their attacks and began to fortify their positions.

The fortunes of war had been even harder at Cassino. After some initial gains north and east of the town, 34th Division launched a major attack during the first week of February, but by the 12th it had to admit defeat. The New Zealanders then took up the challenge, courageously, but with equal lack of success. In an attempt to break the rapidly solidifying Italian stalemate, the Allies organized a third assault on Cassino. Massed air power and artillery battered Cassino for hours before the infantry and armor went in, only to find that the preparatory bombardment had turned the place into an almost impenetrable maze of rubble, perfectly suited to the die-hard German paratroopers of 1st Parachute Division, who fought the Allies to a standstill by the 23 March.

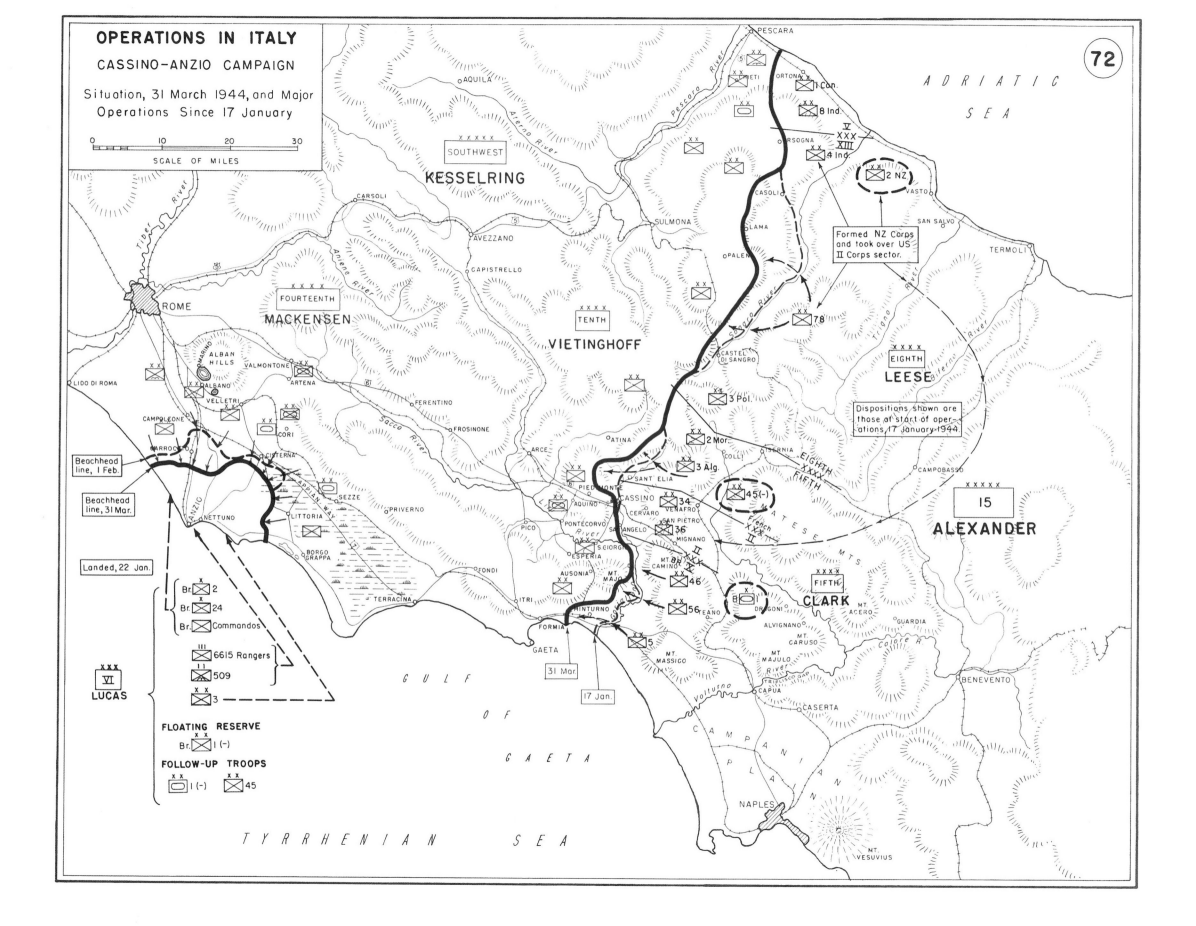

OPERATIONS IN ITALY
CASSINO–ANZIO CAMPAIGN

Situation, 31 March 1944, and Major
Operations Since 17 January

SCALE OF MILES
0   10   20   30

ADRIATIC SEA

PESCARA

AQUILA

SOUTHWEST

KESSELRING

CARSOLI

SULMONA

AVEZZANO

CAPISTRELLO

Formed NZ Corps and took over US II Corps sector.

SAN SALVO

TERMOLI

VASTO

2 NZ

4 Ind.

ORSOGNA

CASOLI

LAMA

OPALEN

78

CASTEL DI SANGRO

ROME

FOURTEENTH

MACKENSEN

TENTH

VIETINGHOFF

EIGHTH

LEESE

Dispositions shown are those at start of operations, 17 January 1944.

CAMPOBASSO

15

ALEXANDER

ALBAN HILLS

MARINO

VALMONTONE

ALBANO

ARTENA

VELLETRI

LIDO DI ROMA

CAMPOLEONE

CARROCETO

CISTERNA

CORI

FERENTINO

FROSINONE

3 Pol.

2 Mor.

ATINA

COLLI

ISERNIA

EIGHTH

FIFTH

Beachhead line, 1 Feb.

Beachhead line, 31 Mar.

APPIAN WAY

SEZZE

PRIVERNO

SACCO River

ARCE

SANT ELIA

3 Alg.

PIEDIMONTE

AQUINO

CASSINO

34

VENAFRO

45 (−)

Landed, 22 Jan.

NETTUNO

ANZIO

LITTORIA

BORGO GRAPPA

CERVARO

SAN PIETRO

36

MIGNANO

PICO

PONTECORVO

SAN ANGELO

S.GIORGI

Liri River

CLARK

FIFTH

MT. ACERO

GUARDIA

Br. 2

Br. 24

Br. Commandos

6615 Rangers

509

3

ESPERIA

AUSONIA

MT. MAJO

MT. CAMINO

46

DRAGONI

ALVIGNANO

MT. CARUSO

TERRACINA

FONDI

ITRI

MINTURNO

FORMIA

56

TEANO

8

MT. MASSICO

MT. MAJULO

Volturno River

Colore R.

BENEVENTO

FLOATING RESERVE
Br. 1 (−)

FOLLOW-UP TROOPS
1 (−)   45

LUCAS

VI

31 Mar.

17 Jan.

GAETA

5

MT. CARUSO

TRIPLICE GAP

CAPUA

CASERTA

GULF

OF

GAETA

CAMPANIAN PLAIN

NAPLES

MT. VESUVIUS

TYRRHENIAN SEA

72

ROME CAMPAIGN

★

Alexander at last had secured sufficient reinforcements to give him a definite numerical superiority over Kesselring. He now planned an overwhelming offensive designed to destroy the right wing of the German Tenth Army.

Eighth Army would make the main attack against Cassino and up the Liri and Sacco Valleys, along the general axis of route 6 to Valmontone. Simultaneously, Fifth Army would attack out of the Garigliano bridgehead to Anzio to link up with its VI Corps, which would hold itself ready to attack inland to Valmontone on or after D+4, thus trapping the Germans retreating before Eighth Army. An elaborate cover plan deceived the Germans into thinking that a large amphibious operation was being mounted against Civitavecchia.

During the winter the Germans had begun two new defense lines: the Hitler Line (still incomplete) ran from Terracina inland to Piedimonte, with its strongest defenses extending across the Liri Valley. The Caesar Line (apparently barely begun) lay across the highways south of Rome in the Alban Hills region.

The Allies attacked late on the evening of 11 May, attaining complete surprise. The German, however, was too good a soldier—and his defenses too strong—to permit any sudden breakthrough. The British, French, and Americans found their initial gains followed by stiffening resistance, and the Polish Corps was defeated in its spirited attempt to envelop Cassino from the north. But in the Mount Majo area (a different Mount Majo to that mentioned earlier), the French discovered that the Gustav Line was relatively weak, the Germans having decided that the rugged terrain would not require extensive fortification.

Clearing this area by 13 May, the French drove forward the next morning across roadless mountain country. Spearheaded by parties of *goumiers* (Moroccan irregulars), their progress was unexpectedly swift, and by 17 May they threatened the road running north from Itri, thereby dislocating the whole German front. British XIII Corps, supported by the Canadians, pushed forward west of Cassino, which fell at last to a renewed Polish assault on 17–18 May. Failing in an attempt to rush the Hitler Line on 18 May, XIII Corps breached it by a coordinated attack on the 23rd. The Germans retired doggedly northward.

VI Corps attacked from the Anzio beachhead on 23 May and made good progress toward Valmontone. Momentarily, the German Tenth Army appeared doomed. On the 26th, however, Clark, abruptly shifted the weight of Fifth Army's advance northwest, toward Rome, and as a result, small, skillfully handled German rearguards were able to check the Americans at both Valmontone and Velletri until 2 June. Then, their mission gallantly discharged, the Germans broke contact and withdrew. American troops entered Rome on 4 June, and the Tenth Army escaped.

Kesselring now faced a problem. The last remaining German defensive system in Italy, the Gothic Line (running generally from Pisa northeast to Rimini), which would have to shelter his Tenth and Fourteenth Armies, was not yet complete, and in order to give himself time, he would have to conduct a slow, fighting retreat—and all of it in the teeth of absolute Allied air superiority

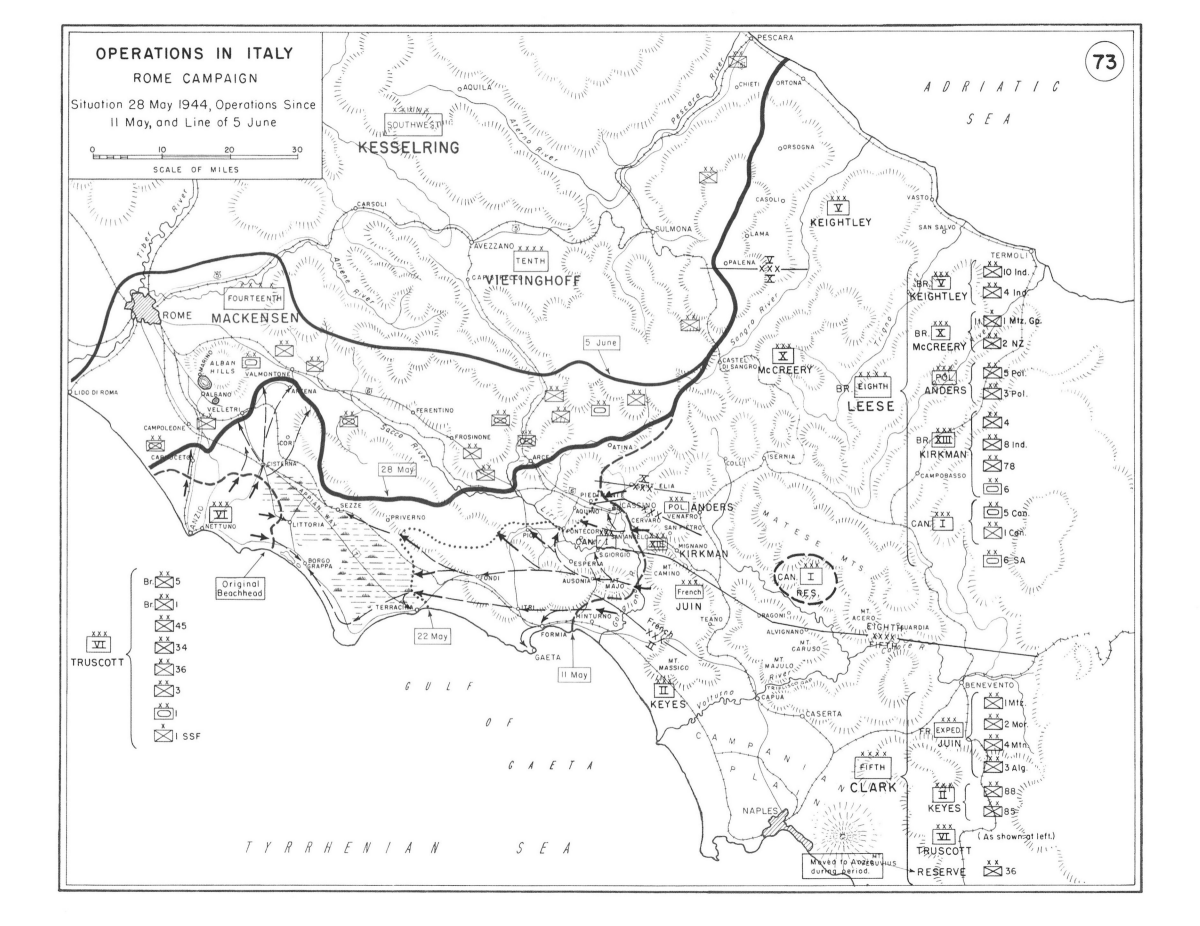

OPERATIONS IN ITALY
ROME CAMPAIGN
Situation 28 May 1944, Operations Since
11 May, and Line of 5 June

SCALE OF MILES

THE ATTACKS ON THE GOTHIC LINE

★

Initially, the Allied pursuit swept the Germans northward, especially in the flat coastal plain north of Rome (Civitaveccia fell on 7 June). Everything promised a major triumph, and the Allies could practically taste victory. Alexander was confident that his forces could shatter the Gothic Line and break into the Po Valley during August. Once there, he could attack either westward in southern France or eastward through Venice into Austria. British leaders favored the latter as offering the most direct threat to Germany, but the Americans favored the invasion of southern France and considered the capture of the port of Marseille essential for the support of operations in Western Europe. Following prolonged (and occasionally sharp) consultations, Churchill yielded to Roosevelt's insistence.

Meanwhile, Hitler had reinforced Kesselring with eight more divisions of varying quality, and allowed him to retain the redoubtable Hermann Göring Panzer Division, previously scheduled for transfer to France. Thus reinforced, Kesselring reestablished his front, covered it with hastily sewn minefields and demolitions, and sacrificed his second-rate units ruthlessly in order to buy time to concentrate and organize his crack divisions. Kesselring and his subordinates waged a masterly delaying action, but by 4 August, the Allies had reached the outworks of the Gothic Line, where winter and exhaustion halted them. They had advanced 270 miles in sixty-four days, including the penetration of the Gustav and Hitler Lines

The Gothic Line had been shrewdly located to take advantage of the mountain chain which divides central Italy from the Po Valley. On the west coast, the corridor between these mountains and the sea is extremely narrow; the corridor along the east coast, while much wider, is cut by many rivers. Although not yet complete, the existing defenses of the Gothic Line still represented a serious obstacle. From a point on the west coast southeast of Spezia it ran through the mountains north of Pistoia to the Foglia River and Pesaro on the Adriatic. An outpost line ran through Pisa and along the Arno River; particularly strong fortifications guarded the Futa Pass, on the direct road to Bologna.

Alexander had originally intended to take the Gothic Line in his stride, utilizing his Moroccan units (considered by the Germans to be, with the New Zealanders, the best troops they faced in Italy) to clear the Florence–Bologna road by operating through the mountains on either side of Futa Pass; but they were now too weakened, and so he paused for three weeks to regroup for a new offensive. Most of Eighth Army was diverted, swiftly and secretly, to the Adriatic coast for a drive through Rimini toward Ravenna and Bologna where, it was hoped, this sudden shift of the main Allied effort would catch Kesselring off guard. Fifth Army, now reinforced by the British XIII Corps, would carry on overt preparations to convince the Germans that the main attack would be launched along the Florence–Bologna axis; then, once Eighth Army's offensive began to draw in German reserves, it would launch its own offensive, employing its II and XIII Corps, toward Bologna and Ferrara.

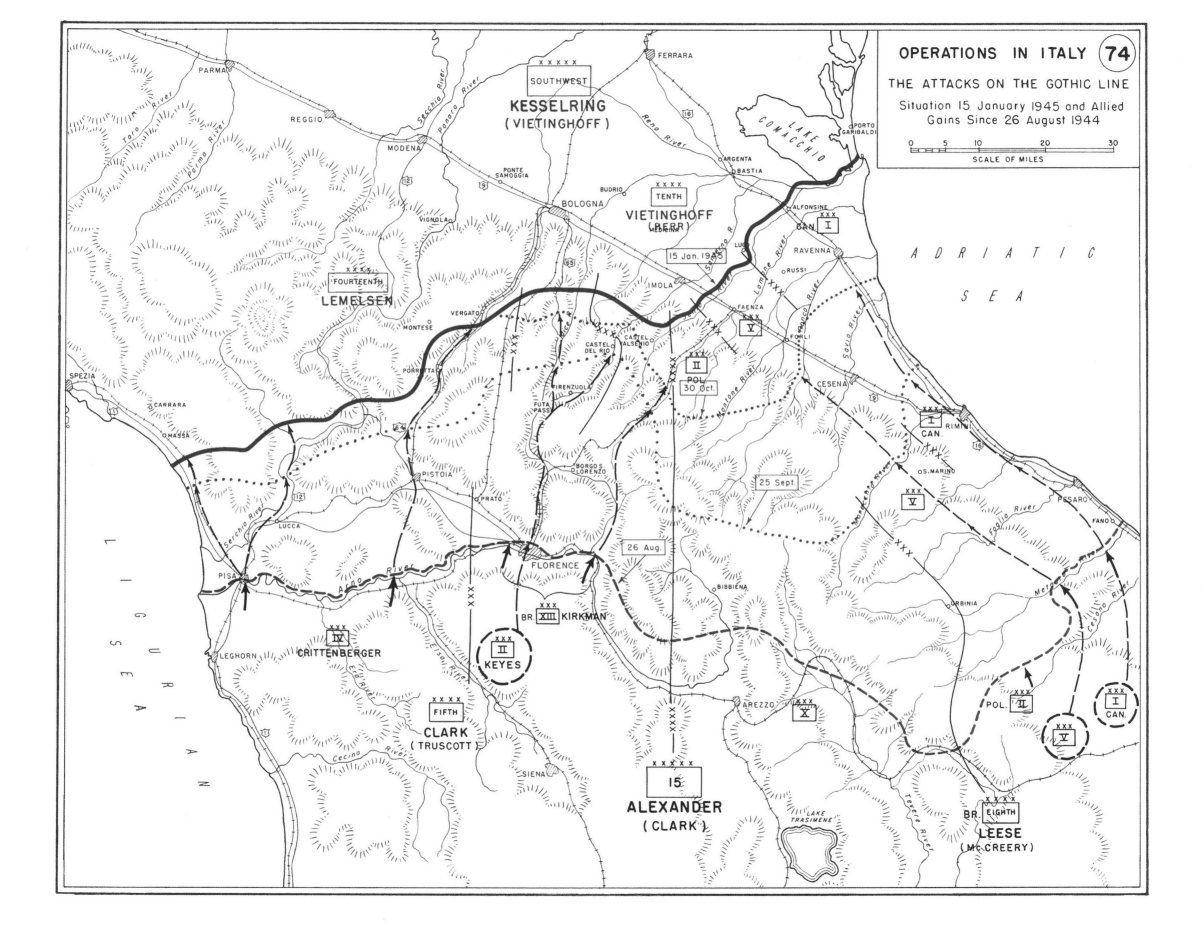

SCALE OF MILES

KESSELRING
(VIETINGHOFF)
SOUTHWEST

TENTH
VIETINGHOFF
(HERR)

FOURTEENTH
LEMELSEN

15 Jan. 1945

ADRIATIC

SEA

LAKE
COMACCHIO

CAN. I

FERRARA

PORTO
GARIBALDI

ALFONSINE

RAVENNA

ARGENTA
BASTIA

BUDRIO

BOLOGNA

IMOLA

FAENZA V

FORLI

CESENA

ORUSSI

V

II
POL.
30 Oct.

XXX
CASTEL
DEL RIO

CASTEL
ALSENIO

VERGATO

MONTESE

PORRETTA

FIRENZUOLA

FUTA
PASS

BORGO S.
LORENZO

25 Sept.

I
CAN.
RIMINI

S. MARINO

V

PESARO

FANO

26 Aug.

FLORENCE

PISTOIA

PRATO

LUCCA

PISA

BIBBIENA

ORBINA

BR. XIII KIRKMAN

POL. II

I
CAN.

V

II
KEYES

SPEZIA

CARRARA

MASSA

LEGHORN

CRITTENBERGER
IV

L
I
G
U
R
I
A
N

FIFTH
CLARK
(TRUSCOTT)

AREZZO

X

15
ALEXANDER
(CLARK)

SIENA

LAKE
TRASIMENE

BR. EIGHTH
LEESE
(McCREERY)

PARMA

REGGIO

MODENA

PONTE
SAMOGGIA

VIGNOLA

LUGO

ALONFINE

PISTOIA

PRATO

SPRING OFFENSIVE, 1945

★

Eighth Army attacked on 25 August, and the surprise and weight of its initial assault carried it through the Gothic Line; by 4 September it was attacking Rimini. Utilizing his excellent east-west road network, Kesselring rushed up reinforcements to check Eighth Army there. This, however, weakened his right flank and center to such an extent that the outpost line along the Arno had to be evacuated, following which Fifth Army advanced rapidly northward until it struck the main defenses on 13 September. Fighting there was stern, but the German units in the line were too stretched to man their extensive defenses. Backed by concentrated artillery fire, the Americans found an opening near Firenzuola that enabled them to outflank Futa Pass. In the west, IV Corps advanced against relatively light resistance. Both Allied armies were now going through the Gothic Line in many places, but could only make slow progress against improvised defenses in the hills beyond.

Eighth Army finally took Rimini on 21 September, and on 1 October Clark committed his reserves in a final bid for Bologna. His attack carried to within nine miles of the city before a concentration of picked German divisions stopped it on 20 October. Profiting from this shift of German troops, Eighth Army was able to increase its gains. Both armies, though, were by now exhausted. Casualties had been heavy and replacements few. Ammunition stocks were dangerously low, and the weather worsened steadily. Thereafter, the Allies halted for the winter, bitterly aware that final victory had just eluded them.

The ensuing stalemate on the Italian front (from early January through March) was the longest period of quiet it had known. But, though the Russians were within forty miles of Berlin on 1 April 1945, and the armies of the Western Allies were thrusting deep into Germany, Hitler still clung to northern Italy. There, the depleted armies of Army Group Southwest stoically and methodically strengthened their front and built new defense lines to their rear along the Po and Adige Rivers while Fascist Italian troops of the Ligurian Army guarded the passes into France (and deserted at every opportunity). Allied air attacks were constant and unanswered; supplies of motor fuel were dwindling to dangerously low levels, and so, in view of these factors, Gen. Vietinghoff requested the authority to begin a secret withdrawal north of the Po; Hitler's reply was the standard one: the position was to be defended to the last man.

The Allied armies (now rested and reorganized) knew that only a few more miles of mountainous terrain separated them from the open country of the Po Valley, where massed armor could operate effectively. Alexander and Clark ordered Eighth Army to open the 1945 offensive with an attack up the Adriatic coast, pushing northwestward toward Ferrara. Fifth Army would then drive northward, capture Bologna, and continue to Bondeno for a rendezvous with Eighth Army. Thereafter, the Allies would strike north across the Po Valley, blocking the last escape route into Germany. The result seemed a foregone conclusion, but Vietinghoff's command had made a career of forlorn hopes, and it would meet the Allied offensive as resolutely as it had earlier ones.

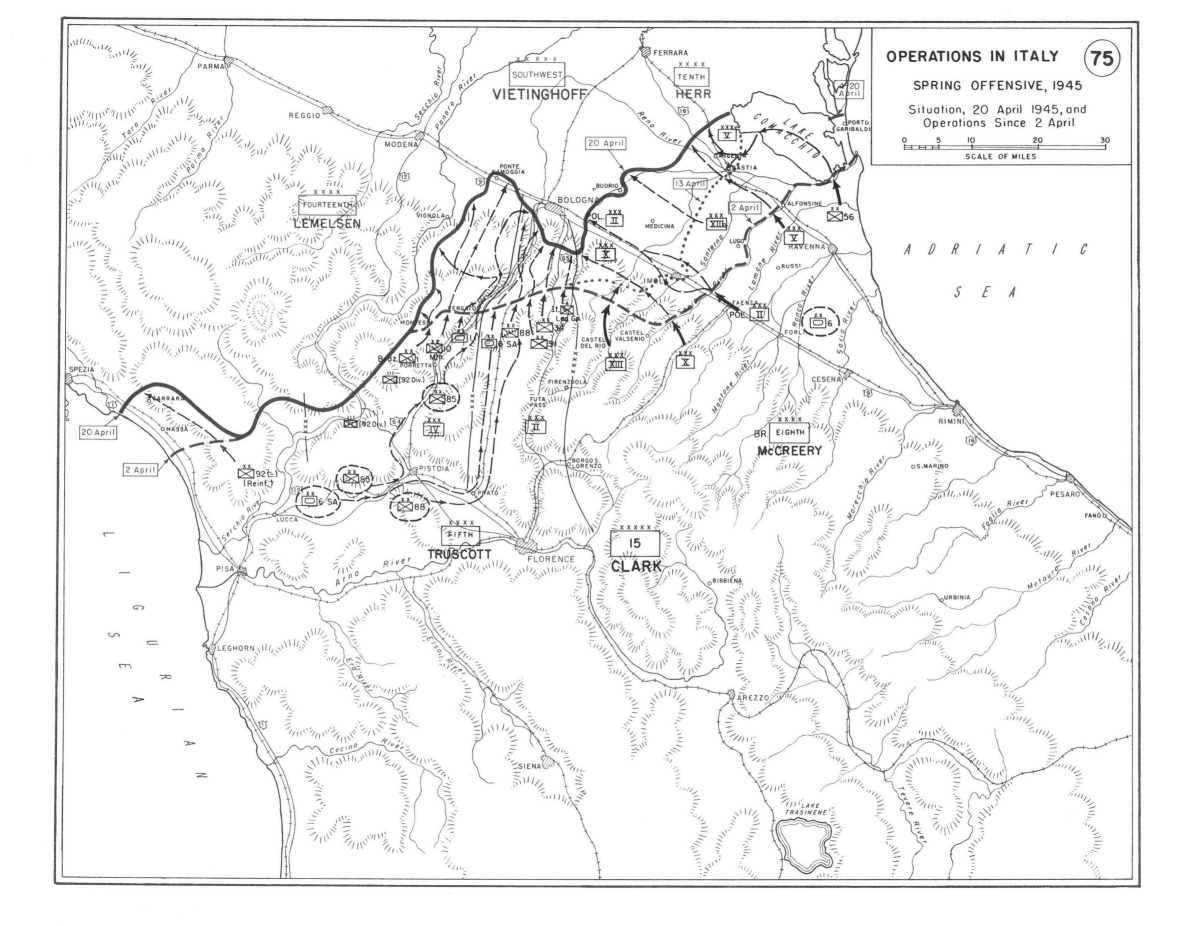

OPERATIONS IN ITALY 75

SPRING OFFENSIVE, 1945

Situation, 20 April 1945, and
Operations Since 2 April

0   5   10   20   30
SCALE OF MILES

SOUTHWEST
VIETINGHOFF

TENTH
HERR

FOURTEENTH
LEMELSEN

FIFTH
TRUSCOTT

BR. EIGHTH
McCREERY

15
CLARK

A D R I A T I C   S E A

L I G U R I A N   S E A

LAKE COMACCHIO

PARMA
REGGIO
MODENA
FERRARA
PORTO GARIBALDI
BOLOGNA
IMOLA
FAENZA
RAVENNA
FORLI
CESENA
RIMINI
PESARO
FANO
PISA
LEGHORN
FLORENCE
PRATO
PISTOIA
LUCCA
SPEZIA
CARRARA
MASSA
VIGNOLA
FIRENZUOLA
AREZZO
SIENA
BIBBIENA
URBINIA
S. MARINO
LAKE TRASIMENE

20 April
2 April
13 April

THE PURSUIT

★

The final phase of the Allied offensive involved the British V Corps of Eighth Army pushing up Highway 16, through the Argenta "gap." A breakthrough here would unhinge the entire German line. Fifth Army would attack later, to the west of Bologna. In the early afternoon of 9 April, a massive air and artillery bombardment preceded V Corps' attack. The Germans fought stubbornly, but by the 14th the gap had been forced. All along its front, Eighth Army had reached the plain. Vietinghoff had committed his last reserves, but in vain. Also on the 14th, Fifth Army also began its assault, and with their defenses ruptured all along their front, German resistance collapsed by the 19th, and American and Polish columns converged on Bologna on the 21st. The pursuing Allies now raced for the Po, which the U.S.10th Mountain Division crossed on the 23rd. Die-hard rearguard actions checked II Corps for just enough time to enable several German divisions to escape the trap at Bondeno. Using every kind of pontoon and boat, the Germans made a desperate scramble to cross the Po, having to abandon most of their heavy equipment in the process. Around Ferrara, however, the Germans fought desperately to protect their withdrawal.

Against all odds, Vietinghoff had saved a surprisingly large part of his army, but it was stripped of most of its equipment and ammunition. Once across the Po in large numbers, Allied columns thrust through collapsing resistance all across northern Italy, and by 25 April major German resistance had evaporated, Eighth Army having crushed the hard core

of Tenth Army up against the Po on the 24th. On 29 April, Vietinghoff agreed to an unconditional surrender, effective at noon, 2 May. Allied troops, however, pressed forward to the Austrian border where men from the 88th Division established contact with elements of the American Seventh Army, coming south, at Vipiteno on 4 May.

Throughout the war, Italy had been a poor relation among the various theaters. The Allies' prime purpose there had been, bluntly, to attract and consume German units which might otherwise have been employed on the Western Front or in Russia. In this, the Italian Campaign, for all its disappointments, was an obvious success. Fighting in Italy was slow and difficult. It was a war fought with what was left over, with what could be spared, and it is doubtful if Alexander, Clark, and their subordinate commanders have received sufficient credit for their ability to carry forward an aggressive, eventually victorious campaign under such difficult circumstances.

The success of the Italian campaign reached far beyond the mountain battlefields. Italy became a huge airbase delivering heavy blows against the Reich. Furthermore, Hitler was forced to divert troops in order to protect the Balkans. And, by his original decision to fight for Italy south of Rome, he was forever forced to keep divisions idle in northern Italy to guard both coasts against possible amphibious landings, while his Atlantic Wall remained only a shell, and his commanders in Russia pleaded for reinforcements. In no small way, Italy was to Hitler what Spain had been to Napoleon—an ulcer that became a cancer.

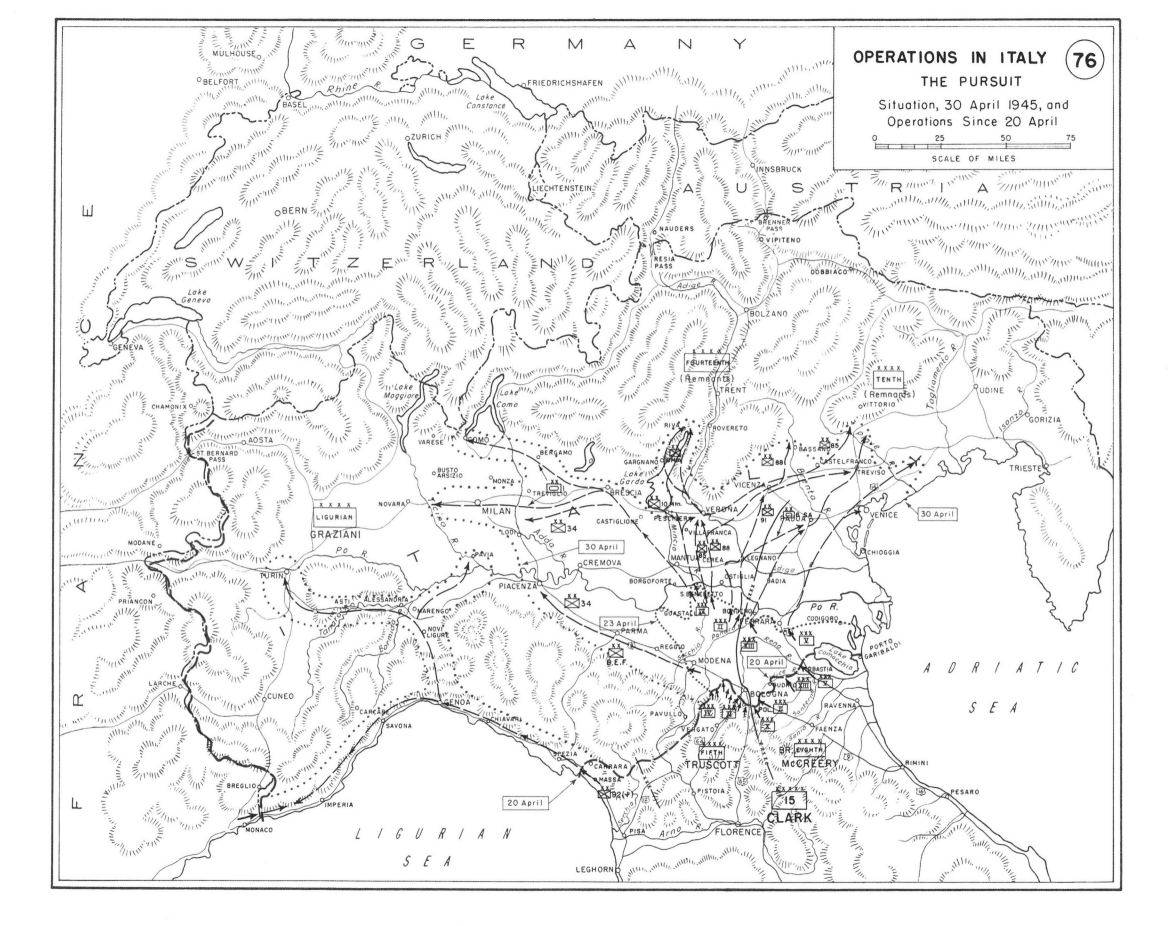

OPERATIONS IN ITALY (76)
THE PURSUIT

Situation, 30 April 1945, and
Operations Since 20 April

0   25   50   75
SCALE OF MILES

GERMANY

MULHOUSE

BELFORT

FRIEDRICHSHAFEN

Rhine R.

BASEL

Lake Constance

ZURICH

S W I T Z E R L A N D

A U S T R I A

BERN

LIECHTENSTEIN

INNSBRUCK

NAUDERS

BRENNER PASS
VIPITENO

RESIA PASS

Adige R.

DOBBIACO

Lake Geneva

BOLZANO

GENEVA

CHAMONIX

GORIZIA

Lake Maggiore

Lake Como

FOURTEENTH
(Remnants)
TRENT

TENT
(Remnants)
VITTORIO

UDINE

Tagliamento R.

Isonzo R.

AOSTA

ST. BERNARD PASS

RIVA

ROVERETO

BASSANO

85

Adige R.

Brenta R.

TRIESTE

MODANE

VARESE

COMO

BERGAMO

GARGNANO

Lake Garda

88

VICENZA

CASTELFRANCO

TREVISO

Piave R.

30 April

F R A N C E

NOVARA

TREVIGLIO

MILAN

BRESCIA

CASTIGLIONE

PESCHIERA

VERONA

VILLAFRANCA

91

PADUA

VENICE

CHIOGGIA

LIGURIAN
GRAZIANI

MONZA

BUSTO ARSIZIO

34

110 Mtn.

88

CEREA

LEGNANO

Po R.

MODANE

LODI

Adda R.

Ticino R.

MANTUA

OSTIGLIA

BADIA

30 April

MODENA

CREMONA

BORGOFORTE

S.BENEDETTO

IV

II

PORTO GARIBALDI

TURIN

PRIANCON

ASTI

ALESSANDRIA

MARENGO

PAVIA

PIACENZA

34

GUASTALLA

BONDENO

FERRARA

CODIGORO

XIII

V

20 April

Po R.

Reno R.

Lake Comacchio

ADRIATIC
SEA

LARCHE

CUNEO

NOVI LIGURE

BORMIDA

23 April
PARMA

REGGIO

B.E.F.

20 April

FORLI

BASTIA

XIII

V

CARCARE

GENOA

SAVONA

CHIAVARI

PAVULLO

BUDRIO

II

RAVENNA

BREGLIO

IMPERIA

SPEZIA

CARRARA

MASSA

92(+)

VERGATO

BOLOGNA

POL

II

FAENZA

FIFTH
TRUSCOTT

BR. EIGHTH
McCREERY

RIMINI

MONACO

20 April

PISTOIA

15
CLARK

PESARO

PISA

Arno R.

FLORENCE

LEGHORN

L I G U R I A N   S E A

PERSONALITIES OF THE EUROPEAN THEATER: ALLIES

★

General Dwight Eisenhower meets with Airborne troops just before they board their aircraft for the assault on Europe, June 6, 1944.

American and British military leaders confer during World War II. From left: General George S. Patton Jr., General Omar Bradley, and British commander Sir Bernard L. Montgomery.

U.S. General Mark W. Clark riding in a PT boat that carried him to the Anzio beachhead south of Rome in February 1944. Clark commanded the American Fifth Army that eventually captured Rome.

Commanders of the American forces in Europe pose for a group portrait in 1945. Seated from left: William Hood Simpson, George S. Patton Jr., Carl A. Spaatz, Dwight Eisenhower, Omar N. Bradley, Courtney H. Hodges, and Leonard T. Gerow. Standing from left: Ralph F. Stearley, Hoyt Vandenberg, Walter Bedell Smith, Otto P. Weyland, and Richard E. Nugent.

The Allies Big Three meet in Yalta in February 1946 to make final plans for the defeat of Germany. From left: Prime Minister Winston Churchill, President Franklin D. Roosevelt, and Premier Josef Stalin.

Russian commander G. K. Zhukov, center in lighter uniform, meets with General Eisenhower and British General Montgomery at Eisenhower's headquarters in Frankfurt, June 10, 1945. Zhukov presented the Russian Order of Victory to Montgomery.

PERSONALITIES OF THE EUROPEAN THEATER: AXIS

★

Field Marshal Karl Gerd von Runstedt, who was Germany's Commander-in-Chief, West, as Allied forces invaded Normandy and moved across Europe.

Italy's Benito Mussolini and Germany's Adolf Hitler ride through Munich during a meeting of the two Axis leaders in June 1940.

Field Marshal General Erwin Rommel reviews German coastal defenses on the English Channel in March 1944, just months prior the Allied invasion of Normandy.

German Field Marshal General Walter Model, left, confers with a tank commander on the Eastern front in the spring of 1944.

Defendants sit in the courtroom and listen to the proceedings during the war crimes trials at Nuremberg in 1945. In the front row are, top to bottom, Hermann Goëring, Rudolf Hess, Joachim von Ribbentrop, and Wilhelm Keitel.

Field Marshal Wilhelm Keitel signs the surrender terms for the German Army at Russian headquarters in Berlin, May 7, 1945.